THE AMERICAN
ROSE ANNUAL

THE AMERICAN ROSE ANNUAL

THE 1919 YEAR-BOOK OF ROSE PROGRESS

Edited for the American
Rose Society, by

J. HORACE McFARLAND

1919
AMERICAN ROSE SOCIETY
EDITOR'S OFFICE
HARRISBURG, PA.

THE American Rose Annual is supplied to all members of the American Rose Society whose dues are paid for the current year. Additional copies are supplied to members only at $1 each, postpaid. When sold separately, the price of the Annual is $2, and includes annual membership. Members may obtain copies of the 1917 and 1918 Annuals, so long as in print, at $1 each, and of the 1916 Annual (the first issue), at $2 each.

Address, E. A. WHITE, SECRETARY, ITHACA, N. Y.

COPYRIGHT, 1919
By J. HORACE MCFARLAND, Editor

The 1920 American Rose Annual will be issued in March, 1920

Completely prepared, illustrated and printed by the
J. HORACE MCFARLAND COMPANY
Mount Pleasant Press
Harrisburg, Pa.

YOUR ROSE-GARDEN?

"You may be rich enough to buy a rose-garden as big as the Garden of Eden, . . . but unless you, with your own hands, participate to a greater or less degree in the care of your flowers, there may be a rose-garden, even a beautiful rose-garden, but it will never be YOUR garden."

THE LATE ADMIRAL AARON WARD.

(From article on page 103, 1918 Annual.)

THE AMERICAN ROSE SOCIETY
ORGANIZED MARCH 13, 1899

"To increase the general interest in the cultivation and improve the standard of excellence of the Rose for all people"

OFFICERS, 1918–1919

President	BENJAMIN HAMMOND
Vice-President	W. J. KEIMEL
Honorary Vice-Presidents	E. M. MILLS, D.D.
	J. HORACE MCFARLAND
	DR. ROBERT HUEY
	W. G. MCKENDRICK
Treasurer	HARRY O. MAY
Secretary	E. A. WHITE, Ithaca, N. Y.

Executive Committee:

E. ALLAN PIERCE (1919)	WALLACE R. PIERSON (1921)
ROBERT PYLE (1919)	ROBERT SIMPSON (1921)
GEORGE H. PETERSON (1919)	JOHN H. DUNLOP (1921)
LOUIS J. REUTER (1920)	J. HORACE MCFARLAND
JESSE A. CURREY (1920)	O. P. BECKLEY
S. S. PENNOCK (1920)	

Publication Committee:

E. A. WHITE   ROBERT PYLE   ROBERT SIMPSON

Former Presidents:

*WILLIAM C. BARRY	ALEXANDER MONTGOMERY
ROBERT CRAIG	F. R. NEWBOLD
BENJAMIN DORRANCE	WALLACE R. PIERSON
W. H. ELLIOTT	AUGUST F. POEHLMANN
ADOLPH FARENWALD	ROBERT SIMPSON
S. S. PENNOCK	

MEMBERSHIP

Life Members ($50) and Annual Members ($2) receive all publications, tickets to all exhibitions, and are entitled to vote at all meetings.

Affiliated membership can be secured for associations and societies interested in rose culture, at the rate of $1 per member each year, receiving in consequence the current American Rose Annual, supplied through the secretary of the affiliating organization.

Remit, with full address, to E. A. White, Secretary, Ithaca, N. Y.

---

*Deceased

EDITOR'S PREFACE

FACING, after the most destructive war the world has ever known, a peace which should set mankind in general far ahead in the scale of possibilities of human development, this fourth American Rose Annual makes its hopeful bow. Hopeful it is, because, during the Great War, no day passed in which somewhere the rose did not help to cheer the living or soothe the bereaved; and yet more hopeful, because a freed world will turn more surely from fighting to flowers as it works its onward and upward way of development.

The war has drawn all nations, save the sorrowful autocracies, closer together, and this 1919 American Rose Annual is almost an International Rose Annual in consequence of this feeling of community in the rose. England and her great colonies of Canada and Australia, her lesser colony in Bermuda; France and Italy, and even little, just-released Luxemburg, are heard from in these pages upon the world-subject of roses.

Roses seem to incite always the effort to improve, for all the nations, all the writers, are trying for better roses, to serve the better world we are now to make.

While the Editor has prepared this 1919 Annual under the peculiar handicap of service in Washington,—where he has been heeding the call of Uncle Sam for many busy months,—he believes the rose-presentation has not suffered in consequence, simply and only because his rose friends have done unusually well "their bit" in patriotic as well as in capable helpfulness. His thanks to them are at the same time a congratulation upon the result—their result.

In this Annual the record features begun in the first issue, that for 1916, have been continued and amplified. Perhaps the statistical form of presenting rose records, though undoubtedly compact, is less desirable than the chatty and narrative form? Only the readers of the Annual can decide!

Rather especial emphasis may be put on the survey of the nation's rose-supply, with its appurtenant presentation of a letter from the Chairman of the Federal Horticultural Board (on page 115), because of the importance of sustaining that same rose-supply by American production. As much emphasis may also be given to the encouraging advances in rose-hybridization reported in this volume.

The American Rose Society has weathered the war-storm in safety and in strength, and is facing, with confidence, a great advance in rose-love, rose-knowledge, and rose-culture. It has hopes, bright hopes, of more membership and consequently of more strength, warranting it in research work and in increased publication effort—the latter to be evidenced in a much-needed Rose Manual and a hardly less-needed Rose Catalogue. The Editor especially asks those who care to help in either effort to write him, particularly in relation to willingness to fill out and return a peculiarly complete and convenient description card of varieties that has been prepared.

What of the rose-future? "Better roses," say our friends; "roses better adapted to the variable climates of this land, of undoubted hardiness and vigor; roses blooming more finely and more freely; roses good to look at for habit and foliage when flowers are few. Better roses indeed!" So it may be, as our friendship for the Old World becomes less dependent and more brotherly, forcing upon us efforts here and results here. We should have men in America making roses as well as Paul and Dickson and McGredy, as finely as Guillot and Pernet-Ducher and Barbier, to the end that America may feed new rose-blood into the gardens of Europe from which she has long drawn in careless ease.

The rose-future is bright with rose-promise!

As the Annual is closing, a plantsman supporter of its issues comes in with the pleasing word that his advertisements in the book have been most effective in bringing about sales. Why not? Only honest tradesmen of the rose are admitted, and the Annual goes only to rose-hungry folks who believe in it. Thanks are due, both ways!

J. HORACE McFARLAND

Harrisburg, Pa.,
March 15, 1919.

CONTENTS

	Page
DEDICATION	3
EDITOR'S PREFACE	5
SILVER WEDDING ROSES . . . . *Barbara* Author of "The Garden of a Commuter's Wife"	9
FRAGRANT ROSES . . . . *Dr. W. Van Fleet*	14
ON A SUN-DIAL WREATHED WITH ROSES. Poem *Frederick F. Rockwell*	21
THE NORTHERN CHEROKEE ROSE . . . . *W. C. Egan*	22
AN ANNIVERSARY CANADIAN CIVIC ROSE GARDEN *The Editor*	24
PORTLAND'S NEW TEST-GARDEN . . . . . . *Jesse A. Currey*	26
THE FIRST TEXAS ROSE TEST-GARDEN . . . *N. M. McGinnis*	28
ROSE-BREEDING NOTES FOR 1918 . . . . . *Dr. W. Van Fleet*	29
THE PEDIGREE OF OPHELIA . . . . *The Editor*	35
"SPORTS" OR BUD-VARIATIONS IN THE ROSE . *C. S. Pomeroy*	36
FRANK N. MEYER'S ROSE CONTRIBUTIONS . . . *Peter Bisset*	38
THE MAKING OF A ROSE ENTHUSIAST AND HIS GARDEN . *George R. Mann*	42
THE PASSING OF A GREAT ROSARIAN. Tributes to the Memory of Admiral Aaron Ward . . . . *Collected by the Editor*	51
WINTER WORK WITH ROSES . . . . *Alfred W. Greeley*	57
RIDING A ROSE HOBBY IN MONTREAL . . . *Harold W. Nelles*	67
THE SECOND YEAR OF BACK-YARD BLOOM-RECORD . . . *A. P. Greeley*	71
MORE ABOUT CROWN-CANKER . . . . *L. M. Massey*	74
SAVE AND USE THE ROSES . . . . *Mrs. Andrew Wright Crawford*	78
THE 1918 ROSE SEASON IN ENGLAND . . . *Herbert L. Wettern*	80
THE ROSES OF AN ENGLISH LABOR LEADER . . . . *Letters to the Editor*	82
THE NATIONAL ROSE SOCIETY IN WARTIME . . . *The Editor*	83
ROSES IN ITALY. A Letter and a Memorial to M. Pierre Guillot . . *Countess Giulio Senni*	85
ROSES IN BERMUDA . . . . *Mrs. F. St. G. Caulfeild*	89
ROSES IN AUSTRALIA . . . . *George W. Walls*	92
WAYSIDE ROSES IN FRANCE . . . . . . *George C. Thomas, Jr.*	93
A GREAT FRENCH ROSE NURSERY . . . . . *Charles Pennock*	96
THE NEW FOREIGN ROSES	99
THE ROSE CUT-FLOWER SITUATION OF 1918 . *S. S. Pennock*	104
EXPERIENCE AND PROPHECY . . . . *Wallace R. Pierson*	106
ROSES CUT AND ROSES GROWING . . . . . . *Charles H. Totty*	108
WHERE ARE OUR ROSES COMING FROM? . . . . . *The Editor*	111
THE NATIONAL ROSE TEST-GARDEN IN 1918 . *F. L. Mulford*	116

CONTENTS

	Page
ROSE NOTES . . . . *The Editor and Others*	123

Railroad Roses in France—Standing a Hard Winter, 123; Another John Cook Rose Coming—An Experience with Multiflora, 124; Rose Advance in Ohio—A Wise Chamber of Commerce—Roses as Food, 125; The Rose, Climbing Souvenir of Wootton—Dr. Van Fleet's Rose Factory, 126; An American Rose Poet—International Coöperation Increasing—What's the Use of a Long Name?, 127; Los Angeles Takes World Honors—A Thomas Tiplady Story—Protecting Tender Roses, 128; The Toronto Horticultural Society—Flowers Barred from a Hospital—Hard Rose-Luck in Luxemburg, 129; Dr. Van Fleet Does Not Swear!—Turning Roses into Red Cross Cash, 130; What Are Leaves Good For?, 131; The Revival of Rose Interest—Sir Walter Raleigh—The Climbing Rose, Zephirine Drouhin—Climbing Roses Doing Double Duty, 132; Cut-Roses in Great Demand in France—California is "Different"—Harison's Yellow Rose Sets Some Seeds—The Roses We Need, 133.

A PARTIAL LIST OF ROSES INTRODUCED IN AMERICA . .
Charles E. F. Gersdorff 134

THE 1918 WORK OF THE AMERICAN ROSE SOCIETY:
- THE NINETEENTH ANNUAL MEETING 148
- EXECUTIVE COMMITTEE MEETINGS 153
- FOURTH ANNUAL FIELD DAY 156
- THE GARDEN EXHIBIT AT ELIZABETH PARK ROSE TEST-GARDENS, HARTFORD, CONN. 157
- RULES FOR REGISTRATION OF NEW ROSES 158
- REGISTRATION OF NEW ROSES IN 1918 158
- AMERICAN ROSE SOCIETY MEDALS AND CERTIFICATES FOR NOVELTIES . 160
- MEDALS AWARDED IN 1918 160
- SPECIAL PRIZES AWARDED IN 1918 161
- SPECIAL PRIZES AVAILABLE FOR 1919 161
- REGULATIONS AND SCALE OF POINTS FOR JUDGING BLOOMS AND PLANTS . 161
- AFFILIATION OF LOCAL SOCIETIES WITH THE AMERICAN ROSE SOCIETY . 161

LIST OF MEMBERS 162

INDEX 183

INDEX TO ADVERTISERS . . . . 3d cover

LIST OF PLATES

	Facing page
I. E. G. Hill's New American-bred Hybrid Tea, Rose Premier. (Colored plate) . . . . *Frontispiece*	
II. What Madame Plantier Offers the June Bride	9
III. New American-grown Hybrid Tea Rose, Mrs. John C. Ainsworth	24
IV. Method of Rapid Propagation	41
V. The Late Admiral Aaron Ward	56
VI. Rosa xanthina, as Blooming near Washington, D. C.	75
VII. Mr. Courtney Page, Hon. Secretary of the National Rose Society of England	86
VIII. Terminal Twig of Rosa xanthina	105
IX. Rosa xanthina normalis (the Single-flowered Form), as Growing near Washington, D. C.	120
X. Climbing Rose, Zephirine Drouhin, an Unusual Thornless Climber	137
XI. E. G. Hill's New Hybrid Tea Rose, Madame Butterfly (a sport from Ophelia)	152

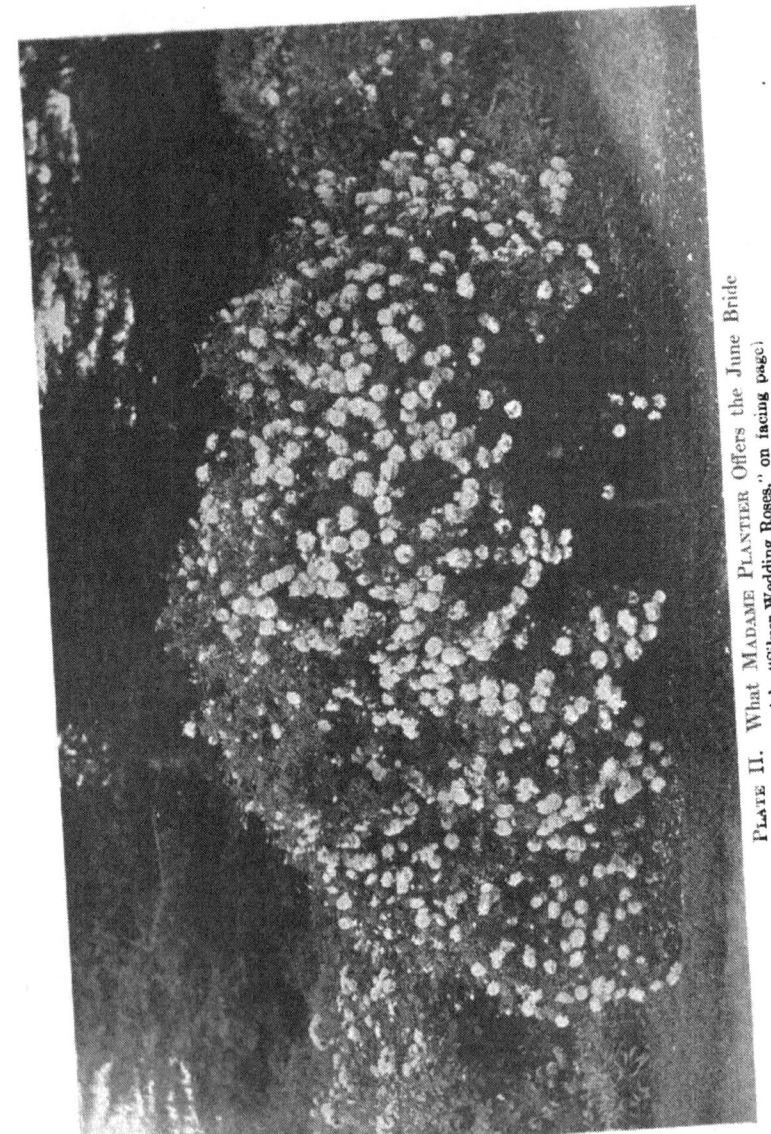

PLATE II. What Madame Plantier Offers the June Bride
(See article, "Silver Wedding Roses," on facing page)

THE AMERICAN ROSE ANNUAL

Silver Wedding Roses

By BARBARA, the Author of "The Garden of a Commuter's Wife"

EDITOR'S NOTE.—Looking up an old friend at what he thought was her sure-enough old home in Connecticut, the Editor found her not, one September day, until inquiry directed him to a new home nearby, already old in the sense of its charm of "homeyness." Here the brilliant author of many books of nature, birds, and the garden had done much more than make a home for herself and the genial "commuter." She had made, nearby, a truly wonderful bird-refuge, with a bird museum attached, to give the folks of Connecticut knowledge of their own feathered treasures, as well as to condense into a little park all the delights of bird-life that would attract the songsters.

It is necessary to write this as a background for Mrs. Wright's delightful essay on roses that rough it and make good "roses to cut and give away."

I WANT from you a little story about your own roses, for the good of the rose and for Auld Lang Syne," wrote the Editor of the American Rose Annual one day in midwinter. A story of my roses that should hold up its head amid the records of rose perfectionists and the pen-pictures of the wonderful rose-gardens of today? Such a thing seemed impossible to me, but then the words "for Auld Lang Syne" made me bold.

So I will tell you the story of what I may call our Silver Wedding roses, fragrant with the memories of the past, but planted in new soil, in a new home-site, new bushes, fresh, vigorous young roots, and set out with as unconquerable hope as of old. Yes, but with this difference: once we strove to have the biggest, best, and most notable of blooms. We courted rivalry; no trouble was too great; for to grow really fine roses one must either have a pocket full of money to pay for skilled labor, coupled with the knowledge of what one wants, or else the will and strength to give to rose-growing entire and single-hearted personal service, both of brain and brawn. *Now* all we seek are the modest roses of satisfaction, not competition—roses in plenty, but not too pampered to rough it a bit—roses to cut and give away without the slightest tinge of remorse at the possibility of having spoiled the symmetry of the bushes—and what greater satisfaction can come from the garden of one's later years than to have something to share in abundance and without calculation of cost? This then is really the only prize-winning quality of our Silver Wedding roses.

Why and how these roses came to be is quickly told. Four years ago, we—then being a family of but two (as often happens at about the time of the Silver Wedding journey!)—forsook a large place with its responsibilities, and set a picturesque and also very comfortable rambling cottage on the rocky bank of a five-acre calf-pasture across the road.

Hereabout a calf-pasture means a stretch of land having shade, water, and sufficient browsing for young cattle that will get their muscular development in searching for their food. This particular bit, in addition to a good spring, had groups of sturdy oak trees, patches of bayberry and barberry bushes. Young red cedars topped little knolls, and circling the rocks and waving above the deep green bays were groups of the pasture wild roses (*Rosa humilis*) and wonderful wands of our naturalized Sweetbrier (*R. rubiginosa*).

While the cottage was a-building, we realized that we had come into a wild garden of the sort where the art lies in knowing what *not* to do. It had been several years since the shrubs and herbage had been cropped, and everywhere lovely possibilities could be discovered, while in middle June wild roses began to dominate and give the keynote. We even curved the path of stepping stones—gathered from an old cellar—which led to the front porch, to protect a natural wild rose-bed.

In May we had gone back to the wild country, where lumbering had bared the land, and rescued from clearing and plowing several wagon-loads of thrifty bushes of mountain laurel and a half hundred white-flowering dogwoods (*Cornus florida*) with which we filled the leaf-mold hollows under and about the great oaks, thus securing a setting of many contrasts.

"Charming," said a friend of the type to whom what has been is always better than what is to be, "But you've no place in this rough land and impossible soil for a rose-garden. When building excitement is over you will be lonely without roses."

But we shall not be without roses—not in a rose-garden, but naturalized. As for the soil, we will make it. I know that we cannot follow the rule of removing the earth to the depth of three feet, putting in drainage, etc., etc. (You all know the professional directions that give amateurs without gardeners the blues!) In the first place, we should quickly strike rock; and, as the whole place is on a gentle slope, south by west, the roses will never have the wet feet that they abhor. We are going to spend this first season grubbing for fertile pockets, filling them with good soil, and then let nature and luck, or rather opportunity, do the rest.

Opportunity, thus challenged, immediately appeared in the shape of a quantity of peaty soil, the concentrated leaf-mold of ages, from a nearby pond that was being deepened. This, being banked up to dry and crumble, was later mixed with manure and lime, and the pocket-filler was ready, proving exactly what the light sandy loam of the place needed.

Then we ordered our roses—100 Hybrid Perpetuals, 150 Hybrid Teas, 50 climbers and creepers, and perhaps 50 odds and ends of the different types. Rootings of old-fashioned varieties, like Harison's Yellow, Thornless Blush, Moss, Cinnamon and Cabbage roses we brought from the old garden; they laid hold hungrily of the new soil and grew apace.

We bought only ungrafted stock with its own roots, in spite of the catalogue lure of "large grafted roses for immediate effect," and the assertion that "most varieties do best on Brier stock." Our ears are forever deaf to this plea, doubtless true from the standpoint of the rose perfectionist, but not so for the amateurs who do their own work, especially for the growers of Silver Wedding roses. The saying that you can always tell wild shoots from the stock because they have seven or more leaflets no longer holds good, since Rambler blood is running riot through the rose family. Of course, instinct and "know how" guide the old rose-grower about this, but if all the roses are on their own roots there is one less worry, and enough roses may be had so grown to keep an even balance of color and perfume.

Iris, peonies, delphiniums, *Lilium candidum*, phlox, and masses of Scotch clove pinks soon gave a settled look to the bit of garden in the swale, and here, in two long borders and some smaller beds, went the majority of the Hybrid Perpetuals and Hybrid Teas. These we planted in such a way that in autumn they might be hilled up, after the manner of corn planted in rows. This, together with a light top-dressing of manure in spring that is forked in, supplemented by a generous sprinkling of bone-dust, is all the protection and food that we find they need. At the time of hilling up we cut down all straggling tops to the height of two or three feet, so that the leverage, when wind-blown, shal not loosen the bushes in the ground. In early May we prune the Hybrid Perpetuals and Hybrid Teas again, according to whether a comparatively few large or many small flowers are wanted.

The climbers and creepers we never prune in the real sense, and only cut out the old wood. The best way to keep the Rambler tribe within bounds is to cut the blooming sprays freely when first in flower. In June and early July there are always weddings and school festivals, to say nothing of Children's Day in the churches, where our Silver Wedding "cut and come again" roses are always welcome for decoration.

A part of our climbers have arches and here and there rough pillars to hold them. One group we have planted into the landscape after the manner chosen by their wild sisters. On a rough bank a quantity of old mossy boulders from a fence lay tumbled in a heap; between these we packed our precious peat-and-loam compound, set in the climbers and creepers, and let them sprawl at will. Last summer, the third after planting, the bloom was riotous, and the long wands lassoed each other to their hurt. This year the tips will be pegged down.

The Hybrid Tea rose is fast pushing out the so-called Perpetual in the more modern gardens, because its blooms may be had all the season. Very good; but in our climate it is difficult to have good roses in late July and August because of the hot sun. The bud of today is faint, panting and overblown tomorrow.

For us the hardy roses of June seem the best. All the old darlings, mixed with the best of the new to keep them from feeling elderly, just like people: Magna Charta, Paul Neyron, Anna de Diesbach (Glory of Paris from now on, please!), *R. centifolia*, Captain Christy, Marshall P. Wilder, Prince Camille de Rohan, Xavier Olibo, Coquette des Blanches, dear old General Jack, the white and pink Crested Moss, the curious parti-colored York and Lancaster; and, above all, we revel in our great shrubs of Mme. Plantier, that in three years' time rival ours of the old garden.* A strong bush of the new "May

*See Plate III, facing page 24.

rose," Hugonis, set last fall in a deep pocket of our treasured soil, is already (February 5) reddening along the stalk, and will doubtless live up to its much-heralded reputation.

Three periods of anxiety come to the growers of even humble Silver Wedding roses, beginning late in May when the first spraying of dilute whale-oil soap is given, to be repeated once or twice before the buds show bright color, to down the green worms. Next, the green or black aphis cries out for dilute "Black-leaf 40." The third pest, the rose chafer, can only be grappled with and routed by the Commuter himself—a fruit-jar partly filled with kerosene in one hand, determination on his face and very old clothes on his body!

At sight of the first chafer, he begins his annual tour of duty among the rose bushes, wherever they may be. The Crimson Rambler, long banished by us because of its deadly monotony and lack of sentiment, is the only rose we have found quite free from chafers, while those roses of the lightest hues—blush, white, and yellow—seem fated; among climbers, Dr. W. Van Fleet and Silver Moon having the hardest struggle.

It is the custom to recommend golf as a suitable form of motiveful exercise for elderly men of business, but I am convinced that a morning and evening walk spent in rose-chafer catching and immersing is quite as beneficial.

Once, in middle October, I sent, with great hesitation, a box of Tea and Hybrid Tea roses, with Sweetbrier sprays for green, to a friend ill in the city—a brilliant woman of the literary world whose room was always a bower of orchids and long-stemmed hothouse roses. My roses looked so small and humble, with their short stems tucked under them in their nest of Sweetbrier, that it seemed foolish to send them forth.

Quickly came a message: "Barbara, please send me some more of your dear roses. I like them best of all; they are so sweet and *human*. Each one has a different face and expression!"

"What is the motive of this long disjointed ramble?" someone asks, as a perfectionist should. "Does the woman wish to discourage the growing of perfect roses?"

No, not that, but rather to keep from discouragement in rose-growing those to whom the having of the Silver Wedding type of rose is the only possibility.

Fragrant Roses

By DR. W. VAN FLEET
Department of Agriculture, Washington, D. C.

EDITOR'S NOTE.—It was a visit to Dr. Van Fleet's interesting perfume-garden at Arlington, under his guidance, that suggested the desirability of an account of fragrant roses. Dr. Van Fleet has kindly provided information and suggestion, and the article which follows is the last word on the subject. Who noted before that there was no odor of musk in the Musk rose, and none of cinnamon in the Cinnamon rose?

AGREEABLE fragrance is one of the most valued attributes of the perfect rose, though many indispensable species and varieties do not possess it in marked degree, and not a few are either odorless or even distasteful to the sense of smell. The name *Rosa fœtida* was given to the wild yellow rose of Persia by Herrmann in 1762, under the impression that the blooms had an unpleasant odor, and this offensive designation has been revived by the later botanists under the rule of priority, but it is safe to say that rose-lovers will continue to use *R. lutea* when referring to the botanical status of the yellow Brier group.

The flowers of the Persian and Harison's Yellow roses are practically scentless, while the foliage gives out, under moist conditions, a perceptible Sweetbrier fragrance. *R. xanthina*, one of the yellow roses of western China, and *R. Ecæ*, of Abyssinia, have, in some of their forms, foliage that emits during damp weather a keen and far from agreeable formic-acid smell that could have suggested the idea of fetor in a rose plant to an unappreciative systematist. The blooms of *R. xanthina*, *R. Ecæ*, *R. Hugonis*, and *R. persica*, or the berberis-leaved rose— all yellow-flowered, Oriental species—are either scentless or possess only a mere suggestion of the unwelcome hawthorn odor apparent in many forms of *R. multiflora* and *R. moschata*.

Passing from the unedifying consideration of roses with unpleasing odors to the really fragrant kinds, one may broadly state that the wild roses inhabiting the coastal regions of the Mediterranean Sea and the eastern shores of the Pacific and Atlantic oceans in the north temperate zone possess agreeable fragrance in the highest degree, while those native to the interior uplands of the respective continents are, to a great extent, devoid of this pleasing attribute. Thus, *R. rugosa*, of Japan and Siberia, *R. gallica* and *R. centifolia*, of the Mediterranean countries, *R. virginiana* and *R. humilis*, of our Atlantic coastal states, typify rose-perfume in its most pleasing form—the true oil or attar-of-rose fragrance. We may well call this the Centifolia odor, as *R. centifolia* and related species form the foundation of the attar-of-rose industry, In the foothills of India grows the gigantic *R. odorata*, which, in its dwarf form, typifies the tea-scented rose varieties of our gardens.

The wild roses of North Europe mostly have faint fragrance or are scentless, and the same may be said of our Middle West and Pacific Coast species, though there are a few exceptions in the extreme Northwest. *R. setigera*, the scentless Prairie rose, is a characteristic example of the lack of fragrance of the rose species of our interior country.

Passing to the various forms of rose-fragrance, the violet-like odor of *R. Banksiæ* may be mentioned. It is faint, but it will be recognized when thousands of blooms are expanded at the same time, as in the enormous plants so common in California. The cinnamon odor ascribed to *R. cinnamomea* and kindred species has never materialized in the blooms or foliage of any of the plants I am familiar with. The cinnamon idea is more easily associated with the color of the twigs than with any odor that arises from flower or foliage.

Mention has already been made of the none-too-agreeable cratægus-like or hawthorn odors that prevail in many wild roses of the Multiflora and Musk rose group. All species do not have it, and it usually is found in diminished intensity in the cultivated forms. I have yet to find a Musk rose, wild or cultivated, that emits anything resembling the real odor of musk.

True rose-fragrance arises from the presence of rose-oil or attar, a volatile oil elaborated in the petals of the blooms just before opening. It appears most abundantly in the cells near the base of the petals, yet is present in such small quantities that it usually requires a ton and a half of fresh-plucked rose petals to produce a pound of oil.

Rose-attar, at ordinary temperatures, more resembles a brownish butter than an oil, and is distinct from any other product of nature. Oils somewhat resembling it in odor are distilled from a species of pelargonium and from a South American wood. A base imitation, only fit for use in cheap soaps and unguents, is manufactured synthetically from coal-tar products, but true rose-attar can always be distinguished by the expert.

The agreeable tea-like fragrance of the tender everblooming roses of the *R. odorata* group is of a different character. It cannot be extracted by distillation, and is only feebly preserved by the grease or *enfleurage* process of recovering flower perfumes, but, when united by hybridization with the attar-scented roses, there results the still more exquisite perfumes found in the various Hybrid Tea varieties.

There is one remaining entrancing rose odor—the despair of perfumery chemists!—that of Sweetbrier foliage after a rain. It cannot be recovered by any known process, and lives and dies with the occasion during which it is perceived. That would be a happy day in which science had been able to fix and preserve this delightful odor! The unpleasant ant-hill or formic-acid smell of the leaves of *R. xanthina* and *R. Ecæ* in the early morning, and after rains, has already been mentioned, and is only to be gotten rid of by choice of the proper varieties of these species, otherwise so desirable for their earliness and for the rare yellow color of the neat little blooms. *R. Hugonis*, also early and yellow-flowered, in my experience does not possess this disagreeable feature, and is in many ways better than either.

Attar of roses is secured from the fresh petals of fragrant roses by the ordinary processes of distillation and condensation used to recover all essential or volatile oils produced in nature, and no very elaborate or costly apparatus is needed for the purpose. It exists in such small quantity, however, even in the best perfume varieties—thirty-five to forty large blooms being required for a single drop—that it remains in solution in the water of condensation that comes over from the still, and must be washed out with ether or redistilled several times before it may be skimmed off, as with more abundant oils. These first waters, however, are most deliciously scented, and, in this country at least, would be more valuable as true commercial rose-waters than the attar itself when extracted from them.

Commercial rose-attar has hitherto been produced in southern France, where it has long been an important industry, and in Bulgaria, Turkey, and Germany in about the order named. Every effort should be made to encourage the industry in France, but the memory of the other countries will long remain a stench in the nostrils of civilization.

The rose varieties used for the purpose in all the countries concerned in perfume production are about the same, mostly natural hybrids of *R. centifolia* and *R. gallica*, the former predominating where quality, and the latter where quantity, of product is most highly appreciated. There is an approach to nature in *R. centifolia minor* and *R. gallica officinalis*, but neither, in all probability, represents the true wild type, and they are little used in practical operations. *R. gallica* in its simpler forms is about as sweet as *R. centifolia* and is a taller and more vigorous grower, but with less abundant petals. In its divergent types, such as *R. alba* and *R. damascena*, the former much grown in Bulgaria, the fragrance is less agreeable than in *R. centifolia*.

The practical perfume varieties all increase by suckers from the large surface-roots, and the usual procedure is to tear apart the clumps after eight or more years of cropping and reset the rooted canes and suckers in new soil. All have but one short season of intensive bloom in spring, giving rise to a great need for labor during picking-hours, which are limited to early morning. This is the most expensive operation connected with rose-attar production, wherefore varieties of equal merit, blooming over a longer period, have long been desired.

The late Monsieur Jules Gravereaux, the famous rose collector of L'Hay in France, sought with marked success to develop continuous-blooming perfume varieties by hybridizing *R. rugosa*, one of the sweetest of wild roses, with the best varieties grown for practical attar distillation. Rose Parfum de l' Hay is the best known of his productions, and has been tried in some quantity in the Arlington perfume experiments of the United States Bureau of Plant Industry. Blooms from 300 plants were collected and distilled for several seasons, in comparison with those of most other perfume roses, the result showing that it is at least equal, under our conditions, in yield and quality to the best of the kind in general use. The amount of attar obtained worked out to more than the general average rate of one pound to 3,000 pounds of fresh petals, and the quality is undeniably high. Only one other variety, Mrs. Curzon, evidently a Centifolia-Gallica hybrid, with the cabbage rose type predominating, greatly exceeded this average, giving almost double the relative yield, but the blooms were rather scantily produced during the usual short spring season. Rose Parfum de l'Hay blooms plentifully in June and at intervals throughout the summer and autumn, the late flowers being especially abundant in August, the seasonal production appearing to be considerably greater than that of the excessive spring bloomers. Thus the labor of collecting and distilling the petals extends over a far longer interval and should be accomplished by a smaller force of workers. In common with many Rugosa hybrids, it can only be obtained as plants budded or grafted on the usual rose stocks, making it more expensive and less useful than sucker-grown varieties that reproduce themselves from rootbuds.

The writer has effected many hybridizations of *R. rugosa* and some of our most fragrant native species with the Old-World perfume roses during the past twenty years, but no varieties of practical merit are yet in sight. If we wish to stock up on commercial perfume producers of this character, we will have to go to the south of France for the start.

The Arlington experiments seem to show that the cultivation of perfume roses in this country and the working up of their products presents no practical difficulty except that of differences in labor costs. There are, doubtless, in the Appalachian region, thousands of acres of well-watered upland soils of the somewhat heavy character favored by deep-rooting roses, as well suited for perfume culture as any in France or Bulgaria, and with requisite persistence the industry could be established here if the promoters were not too keen for quick profits. As with commercial tea-growing, provision would have to be made to gather and care for the special labor needed for picking the blooms when ready.

European chemists, with characteristic cynicism, have devoted much energy to the problem of adulterating rose-attar so that it will pass muster with the importing fraternity, and it is safe to say that very few ounces ever reach this country in its pure state. The production of genuine rose perfume preparations, wholly originating in America, might establish a standard that Europe and the Orient would find it difficult to ignore.

The fragrance of our garden and exhibition roses, without doubt, comes in the first instance from the hybridization of *R. chinensis*, a species naturally of faint fragrance, with *R. gallica*, of Europe, giving rise to the deliciously scented Hybrid Perpetuals of old gardens, and, recently, by the crossing of these with *R. odorata*, to production of the immensely popular Hybrid Teas, some of which are intensely fragrant, while others entirely lack this most desirable quality. Tea roses themselves have their own characteristic fragrance, as is typified by the name, and this, in many instances, blends well with heavier Centifolia odor, rising occasionally to the highest pitch of pungent sweetness. The blend of tea-scent with muskiness in some of the dwarf Polyanthas is agreeable, but the Centifolia fragrance is rarely brought out in hybrids between *R. multiflora* and varieties or species carrying Centifolia odors.

Rose aromas are not congenial to all persons, and occasionally an individual is found to whom they are annoying, and even hurtful, in the way of causing catarrhal symptoms; but to the overwhelming majority of gardeners, fragrance is a prime requisite for the thorough enjoyment of a rose bloom.

We will all continue to grow Frau Karl Druschki until we can get a hardy, white outdoor rose at least as good that includes the fragrance so noticeably lacking in this indispensable variety. There are many lists of fragrant garden roses that vary much with the taste and experience of the compiler. The following species and varieties have proved themselves satisfactory to the writer, but their number could greatly be increased.

SPECIFIC TYPES

Rosa rugosa: Common type *R. rugosa*, *R. rugosa alba* and *magnifica*, Souvenir de Pierre Leperdrieux, Blanc Double de Coubert, Calocarpa, Parfum de l'Hay, Conrad F. Meyer, and New Century.

Rosa virginica, or *lucida*, type and variety *alba; R. humilis*.

R. nitida: R. centifolia in the old Cabbage roses and the Moss roses, Gracilis and Crested Moss; *R. gallica* in Damask and Provence varieties: the typical form of *R. gallica officinalis*.

Rosa bella is the most fragrant of the new Chinese species that has come to my hand, and is well worth growing in any garden in which room can be spared for wild roses.

HYBRID TYPES

Hybrid Perpetuals. Most of the older Hybrid Perpetuals are gratefully fragrant. Among the best are Alfred Colomb, Captain Hayward, Fisher Holmes, Gen. Jacqueminot, Gloire de Margottin, Jean Liabaud, Hugh Dickson, Magna Charta, Marshall P. Wilder, Mrs. Charles Wood, Paul Neyron, Prince Camille de Rohan, and Victor Hugo. There are many others.

Hybrid Teas. The list of highly fragrant Hybrid Teas is a long one, and there are also many that are quite devoid of odor. In a selection for a bed in the perfume-garden, American Beauty (which, to be honest, we should call Mme. Ferdinand Jamain) would take high rank, unless it is preferred to regard it as a Hybrid Perpetual. A few varieties of special excellence are Augustine Guinoisseau, Chateau de Clos Vougeot, George Dickson, Gen. MacArthur, Gruss an Teplitz, La France, Lieutenant Chaure, Magnafrano, and Princess Bonnie.

Tea Roses. Teas are nearly all desirable for the delicate and sprightly tea-like odor exhaled by the blooms. Few are lacking in this respect. Among the best are Bon Silene, Devoniensis, Safrano, and Isabella Sprunt. The yellow Teas are fragrant to a noticeable extent, and this characteristic extends to the hybrid climbing forms, such as Lamarque and Marechal Niel, usually classed as Noisettes. Climbing Niphetos and Climbing Perle des Jardins are most fragrant of the pure Tea climbers.

Fragrant Hardy Climbing Roses. In this class there appears nothing better than Ards Rambler, Birdie Blye, Reine Marie Henriette and Zephirine Drouhin, although Mme. d'Arblay and *R. Wichuraiana* have delicate odors not to be overlooked.

Roses with Scented Foliage. *Rosa rubiginosa*, the Sweetbrier, stands first in the list; *R. agrestis* has a similar quality in less degree, followed by Harison's Yellow, Persian Yellow, and a few other derivatives of *R. lutea*. The Sweetbrier hybrids, with the exception of Lord and Lady Penzance, do not possess fragrant foliage in noticeable degree, though the blooms of several varieties are pleasantly perfumed.

On a Sun-Dial Wreathed with Roses

By FREDERICK F. ROCKWELL*

I have beheld at dawn the fresh blown rose,
With trembling silver at her heart of gold;
And then returned, e'er the first light at dusk
    was burning,
E'er the sun's short half circle reached its
    close;—
Her shattered petals lay upon the mold;
    Dust unto dust returning.

"So frail a thing is Beauty!"—so the dial
Of brass and stone, marking the marching hours
Year after year, whispered—(or was it the
    wind sighing?)
"How brief! how barren! This morn a little
    while
She laughed and nodded to her sister flowers
    Dead now—ere the day's dying!"

The sightless dial, that has not learned to know
For all its years, the shadow from the sun,
How like the world in self-content but warped
    philosophy!
Each silken petal that has fluttered low
Flashed, e'er it fell, a smile from God, and won
    Thereby to immortality!
        —From *The American Woman.*

*See "An American Rose Poet," in Rose Notes, page 127.—EDITOR.

The Northern Cherokee Rose

(*Rosa spinosissima altaica*)

By W. C. EGAN, Egandale, Highland Park, Ill.

EDITOR'S NOTE.—The beautiful hardy rose which Mr. Egan has appropriately christened the "Northern Cherokee Rose" was illustrated in the 1916 Annual, from a photograph supplied by Mr. Charles Downing Lay, who wrote of it on page 18 of the same book. It is one of the comparatively few roses that may be considered as available lawn shrubs, apart from the coddled inmates of the expensively prepared rose-beds.

IN OUR justifiable enthusiasm for the Hybrid Tea roses and the inclined-to-be-tender climbers, we must, nevertheless, bear in mind that there are thousands of gardens in the United States where climatic and pocketbook conditions do not allow their cultivation. These gardens require a rose of unquestionable hardiness and with a rugged constitution.

The owners of these harder-luck gardens love a rose as much as we do, and the "propagating" members of the American Rose Society should endeavor to increase for them the number of varieties and range of colors of definitely hardy roses.

There is a rose of this class that nurserymen seem to have fought shy of. It suckers freely in an open soil, so that a stock could soon be worked up. For the want of a better common name, I call it the "Northern Cherokee rose."

The only objection to its scientific appellation—*Rosa spinosissima altaica*—is that one must be particularly sober when pronouncing it or he may get balled up among the s's! National prohibition will soon eradicate this handicap, but not the s's!

While originally described as a species, it is now considered as belonging to the Scotch group. It is a native of the Altai Mountains in Siberia, has been known to cultivation since 1818, and in 1895 was described as "a rose almost lost to cultivation."

It has, unfortunately, also been known as *R. grandiflora*, a name also applied in European catalogues to a climbing form of the Polyantha rose, thus creating much confusion. In fact, my first effort to obtain this rose was suggested by reading a description of it under the name of *R. grandiflora*. I imported some plants, but received the climbing Polyantha, which went skating

THE NORTHERN CHEROKEE ROSE

the first winter after planting and never returned. I had relied upon the reputed entire hardiness of the Altaica form!

The true *R. spinosissima altaica* is absolutely hardy without any winter protection, and seems free from the attacks of mildew or insects, though it is sometimes troubled with a scale that is easily controlled by spraying.

It forms a bushy shrub about five feet tall and in an open soil spreads freely, just as do the other forms of the Scotch rose. In May and June it is smothered in large clusters of single, paper-white flowers, enhanced in their beauty by the numerous bright yellow stamens in their centers. One vigorous shoot will be crowned by a cluster of these pure white flowers large enough and handsome enough to creditably perform the function of a bridal bouquet at any wedding. I have often thought of this when its blooms were at the height of perfection, but it always happened that no swain of my acquaintance had popped the vital question at an opportune time, such as would bring the culmination of his ardent desire just when the blooms were at their best. Perhaps some loving couple will arrange with me to be married on the day of the maximum bloom of the Northern Cherokee roses; then I can happily provide the decorations.

If I were asked where this rose could be obtained I would have to answer, "I can't tell you." There are groups of it at the Arnold Arboretum and at the Kew Garden, but I know of no nurseryman carrying it in stock. I have had my plant some twenty-five years, always in one "hole" in the lawn. This hole has been kept free of sod for a space four feet in diameter, and as most of its suckers come up in the sod outside this four-foot circle, they are cropped off by the lawn-mower. A few come up within the circle and are tenderly lifted and potted as gifts to friends.

Some years ago I gave a small sucker plant to a friend who, happily, placed it in a large bed of enriched soil. His plant is now not only much larger than mine, but has enabled him, through its offshoots, to present quite a number to his friends.

Enterprising nurserymen should resurrect this rose from the undeserved oblivion in which it rests and offer it to the general public. The beauty of its bloom ought to be enjoyed as well as its excellent quality as a lawn shrub.

An Anniversary Canadian Civic Rose-Garden
By THE EDITOR

THE growth of the municipal rose-garden idea in the United States is easy to note. Usually such gardens are the result of either official or commercial action, through a collective body like that sustaining the effort in Portland, Ore., described by the mayor of that city in last year's Annual and reported upon by Mr. Currey on another page.

The Dominion of Canada, however, is affording us an example of another form of municipal rose-garden, not depending altogether either upon action of the community officials or upon any commercial body.

In celebration of the completion of forty years of business in St. Catharines, Ontario, Hon. W. B. Burgoyne—who has not only been the publisher during that time of the St. Catharines *Standard*, but has been honored as the chief executive of the thriving little city near Niagara Falls which is itself nearly a great rose-garden—has, under date of February 1, 1919, sent his check to the mayor of St. Catharines to be used "toward the establishing of a civic rose-garden in my native town, at such place as the Council may deem best."

Anyone who has been in St. Catharines, especially toward the latter part of June or in the early days of July, and has realized the intense interest of the people of that community in roses, will understand that this gift assures a creditable accomplishment. The mayor and the council of St. Catharines will, undoubtedly, deal with Mr. Burgoyne's generous offer, not as the ordinary and casual officials of the average town, but as those rose-lovers who know what can be done as well as what ought to be done.

In his letter transmitting the gift to Mayor Elson, Mr. Burgoyne mentions the fact that he had provided in his will for the bequest, believing that during the war it was not practicable to undertake the actual work. He evidences the spirit which should animate the whole American continent when

PLATE III. New American-grown Hybrid Tea Rose, MRS. JOHN C. AINSWORTH
(See page 27)

he writes: "The war is now over, and we can begin to turn our thoughts more and more to matters of civic beautification, betterment, and beneficence."

As the Editor well knows, by reason of long acquaintance with Mr. Burgoyne, and also because he has visited St. Catharines, this foundation is sure to work, because Mr. Burgoyne will make it work. Indeed, in his letter he goes further by showing how a design may be had and proposing that immediate action be taken. He also gives so good a reason for a civic rose-garden that it is here transcribed:

"A civic rose-garden would be very valuable in testing out all new introductions for the benefit of all amateur rose-growers, and during the blooming season the hospitals could be daily supplied with an abundance of the Queen of Flowers."

It will thus be seen that not only are the rose-growers of St. Catharines to be advantaged, but the rose is to do more completely its beneficent work among the sick, by reason of Mr. Burgoyne's generosity.

It would be omitting an important corollary to the civic advantage certain to result from Mr. Burgoyne's action if there was not mention made of his activity, not only in the direction of general civic benefit in St. Catharines and in Ontario, but through the Ontario Horticultural Society (of which he has been president) in carrying forward the peculiarly fine work fostered by the government of Ontario for developing a love for everything that grows in the land as part of the civic spirit of the Dominion of Canada. Well-nigh a hundred organizations exist throughout the province, to each of which the Ontario government makes a substantial annual money contribution as well as providing oversight and suggestions. The consequent interest and advantage to the whole people may well serve as an example for emulation in the United States.

Mr. Burgoyne's beneficence is commended to Americans who might well follow it. What better commemoration of some business or special anniversary could there be than the foundation of a municipal rose-garden?

Portland's New Test-Garden

By JESSE A. CURREY, Portland, Ore.

EDITOR'S NOTE.—On page 33 of the 1918 Annual, Hon. George L. Baker, Mayor of Portland, Ore., detailed the plans, rules and support of the remarkable new municipal rose test-garden just then established in the rose city of the Pacific Northwest. Mr. Currey, who originated the plan of this place for the testing of new roses only, details below the experiences of the first season.

ALTHOUGH less than a year old, and despite the difficulties of shipping plants due to the war, the new test-garden at Portland, Ore., has obtained a good start, and many new roses have been sent there to be tested under the favorable climatic conditions of the Pacific Northwest.

This garden is designed for the outdoor testing of new roses only, and none are received which have been in commerce more than a year. The roses are given three tests. In the first section they are given the same kind of treatment as to cultivation, spraying, fertilizing, and pruning as they would receive in the average garden of an amateur. In the second section they are given special treatment to develop them to their greatest beauty. In the third section, which is in another locality, they are given a test to determine their natural disease-resisting qualities.

Owing to the fact that the greater number of roses in the garden were not received until late spring, and therefore had no opportunity to develop, prizes were not awarded in 1918. In 1919 prizes will be awarded, and these will include special awards by the city government of Portland for the best bush and climber, a special prize for the best rose originated by an amateur, and also a special prize for the best rose developed on the Pacific Coast. Booklets describing the garden, entry cards and shipping tags can be secured by addressing the Park Bureau, Portland, Ore. The American Rose Society has appointed a special committee to supervise this garden, and the writer, its chairman, will be pleased to answer any inquiries from members.

The European growers are apparently deeply interested in the new garden, as the entries from England have been very gratifying when the difficulty of shipping plants due to the war is considered. While the rules of the garden provide that each entry must be submitted in three or more plants, the European

PORTLAND'S NEW TEST-GARDEN

growers, to overcome any defects in individual plants, have, as a rule, sent ten or more plants for each entry, with the result that the display of new English roses is quite large.

Hugh Dickson, of Belfast, Ireland, sent the new garden more than a hundred plants, and his entries included Marchioness of Ormonde, H. P. Pinkerton, Ethel Dickson, H. D. M. Barton, and Golden Spray.

Elisha J. Hicks, of Hurst, Berks, England, also sent about 100 plants, including Mrs. Freddie Hunter, Mrs. Dunlop Best, Charles E. Shea, and Climbing Lady Hillingdon.

Another English exhibitor is G. Gibson & Co., of Bedale, they having sent Leslie Gibson, a novelty, rose-pink in color, flaked with white.

The list of American growers is naturally headed by E. G. Hill, of Richmond, Ind., who is having tested in the garden Columbia, Mary Hill, Rose Premier, Rose Victory, Double Ophelia, and Seedling No. 601.

Howard & Smith, of Los Angeles, have a large entry list including Los Angeles, Mrs. F. W. Rindge, Teresa Morley, and unnamed seedlings No. 252, No. 357, No. 1 and No. 211.

Capt. George C. Thomas, Jr., of Chestnut Hill, Pa., the well-known amateur, before his departure for the war front sent to the garden, to be entered in the amateur section, No. 4A, a cross of Aviateur Bleriot and Mme. Caroline Testout; No. 89A, a cross of Sylvia and Dorothy Page-Roberts.

Other entries are May Martin, by Martin & Forbes of Portland; Mrs. John C. Ainsworth* and three unnamed seedlings, by Clarke Bros. of Portland; Florence Chenoweth, a yellow sport of Mme. Edouard Herriot, by C. B. Chenoweth, of Mt. Vernon, Wash.; Bonnie Prince, by James Cook of Boston; Mrs. Charles Gersdorff, by C. E. F. Gersdorff, of Washington, D. C.

Plants will be received at any time by the new test-garden, but the Park Bureau of Portland prefers, when possible, to have dormant plants for late fall or winter planting, as at Portland planting is carried on practically throughout the year.

*See Plate III, facing page 24. Mrs. John C. Ainsworth is a sport of Mrs. Charles Russell, described as an "even shade of rose-pink inside and out, and practically fadeless."

The First Texas Rose Test-Garden
By N. M. McGINNIS
Associate Professor of Horticulture, College Station, Texas

EDITOR'S NOTE.—Most significant is the taking up of rose-study by educational institutions, heretofore confining their efforts to items that satisfy the stomach appetite rather than the eye and soul appetite! Last year the Annual chronicled the advent of a rose test-garden in Ohio, attached to the Ohio Experiment Station, and now Texas joins in.

THE Rose Test-Garden at the Agricultural and Mechanical College of Texas was established in the late winter and early spring of 1917. By the time the planting-season ended we had six plants each of 129 varieties in the garden, representing several species. The plants were given by interested nurserymen who realized the eventual value of the garden.

The garden is located on a rather level tract of land, and can embrace as much as four or five acres if the planting requires that much. The soil is uniform throughout, of the Lufkin fine sandy loam type, and is from ten to twelve inches deep.

When war was declared, the College adopted a policy that all of its energies should be spent along the lines of increased feed- and food-production. Therefore, the sponsors for the garden intermitted its development. During the interim, however, cultivation and care of the 129 varieties were maintained.

The past two years, from December, 1916, to November, 1918, were the driest that this region has experienced, according to the recollections of the oldest inhabitants. This brought out some interesting facts concerning the ability of certain varieties to grow and produce wonderful crops of blooms under trying conditions. The varieties that made the best growth and gave the best crop of blooms during the two years of drought are:

Anna de Diesbach, La Tosca, Papa Gontier, Gruss an Teplitz, Frau Karl Druschki, Maman Cochet, Paul Neyron, Mme. Gabriel Luizet, Magna Charta, Kaiserin Augusta Victoria, President Carnot, Jonkheer J. L. Mock, Prince d'Arenberg, Radiance, and Baby Elegance.

Since peace has been declared, work in the garden has been resumed with renewed enthusiasm and interest. The Texas Experiment Station has joined us in the project, and we have applied to the American Rose Society for recognition.

Rose-Breeding Notes for 1918

By DR. W. VAN FLEET
Department of Agriculture, Washington, D. C.

EDITOR'S NOTE.—As will appear on perusal of these notes, the war excitement has not prevented real progress toward the development of better roses for and in America. Dr. Van Fleet uses rare ability and insight in his patient work, and discouragements do not daunt him. Taken in connection with his articles in the 1916, 1917 and 1918 Annuals, and with his delightful discussion of perfume roses on page 14 of this book, his contributions to recorded real rose knowledge are of unique value.

ROSE-BREEDING, for the development of hardy garden varieties at Bell Experiment Plot, Glendale, Md., was conducted on a more extended and apparently more successful scale in 1918 than in former years. A greater number of new and previously untried rose species becomes available each season and are utilized to the utmost in the hope of gaining characteristics of value.

A collection of rare old garden roses and little-cultivated western species that may come into partial bloom the coming summer has been most kindly supplied by the Arnold Arboretum of Boston. This should open up new fields of endeavor when fully available.

It is, perhaps, not profitable to recount the pollinations made during the past season. The final outcome in the way of blooming seedlings bears such small relation to the hybridizations actually effected and the number of apparently good seeds secured, even under the most painstaking cultural conditions, that disappointment is almost sure to follow high anticipations, while the quality of the offspring of the most promising crosses is apt to fall below expectations. Nevertheless, persistent work in any line of effort is likely to bring encouraging results which may in time measure up to our more reasonable aspirations.

As cheering notes of progress we can report considerable improvement in the newer hybrids of *Rosa rugosa, R. Hugonis, R. Soulieanea*, and *R. Moyesii*. The range of color in *R. rugosa* is steadily being extended, and now covers in single and double, constant-blooming forms about all shades except yellow, from the clearest of whites to glowing crimson.

Yellow flowers may be had by the use of pollen from Persian Yellow, Harison's Yellow, *R. Hugonis*, and *R. xanthina*, but the colorings are far from pure and the blooms leave much to be desired in the way of size and finish. The *R. rugosa* × *R. Hugonis* crosses are very early and vigorous, with remarkably handsome foliage and a profusion of cream- and primrose-tinted blooms, some of which produce seeds. It may be that in time we will get bright yellow-flowered Rugosas, with all the added attractions of the type.

Several exceptionally attractive crosses of *R. rugosa* with Triomphe Orleanais came to notice last year. They are characterized by compact habit, dense glossy foliage and upright shoots topped with immense, broad clusters of bright, cherry-red, semi-double flowers an inch or more in diameter. The spring bloom clothes the entire plant, and this is followed at frequent intervals by other crops culminating in a secondary grand outburst in September. One individual has the petals fringed or laciniated like a dianthus, and the pungent Multiflora fragrance derived from the pollen parent further emphasizes the Scotch-pink effect of the bloom-clusters. A white-flowered hybrid of *R. rugosa* and *R. multiflora* has already been described under the name of *R. Iwara*, and the newcomers should doubtless take their place in this new group about to be formed. The main effort in the development of *R. rugosa* is to secure high-class blooms of the Hybrid Perpetual and Hybrid Tea types on vigorous, hardy, disease-resistant plants, and continuous progress is being made in this direction.

Rosa Hugonis is affording greater encouragement in hybridization than in previous years. The ideal yellow garden rose is far from being in evidence, but some of the *R. Hugonis* hybrids are worth working with. The blend of *R. Hugonis* and *R. spinosissima altaica*, a superior white-flowered form of *R. spinosissima** from the Altai Mountains of southern Siberia, gives rise to strong, erect plants with glossy foliage, densely covered with well-finished single and double blooms, intermediate in size and coloring between the parents. The effect of these elegantly formed bushes, some six feet in height the

---

*See Mr. W. C. Egan's account of this rose on p. 22 of this Annual, and the picture of it facing page 17 of the 1916 Annual.—EDITOR.

third year from seed, is very striking in early spring, and the foliage endures well until early winter, turning a good yellow in autumn. As some of these hybrids produce seeds, it may be possible to develop brighter coloring in future generations, without material loss in habit.

The Scotch rose, or *R. spinosissima* group, appears to "nick" better with *R. Hugonis* than the Rugosas and other hardy species, some of which produce veritable freaks in the way of first-generation hybrids, though succeeding progeny may show improvement.

The first *R. Hugonis* seedling containing Hybrid Tea blood has bloomed for three seasons and is interesting, if not beautiful. The pollen parent was most likely Radiance, and the large, double, pinkish yellow flowers afford strong resemblance to that excellent variety in form and fragrance. The plant is healthy, hardy, and has grown over four feet in height. It fruits sparingly and shows signs of a fair increase by suckers.

Rosa Soulieana, a species from which little was expected, continues to give excellent results. Mention was made in the 1918 Annual of attractive hybrids of *R. Soulieana* with *R. Wichuraiana* and the white-flowered form of *R. virginiana* or *R. lucida*. These have been distanced by a blend of *R. Soulieana, R. setigera, R. Wichuraiana,* and *R. odorata* in the form of the old Tea rose, Devoniensis. In this complex hybrid, *R. setigera* appears to have furnished the hardiness, *R. odorata* the size and finish of the wonderfully numerous, pure white, single blooms that cover the entire plant in season, and the other two species the glaucous, resistant foliage and strong, arching growth that render the vigorous plants practically independent of support. This variety has been given the provisional number of W. S. 18, and as it fruits with great freedom may be of further utility in breeding.

Rosa Soulieana has also produced double blooms, of small size but great perfection of outline, in our breeding experiments, and in the second or F. 1 generation gives rise to very dwarf, everblooming plants of the general character of *R. Pissardii* (*R. moschata nastarana*), a Musk rose hybrid greatly favored in old gardens.

We may yet secure some fine bedding varieties of *R. Soulie-*

ana of the dwarf Polyantha type. The fragrance of *R. Soulieana*, preserved in its hybrids, is faint, but perhaps the most pleasing of any of the species of the Musk rose group.

Owing to its poor seeding abilities when grown as grafted plants on heavy soil, less progress has been made than was hoped for with *R. Moyesii*, notable among wild roses for the deep red coloring and waxy texture of its widely expanded blooms. Now that our plants have been transferred to the sandy loam of Bell Experiment Plot, and have become established on their own roots, seeds are more freely borne, and a fair number of hybrids are under way. Pollen was plentifully produced, even when the fruits failed to mature, and a few early crosses, the result of applying it to the stigmas of other species and varieties, have sufficiently developed to show prospective value.

The most striking is W. S. No. 5, with an unnamed Wichuraiana-Setigera hybrid as seed parent. This, at four years from germination, forms a fine plant with arching shoots six to eight feet high, covered in June with blackish crimson single blooms nearly three inches across. Even the filaments of the stamens are colored, as in *R. Moyesii*, but the petals have a white base, making a striking contrast with the deep coloring of the other portions of the flower. The plant appears exceptionally healthy and hardy, and will be propagated for dissemination and trial.

Of another type is *R. Malyi* × *R. Moyesii*, a compact little upright bush with blooms almost identical with Moyesii, but likely to be produced with greater profusion. *R. Malyi* is a rarity, found only on Monte Santo in Dalmatia, and is thought to be a possible natural hybrid between *R. pendulina* and *R. spinosissima*. It is a most desirable, dwarf, early-blooming wild rose, with bright crimson flowers and of compact habit, but appears quite difficult to propagate. The hybrid with *R. Moyesii* may prove very useful for hedges and rockwork.

Rosa setipoda, until within the last two years, has been an even shyer seed-producer than *R. Moyesii*, notwithstanding its profusion of bloom. A few hybrids, produced by the use of *R. setipoda* pollen on other species, are under way. Only seedlings of *R. rugosa* × *R. setipoda* have yet bloomed, and most of them show imperfect development of the flower-buds. One individual has promise as a dwarf cluster-rose of distinction.

The premier English rose of 1918 appears to be Mermaid, said to be a product of *R. bracteata*, the Macartney rose, and a tea-scented variety. The blooms are described as very large, cream-yellow, with conspicuous anthers. Mermaid has received about all the available honors and medals of the season, and doubtless will be widely grown wherever it is sufficiently hardy. Good varieties are to be expected when *R. bracteata* and *R. odorata* in choice forms are bred together, and many rivals to Mermaid may appear in the future. Our endeavors here, however, are to secure hybrids of *R. bracteata* able to endure the exacting climates of our northern and prairie states.

Thus far, *R. bracteata* × *R. carolina* has given most promising results. Most of these hybrids endure zero weather, and in the single forms develop the longest and most perfectly formed buds of various pleasing shades of pink that we have ever seen, some opening to nearly five inches in diameter, but the plants are scrawny and the foliage easily infected by black-spot at the Bell Experiment Plot. In one hybrid, however, *R. bracteata* so greatly predominates that plant, foliage and flowers almost duplicate that species, *R. carolina* only showing in the sterility of the blooms and in complete hardiness in our locality. The plant came through the dreadful winter of 1917–18 in a very exposed situation, absolutely without injury, though the parent species from which the seed was taken, grown against a south wall, was killed to the soil-line. This hybrid variety should be tested under more severe climatic conditions.

One plant of our three seedlings of Harison's Yellow—the entire outcome of years of seed-sowings—bloomed quite profusely the past season, the third from germination. The plant appears rather nearer *R. spinosissima* than *R. lutea*, one of the reputed parents of Harison's Yellow, and the blooms, though well finished and more double, are lighter in color than those of this most valuable variety. It, however, responds to cross-fertilization and perfects seeds with foreign pollen, which has never been the case in our trials with Harison's Yellow, though countless pollinations have been made extending over a period of twenty years. If the seeds of the new seedling grow, progress may be made toward the evolution of new yellow hardy roses better suited for garden use. The fruits of the seedlings were black and smooth, like those of *R. hispida* and *R. spinosissima altaica*, allies of *R. spinosissima*, instead of bronze-purple and spiny as with the parent plant. About 600 self- or chance-pollinated seeds of Harison's Yellow, from diverse localities, were secured and sown in September, 1918, in the hope of raising more seedlings. Seeds of this variety germinate the following spring, if at all, but the proportion that materializes in plants is remarkably small. Our trials have produced only the three plants mentioned out of many thousands of seeds sown.

The showy fruited rose species are being bred together in the expectation of getting superior varieties, and some attempt will be made to further develop the fragrant foliage of the Sweetbrier, *R. rubiginosa, R. agrestis, R. lutea,* and others. It seems to be within the bounds of possibility that this most agreeable fragrance can be intensified.

In the wind of sunny June
Thrives the red rose crop.
Every day fresh blossoms blow
While the first leaves drop;
White rose and yellow rose,
And moss rose choice to find,
And the cottage cabbage rose
Not one whit behind.
—CHRISTINA ROSSETTI.

The Pedigree of Ophelia
By THE EDITOR

THIS great rose, disseminated in 1912 by Wm. Paul & Son, of Waltham Cross, Herts, England, has not only proved exceedingly valuable in itself as a greenhouse rose, with good reputation also as an outdoor rose, but has been found to be a peculiarly potent parent of seedlings and sports. Much interest has been manifested, therefore, in the parentage of Ophelia. E. G. Hill, who introduced it in America, and who has used it as one of the parents of Columbia, Double Ophelia, Rose Premier, and Mary Hill, confessed himself in ignorance as to its parentage. Inquiry was therefore made of the originator, and a letter from Mr. A. W. Paul, the managing director of the great rose-growing concern in England, gives all the information there is in the following paragraph:

We have no pedigree of the rose Ophelia, which was not raised from artificially fertilized seed, but came from a pod gathered at hazard in the nursery. We know of no reason why it should be so prolific in sports, but its free seeding quality is explained by the flowers not being excessively full of petals. We have often found with garden hybrids that the less double a rose is the more easily it produces seed.

It would seem, therefore, to be definitely settled that Ophelia is a chance seedling, naturally produced. Yet when the above information was transmitted to Mr. E. G. Hill, there came the following reply:

Your note relative to the parentage of Ophelia is quite interesting, to say the least. I was told, when in England last, that Ophelia was seeded from Antoine Rivoire. Everything points to the presence of Rivoire blood in Ophelia. Perhaps I can later throw additional light on the subject, but of course we must credit the Pauls with their statement of its parentage.

There is here a very fruitful matter for investigation for the biologist who will undertake to determine approximate origins through a study of the product. Perhaps knowledge may be advanced by the study proposed in the next article.

"Sports" or Bud-Variation in the Rose

By C. S. POMEROY, Riverside, Calif.

EDITOR'S NOTE.—Just why, in a greenhouse glowing with a thousand roses of one kind, certain individual branches should produce markedly different blooms no one knows. We have come to call such a variation a "sport" from the parent variety, and at present there is much interest concentrated on the "sporting" tendencies of the rose—not the lady!—Ophelia.

Professor Pomeroy is one of the competent workers in the Bureau of Plant Industry of the United States Department of Agriculture, and is now stationed at Riverside, Calif., where he has been studying bud-variations, or "sports," in certain oranges and grape-fruits. To have his keen scientific intelligence turned upon rose variations is very well worth while.

THE occurrence of bud-variations, usually called "sports," in plants propagated vegetatively has long been recognized, but the possibility that new varieties might originate from bud-sports that appeared as individual branches which were more or less decidedly different from the rest of the plant was not fully established until a much more recent date. Florists and propagators of ornamental plants were among the first to recognize the commercial value of bud varieties. Nearly all genera of cultivated flowers and ornamentals are known to have produced sporting forms more or less frequently. The list of varieties known to be of bud origin is very extended, though far from complete. New forms are continually being discovered, but it will manifestly be impossible to determine accurately the origin of many of the older plant varieties.

The rose has probably produced a greater number of recognized bud varieties than any other plant. Carriere's account of bud varieties, written in 1865 (Production et Fixation des Varieties dans les Vegetaux) included fifty standard roses known to have been of bud origin, and he stated that no attempt had been made to make the list complete. In the 1918 Annual of the American Rose Society is a "Partial List of Roses Introduced in America," which I take to include only those originating here. In that list mention is made of ninety bud varieties, none of which was included in the list presented by Carriere, the most of them having been introduced within the last twenty years. Ten other varieties presented in the list in the 1918 Annual are known to have been of bud origin, and it is more than possible that still others were of the same nature. In order to present anything approaching a comprehensive catalogue of rose sports, the foreign varieties originating since 1865 should be added to these two lists.

Every rose-grower knows that, in general, bud varieties are as stable as those produced as seedlings, and they are as constant in the reproduction of their characters under vegetative propagation. Varieties are sometimes found, such as the Killarney, Radiance, and Ophelia, which may be said to be in a mutating stage of development. Such forms may give rise to a number of bud varieties, which in turn may be quite variable in their development or may be practically stable under vegetative propagation. Thus far no method of artificially inducing true bud mutations has been found.

The comparatively high degree of permanence of bud varieties under propagation increases their value to the commercial grower, provided the variation is a desirable one. This presents an economic reason for being careful to determine whether newly discovered forms are of seed or bud origin.

A study of bud-variations in several of our cultivated fruits is being made for the United States Department of Agriculture, and in that connection it is desired to secure as complete a list as possible of varieties of all plants which have originated as bud sports. The writer would be very glad to hear at any time of the occurrence of sporting forms on roses or any other plants, whether or not such forms appear to be of sufficient value to warrant propagation as new varieties. Such information should include the name of the parent variety, a description of the new form, the place where it was found, and the name of the person finding it. This information will be considered confidential if it is so desired.

> *I'll take the showers as they fall,*
> *I will not vex my bosom;*
> *Enough if at the end of all*
> *A little garden blossom.*
> —Tennyson.

Frank N. Meyer's Rose Contributions

By PETER BISSET

Office of Foreign Seed and Plant Introduction,
Department of Agriculture, Washington, D. C.

EDITOR'S NOTE.—When the news was received that the notable plant scout of the Department of Agriculture had died in China under sad circumstances, it seemed only proper that there should be placed permanently on record an account of his relation to certain roses which are coming to have important possibilities in America. In the absence of Mr. David Fairchild, in charge of the Office of Foreign Seed and Plant Introduction, Mr. Bisset, who has handled the dissemination of Mr. Meyer's introductions, and is a very good plantsman himself, has here supplied a brief account of the various rose species involved.

Especial reference is made to the pictures illustrating the roses mentioned, which have been supplied through Mr. Bisset, and which are noted as Plates IV, VI, VIII, and IX.

THE veteran and acute plant investigator who has ranged the East for many years in the interest of American horticulture as field agent of the Bureau of Plant Industry, is no more. His death occurred during June, 1918, and while he was "on the warpath" of science. It is indeed fitting that Frank N. Meyer, a robust and vivid personality, should end in the field the great work he had so well carried on for many years.

Mr. Meyer collected and made available, through the United States Department of Agriculture, and as the representative of its Office of Foreign Seed and Plant Introduction, hundreds of species and varieties, many previously unknown to commerce. Among those already shown to be of definite economic value are a wonderful Chinese form of the well-known Japanese persimmon, and a Chinese pistache nut among numberless other ornamental trees and plants. There is in large use a particularly fine dwarf lemon for which Mr. Meyer was responsible, and the small-leaved elm (*Ulmus pumila*) he sent to America is proving a boon for shade and windbreaks in semi-arid regions, where it replaces the cottonwood. A fine glaucous form of the Chinese juniper is likely to become the model columnar evergreen of the East because Mr. Meyer saw its possibilities. He sent in, also, many cherry and peach varieties that are proving of great value.

But in this Annual it is proper to mention particularly Mr. Meyer's rose introductions, several of which bid fair to be of exceptional value to the United States.

Rosa xanthina, Lindley, as described by Lindley in Rose Monograph 132–1820, is a semi-double, yellow-flowered rose native to China, which was not known to cultivation in our country until after Frank N. Meyer found it in the neighborhood of Peking. He collected 135 cuttings and sent them to the Office of Foreign Seed and Plant Introduction on December 23, 1905. These cuttings reached this country in good condition, and plants were raised from some of them at the Washington greenhouses, and also at the Chico Plant Introduction Field Station, Chico, Calif.

Mr. Meyer's description of this rose, which accompanied the cuttings, is as follows: "A semi-double, yellow rose frequently met with in the gardens here. It is a very thrifty grower and able to withstand long drought; very well fit to serve as a background for smaller plants or to be used as a lining along a path. The straight young shoots, which grow 5 to 8 feet high, might, perhaps, furnish a fine stock for long-stemmed hybrid roses."

This rose has been grown in Washington since its introduction and has proven a valuable addition to our list of hardy yellow roses. The plant blooms early in the spring, beginning to flower several days before the fine, small, yellow-flowered rose, Harison's Yellow, which it resembles quite closely, and, moreover, *R. xanthina* blooms as freely as that well-known, old-fashioned variety. The peculiarly attractive character of the double form of *R. xanthina* is apparent in the illustrations. (Plate VI, facing page 75, and Plate VIII, facing page 105.)

Mr. Meyer also collected and sent to this country the single-flowered form of *R. xanthina*, which has been named *R. xanthina, forma normalis*, by Messrs. Rehder and Wilson in "Plantæ Wilsonianæ." The seeds of this variety were first collected on August 23, 1907, at which time he wrote as follows:

"The beautiful single yellow rose, *Rosa xanthina*, growing in dry, rocky locations and mostly in sheltered places, produces masses of delicate yellow flowers in early summer. It is used by the Chinese as a grafting stock for the Tea varieties of roses. Might be utilized for the same purpose in the United States, and may also be utilized in hybridizing. Seed collected at Shushan, Shantung, China."

This single form of *R. xanthina* is very free in flower, and, blooming early in the season, makes a welcome addition to the roses available for mass effects, or for use as a shrub. The picture accompanying this article (Plate IX, facing page 120) is of a specimen growing at the home of Mr. David Fairchild, head of the Foreign Seed and Plant Introduction Office, just outside the city of Washington.

Another rose which Mr. Meyer sent in from China, and which for several years past has attracted considerable attention, is a climbing or pillar rose he collected in a garden at Pautung Fu, Chihli Province. This has been identified by Messrs. Rehder and Wilson as *R. odorata*. The form that Mr. Meyer collected (known as No. 22449 in the introductions of this office) produces small, double, white flowers with pale pink centers; it blooms quite freely. While an attractive rose, its chief interest at the present time lies in its peculiar usefulness as a stock on which to bud or graft other roses. Cuttings of the young wood grow so readily that with ordinary care 90 to 95 per cent of those put in an ordinary propagating-bench will root. It has also been found that the vigorous young canes, often five to eight feet long, can be used as a stock upon which to insert between each leaf or eye, in the manner of ordinary shield- or slip-budding, buds of any varieties it is desired to propagate. Later, when these buds have united, the canes are made into ordinary cuttings each with a bud of the desired variety, which will root readily in slight bottom heat in an ordinary sand propagating-bench, while the inserted buds will give rise to strong, healthy plants.

Reference was made by Dr. Van Fleet to this surprising facility of propagation in his article on rose stocks, printed on pages 56 to 62 in the 1918 Rose Annual.

Further, this No. 22449 form of *R. odorata* has been successfully used as a grafting stock. The young canes are cut into suitable lengths, and upon these are cleft-grafted or "worked" cions or pieces of wood of the desired variety. The completed grafts are then potted singly in small pots, which are placed in an ordinary sweat-box* used for young grafted stock, and maintained at a temperature of 75 to 80 degrees. Simultaneously,

---

*A "sweat-box" is any enclosure—as a bell-glass, or large inverted jar, or a frame-and-glass affair—in which can be maintained the temperature noted, together with much moisture. Under these conditions, Mr. Bisset informs us the grafts unite and roots are emitted in some ten days, after which the pots are removed for gradual "hardening off."

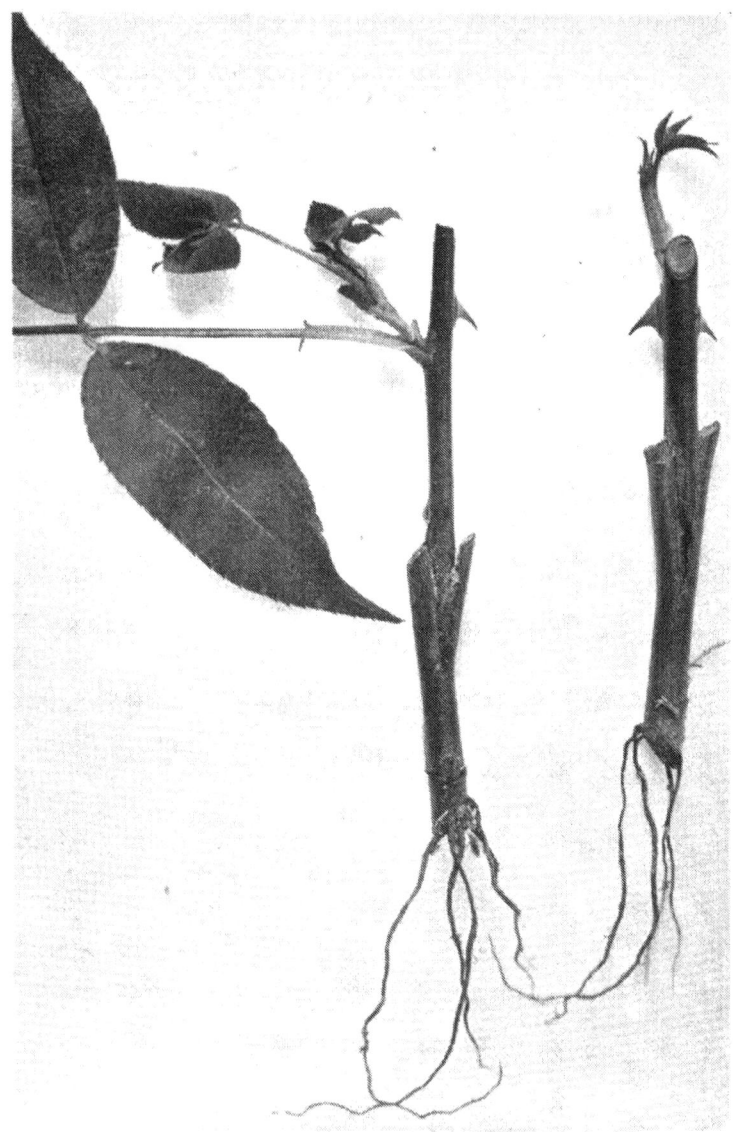

PLATE IV. Method of Rapid Propagation
(The cutting or "stock" is of *Rosa odorata*, No. 22449, introduced from China by the late Frank N. Meyer. See details on page 40. Photograph supplied by Office of Foreign Seed and Plant Introduction, Department of Agriculture.)

the cuttings root and the grafts grow, and as many as 90 per cent of the cuttings thus made have succeeded. Plate IV, facing this page, illustrates the detail of this unique grafting-cutting process of rose-propagation. The grafts are tied with raffia or soft string, but are not waxed.

As yet, the complete hardiness in the colder sections of this form, No. 22449 of *R. odorata*, has not been determined, wherefore we are not now in position to say how much frost it will stand. It is assuredly well worth a most careful test by rose-growers, especially in view of the importance of increasing the propagation of roses in America.

All of these three rose-forms sent to the United States by the late Frank N. Meyer are soon to be commercially available. They will form, among many other similar items, a permanent memorial to rose-lovers of his discrimination and energy. Several other rose species which he collected in China have possibilities, either as rose stocks or as parents in the hybridization work being conducted by Dr. Van Fleet, but it is too soon to judge of their value.

THE ROSE-GARDEN

There is a wine we may not taste till June
Betroths her odors to the throstle's tune.
Deep draughts delicious then each guest
  may drink,
From cups of cream and crimson, white
  and pink,
Such nectar as annihilates desire
For aught less perfect: that begets a fire
Of some strange ecstasy in lovers' eyes,
And lifts the poet-soul to paradise.
—S. C. Thurman.

The Making of a Rose Enthusiast and His Garden

By GEORGE R. MANN, Little Rock, Ark.

EDITOR'S NOTE.—The story that follows will be illuminated when the statement is added that Mr. Mann is a busy and successful architect, to whose credit are many good buildings, notably the new Arkansas state capitol, at Little Rock. Mr. Mann evidently enjoys his roses, and is probably the first recorded case of a conversion from golf to roses! As the result is "probably one hour a week in actual labor, and maybe two hours a day in pursuit of happiness," Mr. Mann will doubtless survive!

The detailed account of how and why, and the well-kept record of what happened, are pressed into this crowded Annual because of the fine human significance of it. Roses mix well with any good profession or business, it seems.

In response to an inquiry, Mr. Mann wrote on January 3, 1919, his Christmas rose experience, which is here added because of its encouraging suggestion in a climate which sometimes presents zero temperatures as well. There might well be a million more Christmas roses in the Southwest, following this example. Mr. Mann's letter follows:

"Upon Sunday, December 22, 1918, I cut a large number of roses from my garden; and upon the 24th, as the weather-man called for a cold wave, which duly arrived Christmas day, I cut all the remaining roses and buds. In the warmth of the house many of the buds opened, and I had a fine display of roses during Christmas time. These late roses are always the most beautiful and are darker and more highly colored than at any other season. The varieties giving the late bloom are as follows: Radiance, Mrs. George Shawyer, Mme. Leon Pain, Jonkheer J. L. Mock, Duchess of Wellington, Wm. R. Smith, White Killarney, Old Gold, Mme. Jules Grolez, Cardinal, Red Radiance, Robin Hood, Francis Scott Key, Gruss an Teplitz, Ecarlate, Chateau de Clos Vougeot.

"It is interesting to note that from about one hundred varieties of roses growing in my garden, it was mostly the red roses that gave Christmas bloom."

LITTLE ROCK was long known as the Rose City, but in February of 1901 the temperature fell to 15 degrees below zero, and practically every rose bush in the city was killed. It is only now, after half a generation of time, that the town is again becoming worthy of the name.

While I have always been fond of flowers, and have greatly admired the roses about the town, they were only "pink, white, yellow and red" roses to me until early in 1915, when my daughter, remembering my love for flowers, sent me Capt. George C. Thomas' "Outdoor Rose-growing." The book was a revelation to me, and as I read and re-read it the rose-fever got into my veins, wherefore I sent for his "sixteen best roses."

The question now was, where could I plant them? When my

residence was built, the lot immediately back of the house was low, and, to give me a level back yard, I built a five-foot retaining wall on the eastern and northern lines, filling in with a stiff clay. I then formed beds along these walls and next to the residence for old-fashioned flowers, and on the north I built a trellis upon which I placed trained fruit trees. Between each tree I planted a Dorothy Perkins rose, training the stems straight up and spreading out the shoots at the top into a broad cornice along the top of the trellis. The central space I formed into a putting-court, separated from the surrounding beds and garage by a gravel walk. This was the condition of my grounds when my roses arrived, and the only place I had to plant them was in a single row around the putting-court.

The roses did well, and the sight of their beautiful blooms fanned the rose-fever in my blood until it became stronger than my love for golf. That fall I gave up my court, forming five-foot beds on its four sides, with narrow grass walks coming in from the corners to the central space, which remained in grass. These beds were filled with roses, many of which were own-root greenhouse plants from our local nursery. In the spring of 1916 I inveigled Mrs. M. into giving me her old-fashioned flower-beds, and in these I planted budded two- and three-year-old plants, those received from Mr. Peterson, of Fairlawn, being budded on Multiflora. These plants showed such fine growth and bloom that I now use Multiflora stock exclusively when the varieties I wish are available on that stock.

The season of 1916 was very wet, and while the roses in the outside beds did well, as they had drainage between the earth and the outside walls, those in the central beds were poor, as the clay fill held water like a cup. During the winter of 1916–17, to obtain better drainage, I took up the roses in the central beds, discarding many of the own-roots plants, and "heeling in" those retained. I then excavated the beds to a depth of two feet, digging in the bottom a trench one foot deep in which I laid farm drain-tile (connected same with the house sewer), filling up this trench with broken stone. The beds were then refilled with a mixture of two-thirds old clay sod, and one-third well-rotted cow-manure. I also added a large pail of ground limestone and one of bone-meal to each twenty square feet of bed.

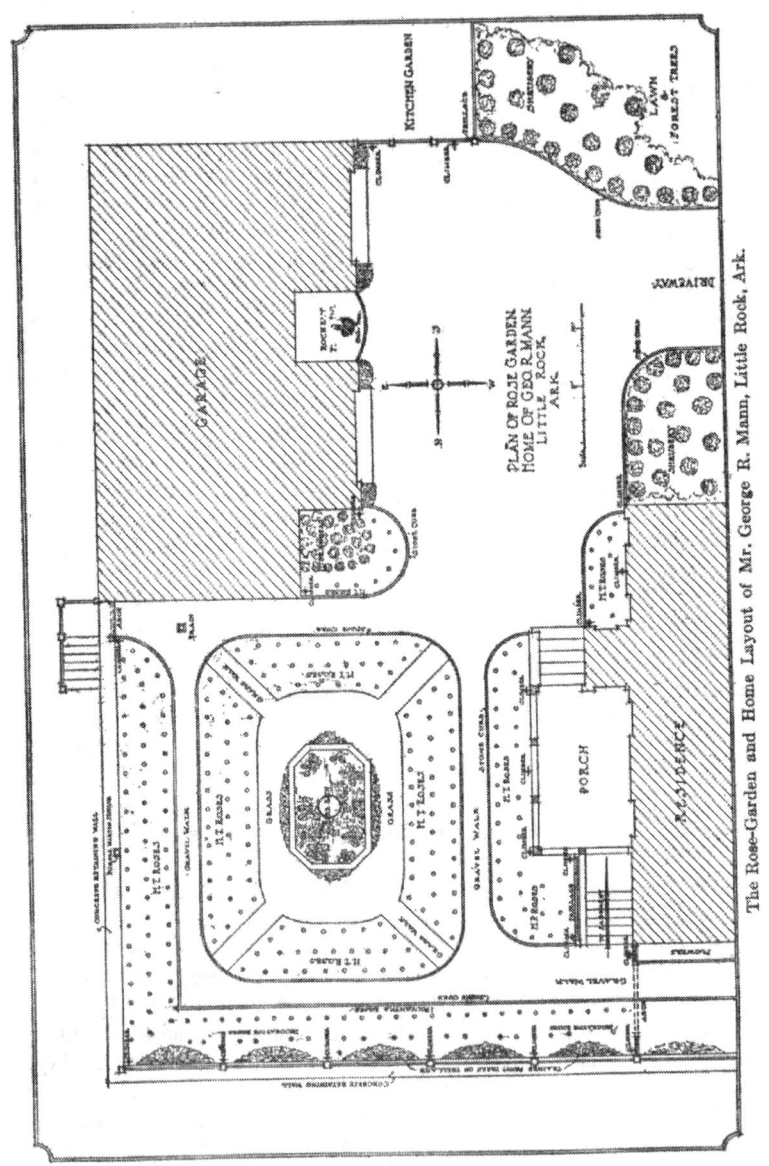

The Rose-Garden and Home Layout of Mr. George R. Mann, Little Rock, Ark.

In the central space I built a lily-pool, designing a terra-cotta bird-bath for its center. This pool has added greatly to the beauty of my garden, and the pink, white, yellow, and blue lilies, with the goldfish in the pool, are an added attraction for both old and young. (See plan on facing page.)

I was late in finishing the beds, and, when ready, my heeled-in plants, including a lot of new plants received March 1, were out in full leaf. This set them back badly; a number died and I had little spring bloom.*

My dairyman each day throws out fresh cow-manure and immediately sprinkles it with lime. In a short time this material fully disintegrates, forming a loose, light mass, cleanly and easy to handle if kept under cover, as it should be. I had been in the habit of sprinkling this material about the plants between each blooming period, taking the place of liquid manure. This had given such good results that, with a feeling of "kill or cure," I decided to give my new beds a heavy mulch of this material, and it was put on July 1, to a depth of about one and one-half to two inches. The result was marvelous. The plants started into strong growth, and I had a very large amount of bloom the remainder of the season.

November was very mild, many of my plants making strong new growth, and on December 1 a number were in bloom. Early in December we had snow, and the next day the thermometer stood at 7 above zero, and from that time on until the end of January there was a succession of storms, the thermometer seldom registering as high as freezing, and going as low as 8 below. February 2 was cloudy, and as Mr. Groundhog failed to see his shadow, he remained out and we had no more killing frost throughout the season. I found that all my Teas, Hybrid Teas and Noisette climbers were frozen to the ground. The bush roses that had had late bloom were generally killed to the ground, and the remainder (with few exceptions) were killed to the top of the first snow—about three or four inches, the exceptions being Mme. Herriot, Willowmere and Gorgeous.

I had received a number of plants about December 1, but as it was not convenient for me to plant, they were heeled-in

*Here is another confirmation for the theory that there is "a critical date" for transplanting roses in spring, after which success is much less likely, despite elaborate care. See note on page 104, 1918 Annual.—EDITOR.

and were not planted until February. As they were dormant, they were not damaged by the cold, and have all done well. This spring the roses quickly started into growth, and upon April 8 I cut my first rose—a Mme. Herriot, and by April 15, many varieties were in bloom, almost a month earlier than usual, as we generally have hard frosts in March that kill back all early growth.

I now decided to keep a record of the season's bloom. This has been done very faithfully, with the exception of the July-August period, when I was obliged to be in Washington. As I am the only one who has a speaking acquaintance with all the roses in my garden, the record was not kept during that period. The record was kept until November 15, but there will, probably, be bloom through November, and, possibly, in December, as I have seen roses blooming here at Christmas time. I have not counted the blooms of such roses as Gruss an Teplitz, Ecarlate, the Irish singles and Polyantha types, that are grown mostly for decoration; they are all great bloomers, but do not stand hot weather very well.

It is interesting to note that, with the exception of Radiance, the first forty-four varieties in the list are growing in the specially prepared central beds.

While I believe that practically all the roses in my list will do well in this climate, the opinion of one, unless he grows many plants of the same variety, is not worth much. For example, I have one White Killarney which makes fine growth and has perfect foliage, is always in bloom, and is probably way above its class, while my lone Killarney has not done well. Consequently an opinion based upon either of these plants would probably be an incorrect one.

In reds, General MacArthur is fine in spring and fall, but comes small and burns quickly in hot weather. Francis Scott Key is a strong-growing, large, full, very high-centered rose, stands the heat well, and is a wonderful keeper, both on or off the bush. When perfect, it is the peer of all reds, but it sometimes fails to open. Red Radiance has beautiful color and is little affected by hot weather. George C. Waud, Laurent Carle, Ben Cant, and Mary, Countess of Ilchester do well. Cardinal, Lieut. Chaure and Robin Hood, new roses in my garden, are very promising—and Lieut. Chaure especially so. National Emblem has shown but little growth. Old American Beauty does well here as an outdoor rose. I have noted a number of fine plants throughout the town with bloom about equal to greenhouse-grown. Upon inquiry, I have found that in many cases these plants were started by "slipping" cut greenhouse roses after the bloom had fallen. My own plants are on Multiflora. In spring the flowers come on short stems, but in late summer, and again in late fall, they throw up three-foot shoots that are tipped with blooms that are all that one could ask. While I am a great believer in budded plants, this rose is probably best on its own roots.

Yellow roses in this climate generally show but little color, except in fall. Duchess of Wellington is very beautiful in cool weather, but comes single and white in heat. Lady Hillingdon and Mme. Charles Lutaud hold their color very well. Rayon d'Or is always yellow, in fact, it is almost too vivid a yellow, as to me it somewhat lacks the delicacy and softness of color that one associates with the rose. Its great fault is its dying back proclivities in the fall.

In pinks, Radiance is good in every way. Lady Alice Stanley is beautiful at all times—a perfect cut-flower. Mrs. George Shawyer, J. J. L. Mock, Lady Ashtown and Mme. Segond Weber do well. Mme. Leon Pain is as good as Radiance, and the bloom to me is more attractive. Mme. Jules Grolez has fine growth, foliage, and color here, and is a wonderful bloomer. In light-colored roses, Ophelia is always beautiful in half-open bud, and in open flower in the spring and fall. President Carnot, Pharisaer, Mme. Jules Bouche, and Mrs. Harold Brocklebank do finely, and an especially attractive rose is Antoine Rivoire. I have a Radiance sport, milky white, with delicate blush center. It is semi-double and very beautiful, especially in the half-open bud, but has not shown the amount of bloom of its parent.

Where all are so good and beautiful, preference is much a matter of personal taste. If I have a preference, it is for Willowmere and Joseph Hill. Willowmere is a strong grower, always beautiful, good in heat, and very long lasting, both on and off the bush; and Joseph Hill is a most charming flower.

Los Angeles is much the same as Willowmere, but has so far shown but little growth or bloom. My Titania plants received this spring were very, very small, and pot-grown. They have made wonderful growth and are going to be great bloomers. It is a most attractive little rose.

Such success as I have had in my garden, I owe, first, to Captain Thomas and his book, and, second, to thorough preparation of beds and proper feeding, pruning, and watering. Rose bushes must have food, and lots of it, to make flowers, and the best food is cow-manure. Too many times manure that has laid out in the rain for months is used, after the best of its fertilizing qualities have leached away. It should be kept under cover.

I prune my plants to four or five eyes. (This year they were pruned from the ground-level to three or four inches by last winter's cold!) In connection with the cutting of roses, which are all cut with long stems, I do quite a lot of pruning. I find that when a plant sends out a blind growth, generally evidenced by its being tipped with two small leaf-stalks that come directly opposite each other, with no growth between, if it is left whole on the plant, it will never have a bloom, but if cut back as one would a blooming shoot, a new shoot will be thrown out that will probably be productive.

Sprinkling is worse than useless. When you *know* the plants need water, take off the nozzle of your hose and let the water run until the beds are saturated to the bottom. I occasionally sprinkle, but it is only to freshen up the foliage.

I have little insect trouble. In spring and late fall there are aphides a-plenty, but spraying with a Kirk's tobacco cartridge, applied with the garden hose, eliminates them. About the worst trouble is a hairy black fly that bores down into the stem as soon as one of any size is cut. The boring out of the pith does not greatly injure the plant during the present season, but the shoot will generally be found dead in the spring. The remedy is to rub on the stem, as soon as cut, a little pruning compound. Black-spot has caused me much trouble, but last spring, after pruning, I dosed my plants with a strong solution of bordeaux mixture, put on with a sprinkling-can, until the plants and ground were blue; and at its first appearance I used the 10–90 arsenate-sulphur dust recommended in the 1918 Annual, so that this season I have almost escaped the pest.

The first half of September (1918) was very warm, while the last half was unseasonably cold. This change in temperature of from 35 to 40 degrees caused the plants to mildew badly—the first I have had to any extent in my garden. As a remedy I used the 10–90 arsenate-sulphur dust. This stopped its ravages, but the mildew seriously affected my fall bloom—at least I have had less bloom this fall than last.

When once established, the actual labor entailed in the care of roses is very little. If plenty of fine manure has been used, the ground will not bake, and weeding and an occasional stirring of the surface soil are all that is necessary.

I have the entire care of my garden, and devote to it probably one hour a week in actual labor, and maybe two hours a day in the pursuit of happiness!

MONTHLY ROSE BLOOM—SEASON OF 1918

Roses budded to 6-inch stems. Abbreviations: O. R., Own Root; M., Multiflora; B., Brier.

Name of Variety	Stock	Apr. 15 to May 15	May 15 to June 15	June 15 to July 15	July 15 to Aug. 15	Aug. 15 to Sept. 15	Sept. 15 to Oct. 15	Oct. 15 to Nov. 15	Total	Season
Chrissie MacKellar	O. R.	3	16	16		13	20	4	72	Second
Mme. Jules Grolez	M.	8	16	18		12	7	11	72	Third
Lady Pirrie	M.	14	20	8		12	3	9	66	Third
White Killarney	M.	12	14	12		11	5	10	64	Third
Florence Pemberton	M.	6	16	15		13	6	6	62	Third
Mrs. B. R. Cant	M.	6	6	17		15	5	10	59	Second
Mrs. A. R. Waddell	M.	7	12	14		13	6	7	59	Third
Radiance	M.	8	14	14		8	6	5	55	Third
Old Gold	M.	2	13	14		12	8	6	55	Second
General MacArthur	B.	12	17	10	Blooms not counted	6	7	2	54	Fourth
Etoile de France	O. R.	11	16	12		10		5	54	Third
Mrs. Aaron Ward	B.	4	13	12		11	6	8	54	Fourth
Etoile de Lyon	B.	7	11	8		12	6	10	54	Second
Souv. du President Carnot	M.	7	14	12		8	5	8	54	Third
Duchess of Wellington	B.	7	8	14		11	4	9	53	Fourth
Mme. Maurice de Luze	M.	7	10	14		12	6	1	50	Second
Mme. Jules Bouche	B.	1	13	10		12	5	9	50	Fourth
Lady Ursula	O. R.	8	10	12		12	5	2	49	Third
Willowmere	M.	11	10	11		6	5	6	49	Third
Mme. Leon Pain	B.	7	11	12		8	4	6	48	Fourth
Mme. Ravary	M.	6	6	15		10	3	7	47	Second
Lady Ashtown	M.	7	8	10		9	6	4	44	Second
Lady Hillingdon	M.	2	9	10		12	3	8	44	Third
Ophelia	M.	5	9	10		7	4	9	44	Third
Pharisaer	M.	4	12	9		7	3	8	43	Third
Souv. de Gustave Prat	M.	5	8	13		10	2	5	43	Second
Grace Molyneux	B.		9	10		9	5	10	43	Third
Ellen Willmott	B.	5	11	10		9	8		43	Fourth

MONTHLY ROSE–BLOOM—SEASON OF 1918, continued

Name of Variety	Stock	Apr. 15 to May 15	May 15 to June 15	June 15 to July 15	July 15 to Aug. 15	Aug. 15 to Sept. 15	Sept. 15 to Oct. 15	Oct. 15 to Nov. 15	Total	Season
Senateur Mascuraud	M.	4	7	9		10	3	8	41	Second
Geo. C. Waud	B.	5	13	7		11	3	2	41	Third
La France	O. R.	7	11	10		7		6	41	Third
Mme. Charles Lutaud	B.	3	12	13		8	5		41	Third
Mary, Countess of Ilchester	M.	3	9	12		9	5	2	40	Second
Cardinal	M.	3	9	11		8	2	5	38	First
Mme. Edouard Herriot	M.	6	9	9		5	6	3	38	Second
Betty	B.	2	6	7		14	2	6	37	Fourth
Laurent Carle	B.	3	12	11		8		3	37	Fourth
Killarney Queen	M.	6	10	8		7	4	2	37	Third
Mrs. Harold Brocklebank	M.	2	6	7		9	5	8	37	First
Jonkheer J. L. Mock	M.	2	11	9		9	2	3	36	Second
Joseph Hill	M.	2	9	7		8	4	5	35	Third
Lady Plymouth	M.	2	9	6		7	7	4	35	First
Lady Alice Stanley	B.	5	4	8		9	6	2	34	Fourth
Mrs. George Shawyer	M.	2	7	8		10	4	2	33	First
Alex. Hill Gray	B.	4	7	9		4	2	6	32	Second
Wm. B. Smith	M.	6	3	5		7	3	7	31	Third
Kaiserin Augusta Victoria	B.	5	7	8		6		5	31	Fourth
Titania	B.		6	6		5	6	8	31	First
Maman Cochet	O. R.	9	5	6		4	4	2	30	Third
Red Radiance	B.	3	5	6		8	3	5	30	Second
Lieutenant Chaure	M.	4	5	6		7	1	7	30	First
Gorgeous	B.	2	10	7		4	4	2	29	Second
Mme. Edmond Rostand	B.	5	8	7	Blooms not counted	5	1	2	28	Second
Duchess of Westminster	B.	4	7	5		7	3	2	28	Fourth
Robin Hood	M.	4	3	6		7	3	5	28	First
Francis Scott Key	B.	3	4	7		8	2	4	28	Second
Harry Kirk	M.	4	6	7		6	2	2	27	First
Mme. Caroline Testout	B.	3	6	9		5	1	3	27	Second
Mme. Segond Weber	M.	1	5	7		7	4	2	26	First
Farben Konigin	B.	5	5	6		3	5	2	26	Third
Chateau de Clos Vougeot	M.	6	4	6		5	3	2	26	First
White Maman Cochet	O. R.	7	4	6		5	1	3	26	Third
Col. R. S. Williamson	O. R.	5	4	5		6	4	1	25	Discarded
Rayon d'Or	M.	3	10	6		5		1	25	First
American Beauty	M.	10	8			5		2	25	Third
President Taft	O. R.	5	4	7		4	2	3	25	Fourth
Killarney Brilliant	M.	1	7	4		6	2	4	24	Third
My Maryland	B.	4	4	5		5	3	2	23	Third
Antoine Rivoire	B.	2	4	5		6	5	1	23	Fourth
White Radiance	O. R.	5	4	6		5	2	1	23	Second
Mrs. John Laing	M.	12	8					2	22	Third
Killarney	B.	3	4	5		6		4	22	Fourth
Hadley	M.	4	4	5		4	2	2	21	First
Natalie Bottner	B.	2	5	6		5	2		20	First
Richmond	O. R.	6	1	5		4	2	2	20	Discarded
George Arends	M.	8	10				1		19	Third
Frau Karl Druschki	B.	11	7						18	Fourth
Louise Catherine Breslau	B.	1	7	5		3	2		18	First
Franco-Russia	O. R.		4	5		4	4		17	Discarded
National Emblem	B.		4	5		4	4		17	First
Dean Hole	B.	1	5	5			3	1	15	Discarded
Helen Gould	O. R.	3	1	3		4	2	2	15	Discarded
Ulster Gem	B.	3	3	3		2	3	1	15	Second
Mrs. Joseph H. Welch	O. R.	1	3			5	3	1	13	Discarded
Mme. Lambard	O. R.		3	4		5	1		13	Discarded
Mme. Melanie Soupert	M.	2	1	3		2	3	1	12	First
Los Angeles	B.	1	2	3		3			9	First
H. V. Machin	B.	3	3						6	First
George Dickson	B.	2	4							Discarded

The Passing of a Great Rosarian
Tributes to the Memory of Admiral Aaron Ward*
Collected by THE EDITOR

ALTHOUGH blessed with some sixty species of the genus Rosa native to the mainland, and notwithstanding the cultivation of the rose in gardens for at least two centuries, the Queen of Flowers is too young in America to have at her court many really great rosarians. In each generation, less than a half-dozen men have been preëminent in that unselfish attention to the rose which is a major part of greatness in rose-growing. Admiral Aaron Ward, by profession and by success a great naval officer, was by avocation, and equally by success, the most notable figure of his time in attention to the rose.

Those of us who met him at his Willowmere home, or at sessions of the American Rose Society, which he served so admirably, or in attendance upon a great rose show, or who came to know how he made his loved roses serve the cause of mercy and help through the use of his garden in promoting ambulance work in France, recognized in him a leader and a friend, a kindly critic and a helpful instructor.

His rose-fame was world-wide, as the letters below will testify. When he died, on July 5, 1918, the nation lost a devoted sailor and the earthly kingdom of the rose its prime minister.

His loving friends can tell the story better than the Editor of the Annual which he helped. Let the "grand old man" among American rose-producers speak first:

> Admiral Ward was one of the most interesting and delightful gentlemen I have ever known. Of genial, kindly disposition, combined with a foundation of firmness and quick decision wherever prompt action was necessary, he had the unusual combination of gentleness and stern control that made him the successful commander of a battleship and a friend after one's own heart.
>
> My acquaintance with Admiral Ward came about through correspondence with our mutual friend, Monsieur J. Pernet-Ducher, of Lyons, France, in the discussion of the parentage of certain varieties of roses originated by M. Pernet-Ducher.
>
> The Admiral was a warm admirer of the French rosarian and made frequent visits to Lyons to study minutely the progress made by him in his work, especially in the introduction of Austrian copper blood into the Tea sections. In this line

*See portrait, Plate V, facing page 56.

of crosses, Willowmere, one of the finest examples, and a grand garden variety, was named for Admiral Ward's beautiful home-place at Roslyn, L. I.; while Constance, a dazzling yellow, of similar type, was named for the Admiral's little daughter who died in early childhood, and Mrs. Aaron Ward, known to every florist, and the later crimson-scarlet garden rose, Admiral Ward—all were raised by M. Pernet-Ducher. The Admiral was very happy over the fact that Mrs. Aaron Ward had become a standard and popular variety.

It was hinted by some of the Admiral's naval friends that the Admiral's flagship had a curious way, when on a cruise, of "happening into" French harbors which were within easy distance of Lyons, and he never explained or denied!

He had a delightful sense of humor, and his letters were rippling with pure fun. His visit to Richmond is one of the pleasantest incidents in our rose-growing career. His kindly good cheer, his interest in roses, and in the men who originated them, and his warm friendship for M. Pernet-Ducher, his live acquaintance with hundreds of varieties as he knew them in his own rose-beds, his humorous characterization of their peculiarities, his keen interest in the seedlings that were "coming" on both sides of the water, made the occasion memorable.

I had the pleasure of going through his garden with him in June of 1917. We talked of the roses, but his heart was full to overflowing with the war, and sorrow at the loss of both M. Pernet-Ducher's boys in battle. When we parted, it was with the expectation of seeing him this year, again, at Richmond. But our Admiral is now among the flowers immortal!

Mrs. Ward is quite as well "up" in roses as was her distinguished husband, and she it was who oftenest decided as to the use of the pruning shears, about which frequent good-natured arguments arose. That the little lady was nearly always right was proven by the great showing of bloom at Willowmere.

The heartfelt sympathy of all who knew the Admiral and Mrs. Aaron Ward goes out to the lady of Willowmere in her bereavement, and we share in her irreparable loss. E. G. HILL.

The President of the American Rose Society, Mr. Benjamin Hammond, who well knew the wisdom in counsel of the sailor-rosarian, has thus written:

Admiral Aaron Ward was a true-hearted, able man, with the vigor and clear vision of a good sea captain.

At the beginning of this war he took charge abroad of the ship "Red Cross" on its errand of noble mercy. In New York he was at home, having had several terms of duty at the Brooklyn Navy Yard, and as supervisor of the harbor. He had sailed the oceans from land to land in all latitudes, but his name, however, is far wider known among the people of America for his connection with the Queen of Flowers—the rose. When Pernet-Ducher named the beautiful yellow rose, which grows to perfection from Long Island to Vancouver, it was after the one the Admiral loved best—his wife. Here lay in his character the sentiment for that which is beautiful—the strong man for whom the great winds and rough waves had no terrors. He had the love of home and beauty in the very fiber of his being. In the American Rose Society, as far as his duties permitted, he was always ready to give a guiding hand.

At its first meeting after his death, the Executive Committee of the American Rose Society took suitable action, as recorded on page 148 of this Annual.

THE PASSING OF A GREAT ROSARIAN 53

Because he had had so much to do with the rose in France, and with service to the wounded of the French army and the Allies, it is well now to read from Admiral Ward's friends of the tricolor:

Indeed, Admiral Ward was one of my best friends, and I should have been pleased to write a note about his love for rose-growing, but I am not in spirit to do so, now less than ever. I would have written this sooner, but on the 15th of October I have had my house half destroyed by the explosion of a munitions factory situated near it. Fortunately, my family and I had just time to escape; but since that date I have been worried to look after everything being repaired—it is so very difficult to find materials just now, and labor is so scarce.

But, thanks to you, our brave Allies, thanks to your gallant soldiers, this terrible war is over, and I hope we shall soon get back to our old ways.

With my regrets, please accept my best wishes. J. PERNET-DUCHER.

The last time the Editor saw Admiral Ward, he was full of concern at the silence of his friend, Pernet-Ducher. Later, he came to know the sad reason for this silence, in the sacrifice in the war of two sons of the French rosarian. The tender regard in which these men held each other is in evidence in the subjoined letter from the Director of the great rose-gardens of Bagatelle, in Paris:

During his life, full of military labors, Admiral Ward did always find time to devote his leisure to the culture of roses, and since he retired from active service, in 1913, this became his principal occupation. He rapidly established friendly relations with all the French rose-growers, but with one of them, whom he met more frequently during his trips to Europe, he entertained an intimate friendship.

On the rose-culture fields at Venissieux, near Lyons, whence so many beautiful new varieties have come to us, there is the little house of Pernet-Ducher, which is filled with souvenirs from Admiral Ward.

It is a heart-touching affair, this friendship between a French rose-grower and an American naval officer, and the most beautiful varieties recently produced by M. Pernet-Ducher bear the names of either the native country or of members of the family of Admiral Ward. Any lover of roses today knows the varieties Mrs. Aaron Ward, Willowmere (the name of the locality where Admiral Ward had his rose-gardens), Constance, a daughter; Raymond, and Franklin, the latter two being the names of the Admiral's regretted sons; and all these species will appear in the rose contest next fall.

When the Bagatelle Rose-Garden was established in 1906, Admiral Ward took a great interest, and came to visit it. He did so another year, and before minutely examining all the square rose-beds, he asked for the bed of Pernetiana rose bushes, and the place where the Mrs. Aaron Ward roses were planted.

The interest he showed in the Paris rose-gardens, his broad experience in the culture of this plant, combined with the thorough knowledge and appreciation he had for roses, and furthermore his high social standing, which offered a guaranty for his impartiality, and, above all, the admiration we had for American sympathies, decided us to ask him to extend to us the honor of taking a seat in the Jury of the Bagatelle Rose Contests.

He readily accepted, but, unfortunately, political events were at that time in their most critical condition, and his illness also prevented his coming.

It was last summer at Lyons, in the dining-room of the Pernet-Ducher mansion, where I found an opportunity to have a little chat with the great rose-planter, and, before I went, to admire all his new wonders, I learned the sad news of the Admiral's decease. M. Pernet-Ducher, when telling me of this event, had tears in his eyes, as he said that all the triumphs he had within these last years with his roses had been embittered by the most cruel happenings, namely the death of his two sons on the field of honor and the loss of one of his best friends. J. C. N. FORESTIER.

Admiral Ward made rose-friends everywhere, and he was as welcome among the expert rosarians in England as he was in the gardens of France. From a noted English clergyman, who is equally a noted rose-grower, come these words:

May I say a few words? Admiral and Mrs. Ward paid me the honor of a visit in the summer of 1912. They spent the day with my sister, Florence Pemberton, and myself, and since that date we have corresponded. On that occasion the Admiral had just come direct from Lyons where he had been visiting M. Pernet-Ducher. He was a rosarian above the average, and keenly appreciated the loveliness, of the rose, especially in its two primary attributes, color and fragrance; and in this he was ardently supported by Mrs. Ward. We spent a happy time together, and I greatly grieved to hear of his death. May God rest his soul! JOSEPH H. PEMBERTON.

From the English home of many superb rose varieties, comes this discriminating tribute:

I read with the deepest regret of the death of Admiral Ward. He has visited me on more than one occasion, and the geniality of his manner will remain long in my recollection. As a rosarian I have rarely met his equal; his knowledge of the different varieties of roses was equaled only by his acumen in summing up their distinctive qualities and characteristics, and few cultivators of this beautiful flower could arrive so quickly at a true estimate of the merits of a new variety. His judgment was most accurate.

I am sure that the sympathies of the rosarians of England and France will go out to their confrères of the United States in their loss.

ARTHUR WILLIAM PAUL.
Managing Director of Wm. Paul & Son, Waltham Cross, Ltd.

A great Irish rose-producer writes thus of Admiral Ward:

We are exceedingly obliged for your kind favor of the 25th ult. and regret greatly the death of that great lover of roses—Admiral Aaron Ward. We had many letters from him; he was a keen critic and a great lover of roses. As a matter of fact, we have come across few men who followed up roses with the same keen knowledge, and with that beautiful idea of the best in everything which seemed to impregnate his whole career. It was one of our greatest pleasures to reply to his many queries and the criticisms which he put before us.

His knowledge of roses far exceeded that of the average amateur, and he had a foresight of a new rose given to few growers.

At one time it was our intention to name one of our new dark seedlings after-

THE PASSING OF A GREAT ROSARIAN

him, and it was only owing to the war that we held over exhibiting it. We regarded this seedling rose as our greatest triumph, and being a free-blooming rose, as well as the most wonderful color, we decided that it should bear his name.

His loss will be a great loss to the rose world, his distinguished name being known in probably every climate where roses are grown. His death is regretted not only by ourselves, but, we are certain, by every rose-grower who knew of him. He was of a type seldom met with and one feels the loss of such a personality. SAMUEL McGREDY.

The kindliness of Admiral Ward, his patience with those less well-informed, his delightful willingness to say a good word, was manifested when the 1918 Annual appeared and the Editor was promptly encouraged with a letter so gratifying that it is here reproduced in facsimile:

> Roslyn. April 9 1918
>
> My dear Mr. McFarland:
>
> I am too busy reading the American Rose Annual for 1918 to give you more than a few minutes of my time. But you will please regard those minutes as spent in confectioning my very best mental bouquet in honor of the Editor.
>
> As we say in the Navy, when a drill or squadron movement is thoroughly well done "Good work"!
>
> Yours sincerely,
> Aaron Ward

That Mrs. Ward was a complete associate of her husband in knowledge of and love for the rose some of us knew. Only from her could come the actual rose-history of this notable man, which the Editor transcribes from a letter written at his request:

Rear Admiral Aaron Ward always loved roses, from the time he was a child and had his first little garden. He often spoke of his first rose, which seemed to him the most wonderful rose in the world.

The garden at Willowmere has been in existence as long as I can remember, for I was born here, and my grandmother bought the property about 1837. I remember the York and Lancaster and the Harison's Yellow roses, the moss pinks and the daffodils from my early childhood.

About 1882 we started our real work on the garden, filling the border with the best roses we could get at that time. But the Admiral's garden pursuits were greatly interfered with by much sea duty and his four years as Naval Attaché at Paris, Berlin, and St. Petersburg, where his intimate knowledge of French, Spanish, Italian, German, and Russian, and a notable facility in getting along with other languages, made his services especially valuable to the Government. Indeed, though a Mayflower descendant, he had been mistaken for both a Frenchman and a German!

During 1898 a catalogue of roses fell into my hands which really started our study of varieties. Later, when the Admiral was cruising around the north of Ireland, he went to see the Dickson rose nurseries, leaving them an order for plants; and these were our first importation. One day he said, "France is the home of the rose, and I am going to order plants there," consequently starting his friendship with the greatest rosarian in the world by writing to M. Pernet-Ducher of Lyons.

Whenever the Admiral's sea duty took him within reach of a nursery he went to see it. He obtained formal "leave" to visit the rose nurseries in Luxemburg and Germany, as well as those of India and Japan and our own country.

Roses were not his only floral interest, for he sent home iris, lilies, peonies, lilacs, and various other shrubs from different parts of the world.

After his profession and the nation, flowers and shrubs came first in his heart, and the many friendships he made in this way gave him great pleasure to the day of his death.

Few of the Admiral's friends knew that he was a poet in words as well as a poet in friendship and in his garden. To the Secretary of the American Rose Society, in acknowledging receipt of the resolutions of respect, Mrs. Ward transmitted the poem which had been read at his funeral:

RESPICE FINEM

"Look to the end." No change of tide
Nor fickle breezes should decide
The course we steer across the seas,
That bear our human destinies.
For him who shapes that course aright
The final, beckoning, entrance light
Gleams with a welcome doubly bright.
The slowly quavering harbor bell,
To many but a funeral knell,
For him re-echoes, "All is well."
And wafted to his grateful sense
The Home-wind bears its frankincense,
Myrtle of human sympathy,
Or laurel of posterity.
—AARON WARD

PLATE V. The Late Admiral Aaron Ward
(See "The Passing of a Great Rosarian," page 51)

Winter Work with Roses
By ALFRED W. GREELEY, Williamsport, Pa.

EDITOR'S NOTE.—The experience here detailed and the charts reproduced suggest not only desirable winter work for the rosarian, but a character and quality of test which ought to result in eliminating the unsatisfactory sorts. To follow the ingenious plan worked out by a busy newspaper editor for his winter relation to his garden will give any of us some *real* rose knowledge.

TO THE amateur rosarian the dead winter months have their fascination only in degree less pleasurable than the cultural joys of spring and summer. Winter is the time for reviewing and planning; for the analysis of last year's mistakes and the synthesis of this year's successes. It is under the study lamp, while the snow piles deep over the rose-beds and the thermometer flirts with the nether ranges of the scale, that the strategy of the drive for the coming season's rhythm of rose bloom is perfected, if the rosarian is wise.

Success with roses demands knowledge, experiment and patience—patient, tireless experience that adds ever to the determined desire to know the whys and hows of the never-ceasing miracle of rose bloom. It is an instance of appetite growing by what it feeds upon. He who has watched a rose through its transformation cycle from swelling bud and pulsing green leaf to the burst of beauty in the opening petals of the crowning bloom, and feels no fierce spur to know the why and how of this wonder-work of nature, may be a grower of roses, but a rosarian, never! To the rosarian worthy of the name, the opening rose is an invocation and a benediction, a lyric prayer that springs attuned in beauty from the very heart of nature itself.

As a matter of fact, not one rose-grower in a hundred knows, except in a vague way, whether the roses in his garden, whether his Ophelia, Lady Alice Stanley, or Radiance, are true to type and standard in the unit characters of size, color, substance, number of blooms, and so on, which under average cultural conditions distinguish these varieties. He does not know whether his Mme. Jules Bouche, or Harry Kirk should give him twenty-five or seventy-five flowers during the season, and generally is content if he gets "right smart" of bloom. Lack of knowledge of the standards for bloom is responsible for the fact that the great majority of rose-gardens contain plants that, through inherent inferiority of stock or lack of proper culture, fail to produce either the quality or the average number of blooms characteristic of the variety. Such plants are simply parasites, "free boarders," of the rose-garden. They take as much care and fertilizer as an honest rose, and return only a beggar's dole. The small rose-garden of the average amateur is of too limited space to be cluttered up with under-average plants. They should be scrapped relentlessly.

Profusion of bloom and quality of flowers are the two things which primarily interest the average amateur in rose-growing. Not so long ago, June alone was the month of roses, with only scattering blooms for the rest of the season. The advent of the Hybrid Tea has revolutionized the rose calendar, leaving no excuse for months barren of bloom in the rose-garden.

That which is now true of the dwarfs will soon, let us hope, be likewise true of the climbers. The experts are feeling their way toward this much-desired end. Last year, in my little backyard garden, the first killing frost of November caught Le Mexique rich in hundreds of blossoms, while Ghislaine de Feligonde was not far behind. Growing briers for five-sixths of the season must soon pass out of fashion. For the small garden of the average lover of roses, profusion of quality bloom is the main consideration.

The mere rose-grower plants his roses with more or less careful preparation—sometimes by the signs of the moon—and lets nature do the rest, oftentimes its worst. The enlightened amateur makes almost a religious ceremony of the planting of his roses, which generally occurs late in the fall when the wood is thoroughly ripened and dormant, at which time it feels the minimum of shock from transplanting.

But the chief distinguishing difference between the mere rose-grower and the amateur rosarian is in the matter of keeping intelligent record of the performance of his roses. The small day-book which slips conveniently into the pocket of the old garden coat is the rosarian's *alter ego*. It is the basis of such success as may come to him, for it means recorded observation which later may be analyzed and combined into working rose facts.

Into the rose day-book should go such matters as dates of

bloom, number of blooms cut from disbudded plants, peculiarities of behavior, growth, bloom, etc.; appearance and course of insect and fungus attacks, dates of cultural care; amounts and dates of application of liquid manure, lime and other fertilizers; and temperature readings which should include number of days of sunshine, rainy days, and other data that go to make up the climatic environment. Temperature data, however, generally can be obtained from the local weather observation bureau at the end of the season.

This, in the main, includes the essential facts out of which knowledge of rose habits and behavior is built up and by which local standards of rose-bloom and perfection can be established. Only by this method can the amateur rosarian identify for a certainty those roses which are doing their bloom-duty for him, and, at the same time, discover the lazy, defective plants that are to be weeded out.

A daily bloom-count at the time of cutting in the morning, is about all that is necessary for this purpose, and it is generally as far as the average amateur gets the first season in recorded observation. Afterward his enthusiasm for recorded facts grows. Every addition to rose knowledge brings to us new vistas.

It takes only a few moments each day to transfer the facts from the garden day-book to a set of indexed cards arranged alphabetically under the name of each rose. This card carries the name of the rose, date of purchase and transplanting, age, nursery from which obtained, type, stock, budding and grafting information, and the like. It is a condensed life history of each rose from year to year, with all the facts grouped ready for quick comparison. Another convenient method of permanent record is an indexed loose-leaved book of the right size. It has some advantages over the card system. Other recording methods will suggest themselves to the enthusiast, growing out of individual needs and experiences.

The material for observation and record is virtually limitless, but it is well for the beginner to confine his data to a few relatively simple things at first, such as the discovery of "boarders;" effects of mulching in hot weather; bloom-production of Hybrid Perpetuals, Hybrid Teas, Teas, and Pernetianas; comparisons of various budding stocks; the response to fertilizers of various kinds; special beds; own-root plants compared with budded or grafted stocks; immunity to insect and fungus attacks, etc.

It is only by persistent observation, sturdy questioning and insatiable curiosity that one can attain that almost intuitive understanding of rose character, temperament, and habit that constitutes the rosarian's chief satisfaction.

After the completion of the card-index work comes the tabulation for purposes of comparison, without which the work is relatively valueless. Here comes the test of the year's work in the summation of rose performance. A standard of comparison is necessary, and for Philadelphia and districts of similar climatic conditions, the only available standard is that established by Capt. George C. Thomas, Jr., in his large test-gardens and published in the latest edition of his "Practical Book of Outdoor Rose-Growing." For this pioneering test-garden work and invaluable results American rosarians are under deep obligations to Captain Thomas. The method of comparison is indicated in the following extract from the tabulation of rose performance in my own garden during 1918:

FIRST CLASS: Fifty blooms or more.

No.	Name	1918	1917	Thomas
1.	Mrs. A. R. Waddell, H. T.	84	54	57
2.	Mme. Jules Bouche, H. T.	81	—	71
3.	La Tosca, H. T.	80	—	57
4.	Gruss an Teplitz, H. T.	79	64	107
5.	Harry Kirk, T.	76	31	32
6.	Frau Karl Druschki (No. 1), H. P.	71	64	65
6.	Betty, H. T.	71	21	54
7.	Radiance (No. 4), H. T.	65	—	51
8.	Radiance (No. 2), H. T.	64	—	51
9.	Mme. Segond Weber, H. T.	57	—	49
10.	Lady Pirrie, H. T.	52	—	56
10.	Frau Karl Druschki (No. 2), H. P.	52	45	65
11.	Mrs. Aaron Ward, H. T.	50	20	38
11.	Radiance (No. 3), H. T.	50	—	51

SECOND CLASS. Forty to forty-nine blooms.

No.	Name	1918	1917	Thomas
12.	Wm. R. Smith, T.	49	—	14
13.	Mrs. B. R. Cant, T.	47	—	50
13.	Gen. MacArthur, H. T.	47	23	35
14.	Mme. Edouard Herriot, Per.	46	—	32
15.	Radiance (No. 1), H. T.	45	25	51
16.	Baron de Bonstetten, H. P.	44	13	—
17.	Killarney, H. T.	42	15	—

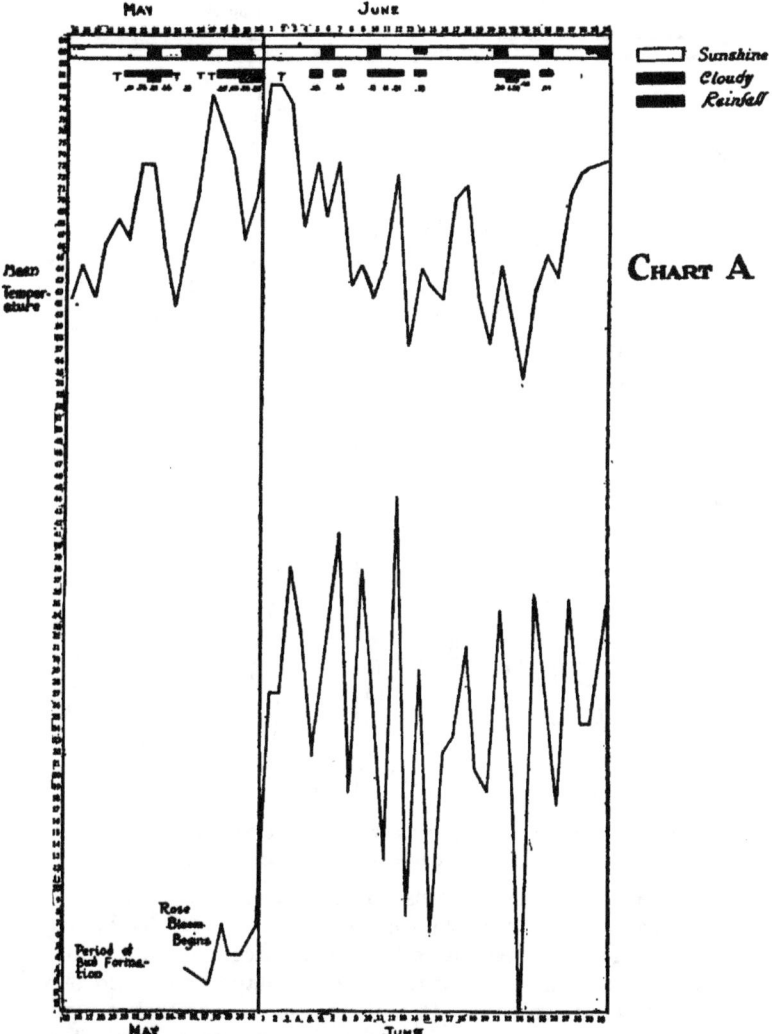

CHART A

Figures top and bottom are days of the month. Figures at left are number of buds, below, and degrees of mean daily temperature (Fahrenheit), above.
Top block indicates sunshine or cloudy; and shaded blocks show rainfall. Small figures below shaded blocks are quantity of rainfall in hundredths of an inch.

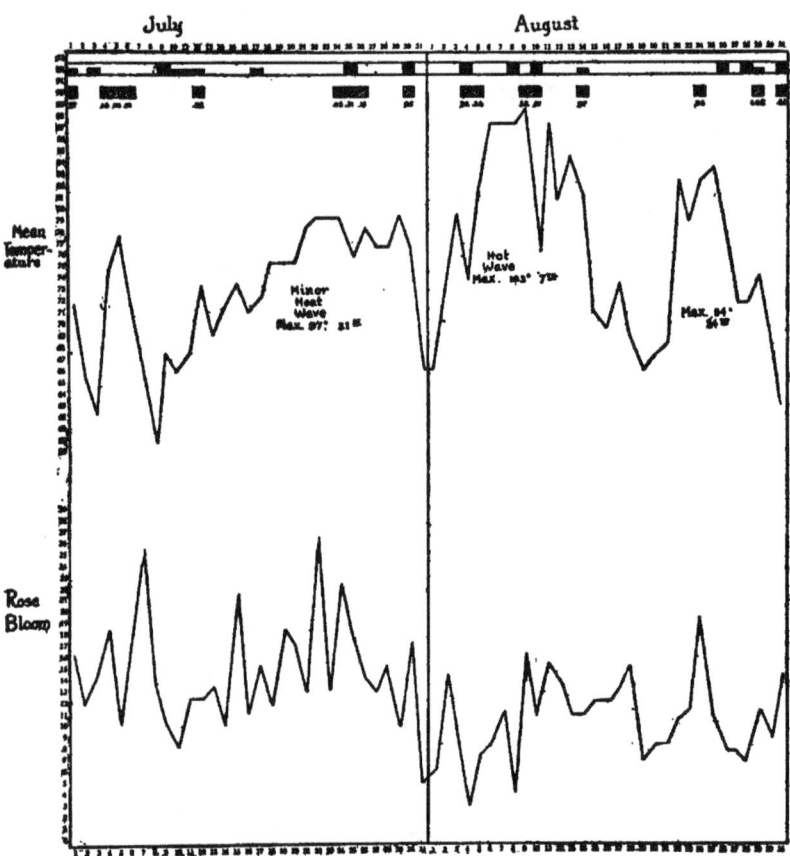

CHART A, continued. See explanation on page 61.

The third class contains all those producing from 25 to 39 blooms, and all under 25 are put in a class of "shy bloomers," from which the weeding-out process takes place after all other expedients of first aid to rose slackers have been tried in vain. This comparison shows at a glance the roses which are able to meet the requirements of a discriminating grower, and it grows in value with the years.

The card-index record also furnishes material for other

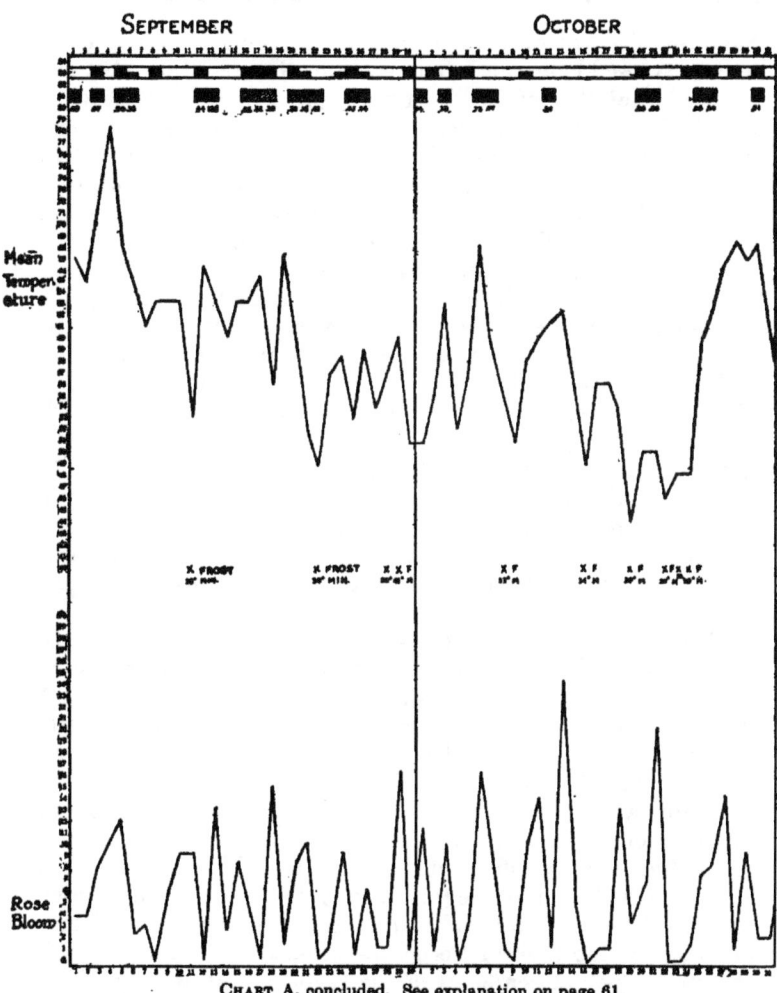

CHART A, concluded. See explanation on page 61.

interesting studies, as, for instance: What are the local weather conditions under which roses thrive best? With the data on the cards, together with the reports of the local weather station, the question is easily answered, as shown in Chart A. Here we have revealed not only the somewhat startling correspondence between rose-bloom and temperature changes, but also the effect of rainfall, sunshine, heat-waves, and frost, which in various combinations are written plainly on the chart. We all know in a general way the dependence of rose-bloom upon a certain range of temperature combined with a definite degree of moisture and sunshine, but few, save the experts, suspect the immediate and sensitive relationship indicated in the quick response the chart shows. Notice how closely the various peaks of rose-bloom fit into the peaks of mean temperature for virtually the entire garden period. The chart likewise emphasizes the optimum bloom-conditions of heat, moisture, and sunshine in June, and the depressing effects caused by the two heat-waves. The discouraging September conditions, an environment of cold, rainy, cloudy days, with a minimum of sunshine, are reflected in the September section of the chart, while the comparatively more favorable conditions which October presented, resulting in an average higher level of rose-bloom, are shown in the section for that month. Throughout the temperature-rhythm and the bloom-rhythm are found in intimate and sensitive correspondence.

The study of a chart of this character enables the rosarian to discover just what local climatic conditions are most favorable to the roses he has under cultivation and development, and it further enables him to approximate, by mulching, culture, shading, watering, and the like, these favorable conditions when he may normally expect unfavorable weather environment.

A further analysis of rose-bloom is presented in Chart B. Here a comparison by months is made of the blooming qualities of the five most prolific Hybrid Perpetuals, Hybrid Teas, and Teas, as established by the tabulation taken from the card-index record. The chart graphically indicates the short period of blooming glory of the Hybrid Perpetuals, so-called, contrasted with the real perpetual character of the Hybrid Teas and the Teas, and it likewise demonstrates, so far as the plants under consideration are concerned, the superiority of both the Hybrid Teas and the Teas over the Hybrid Perpetuals in total bloom and period of efflorescence. The comparison is defective in that the Hybrid Perpetuals were on Brier and Manetti stock,

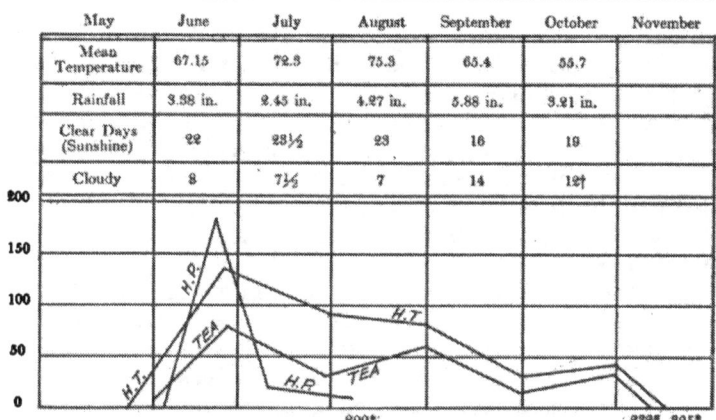

*Total bloom of season. †Eight mornings of dense fog.

CHART B. Comparison of bloom records of five each most prolific Hybrid Perpetuals, Hybrid Teas and Teas, in relation to season, temperature, rainfall and sunshine. (Figures at left indicate number of blooms; below are varieties used with detailed record).

HYBRID PERPETUALS		TEAS	
Frau Karl Druschki (No. 1)	71	Harry Kirk	76
Frau Karl Druschki (No. 2)	52	Wm. R. Smith	49
Baron de Bonstetten	44	Mrs. B. R. Cant	47
Margaret Dickson	19	Lady Hillingdon	30
Mrs. John Laing	14	Maman Cochet	30
	200		232
Average bloom	40	Average bloom	46
(Brier and Manetti stock)		(Selected Multiflora stock).	

HYBRID TEAS			
Mrs. A. R. Waddell	84	PER CENT OF TOTAL BLOOM	
Mme. Jules Bouche	81	Hybrid Teas	48
La Tosca	80	Hybrid Perpetuals	24
Gruss an Teplitz (Manetti)	79	Teas	28
Betty	71		100
	395		
Average bloom	79		
(Selected Multiflora stock).			

Count made at time of cutting. All roses, except Gruss an Teplitz, disbudded to assure perfection of bloom.

while the Hybrid Teas, and the Teas, with one exception, were budded on selected Multiflora stock, from which I have never yet detected a sucker.

But, perhaps, the most significant feature of this chart is

found in the performance of the Teas. August, with its recurrent heat-waves, hot, scorching days, and deficient rainfall, is the month the American rose-grower fears. The August section of Chart A shows the havoc it brings in its trail. But Chart B indicates that August presents a combination of weather conditions of which the Teas highly approve, for in August they nearly equaled their June burst of bloom. Possibly we may find in a development of the hardy Teas a solution of the problem of the August rose-garden!

Chart B also is interesting in indicating in another way the superiority of the Hybrid Teas. The chart shows that the average bloom of the Hybrid Perpetuals was 40 for the season; for the five Teas it was 46; while for the Hybrid Teas the average was 79. This gives a bloom percentage of 24 for the Hybrid Perpetuals, 28 for the Teas, and 48 for the Hybrid Teas. In the development or reconstruction of a rose-garden, it is necessary to establish facts of this character before one can work intelligently and successfully toward rose-perfection.

If America is to become the promised land of roses—a consummation devoutly to be wished—every little rose-garden must become in a way a test-garden, a rose laboratory for the perfection of types and standards suitable to American conditions. Without detracting in the least from the splendid work of American hybridizers and growers, there is yet a big field for the amateur rosarian who brings to the work of rose-perfection a point of view quite different from that taken by the rose-expert, the professional grower, and the technical hybridizer. The standards of rose-perfection are in the hands of the amateur, for he forms the majority of buyers in America. The more exacting his demands upon the rose sellers, the harder will they work to meet them and the higher will the standards of American rose-production become. Probably 50 per cent of the roses in American gardens today, through lack of proper culture, budding on inferior stock, or for many other reasons, fall far below the type average of bloom and are inferior both in quantity and quality. It is only through the self-education of American amateur rosarians, the rose-consumers of the country, that the standards of rose-excellence can be permanently raised to higher levels and the ideals of rose-perfection approximated.

Riding a Rose Hobby in Montreal
By HAROLD W. NELLES, Montreal, Canada

EDITOR'S NOTE.—What is below written ought to encourage any rose-amateur in the United States, for it shows what can be done with actual enjoyment even in a seriously cold climate.

OUTDOOR rose-culture on the island of Montreal presents some difficulties, but none that are insurmountable. The temperature falls low in winter, at times as low as 20 below zero, and, in addition to this, in the spring there are extremes of often 40 degrees in a few hours, accompanied by freezing and thawing, which, as is known, is harder on a rose bush than a steady cold. In the summer we have a dry heat during the day, and the nights lack the heavy dews of the mountains and the moist salt-laden breezes of the coastal regions. These conditions are much better on the lakeshore than they are in the interior of the island or in the city proper. Many times, however, I have thought of my more fortunate rose friends along the seashore, when I have had some promising blooms fail to develop because of a period of dry, hot weather, and I have longed for the cool night-breeze from the ocean, laden with moisture that is so refreshing to gardens and workers alike.

Were we able to grow roses with as little trouble as we can grow sunflowers, I expect we would have no interest in them, and it is good that something within us urges on to attempt the things that are difficult, and that one thrill of pleasure from success under difficult conditions more than compensates for all our previous failures. For example, last year I attempted to grow Montreal melons. My friends told me my troubles were only commencing. They were correct!

The soil on the island of Montreal is a rich, heavy clay, ideal for roses. In some places there is very little top-soil, especially on the hills or near the shores of the lake or river. The under-drainage is splendid, because of the gravelly nature of the soil, but we have, of course, a layer of yellow subsoil which must be removed. As you may imagine, it is considerable work to lay the foundation for a good rose-bed when you must take off the top-soil, get rid of the yellow clay, and then get deep enough into the gravelly soil to permit of a good quantity of prepared soil being filled in. The usual preparation of soil rose-lovers are fully conversant with. I supplement this with liberal dressings of bone-meal.

The location of my rose-bed, I believe, has been particularly fortunate. It is sheltered from the prevailing northwest wind by the house and some bushes. This wind is very cold in winter and would blow all the snow protection off the bed, but, sheltered as it is, the snow remains, to protect. Though the apple orchards in this section were very badly winterkilled, my little garden of Hybrid Teas came through practically intact.

My rose-bed has a southeastern exposure and gets the full benefit of the morning and early afternoon sun, and as the lake is only one hundred yards away, and this lake is five miles wide, it gets the benefit of much of the cool, damp, evening breeze, when there is one. I believe the best protection for a rose bush is earth, piled up high and allowed to freeze, then a good dressing of old manure with some straw in it, and, on top of this, cedar boughs or brush or cornstalks, that will hold the snow and break the force of the spring sun. We had zero weather for weeks, some days the temperature was down to 20 below, and our winter lasted from the middle of November until the end of March. Some few bushes were killed back and some suffered at the roots.

Mrs. Arthur E. Coxhead, a Tea rose which had done very well the previous year, was affected so badly that I had practically no bloom all season—a great disappointment to me. I know nothing finer than Mrs. Coxhead in its clear claret shade. Frau Karl Druschki, the only Hybrid Perpetual in the garden, was practically killed back to the ground, yet before the season was gone I had some good, strong shoots and fair blooms. All these bushes are young. I brought them from Ireland, and they have only been in two seasons. They are all Hybrid Teas and Teas but Druschki. Speaking of Tea roses, I am of the opinion that the winters here are too severe and the changes too abrupt for them. I have some Mme. Edouard Herriot bushes in the garden and I have seen no shade to equal its intense coral-red. I think I have had better success with Lady Alice Stanley than, perhaps, any other bush. This rose won the Gold Medal of the National Rose Society in 1909. The bloom is deep coral-rose on the outside petals, on the inside pale flesh, and is large and full, carried erect on strong stems. For cutting, it cannot be excelled. Mrs. Alfred Tate, in the bud stage, is a joy to look upon—long pointed buds, exquisite coloring of coppery red, shaded fawn. Betty—you all know Betty—another National Rose Society Gold Medal rose, with coppery rose blooms of perfect form, has also done well with me. I put in some British Queen, and for a time thought this rose might equal Frau Karl Druschki, which to my mind is the most perfect white rose, but was disappointed. The wood has been weak and the blooms small and of poor form. The crimson sorts have done the best of all shades, and with less care. King George V, Edward Mawley, George Dickson, all are fine, strong bushes, and bloom all season, producing flowers beautiful in form, sweetly perfumed, and excellent for cutting. Why is it that crimson roses are more heavily laden with perfume than any other shade?

I want to say something about Isobel, a single rose I have. The shade I would say is bright cerise shaded to scarlet, but is hard to describe. To get the full beauty of the flowers, cut them when half expanded and watch the changing form and color. The petals have that exquisite fluting of the edge that you find in a Spencer sweet pea. The bush blooms in profusion all season.

There are many other bushes I could name that are growing well—Mrs. George Shawyer, Mrs. Amy Hammond, Duchess of Sutherland, Robin Hood, Queen Mary, Countess Clanwilliam—all Hybrid Teas of delicate shades, in most cases, and not commonly grown in this climate. Each has its own individuality and charm, speaking to me in its own language during the season and what they say lives with me during the long, cold winter months in town. So many of the beautiful things in life we cannot have with us always—

> "Still may time hold some golden space
> Where I'll unpack that scented store
> Of song and flower and sky and face,
> And count and touch and turn them o'er,
> Musing upon them."

Those lines were written by Rupert Brooke, the English soldier lad who died for his country and the cause of liberty, and lies buried on the Island of Lemnos in the Ægean.

It has seemed to me that all beautiful things should go, one with the other—roses, music, and beautiful thoughts expressed in the music of words—I cannot separate them entirely. Some friends come into my garden who will pass my roses or my sweet peas without a glance, and head straight for the vegetable garden to enthuse over the wonderful growth of the rhubarb or potatoes. I shall leave to some of you who have a penchant for psychology to explain why some minds see more wonder in the growth of a squash than in the beauty of a rose.

To return to the practical side of rose culture in this district, and in connection with the all-important question of insects, I do not think we suffer any more than any other locality in this respect. Eternal vigilance is the price of safety, and prevention is always better than cure. I spray early and often. "Black-leaf 40," whale-oil soap, arsenate of lead—you know them all and their uses for the enemies of your roses. Mildew is prevalent at times. The changes in weather are responsible, I believe, and I use flour of sulphur. There is one little worm that I have found very hard to deal with. It will eat into the promising buds, and once started, the bud is done for. Powdered hellebore will kill it, but it is hard on the bud, and, in any case, it is generally too late, as the damage has been done. Perhaps some of you who read this can tell me some good way to control this pest. I should indeed appreciate it if you could.

People have said to me at various times, "We would like to grow roses, but they require so much care." Yes, that is true if you look at it in that way, but if you are really fond of roses, you do not think first of the care. You will think of your roses as the children of your garden, and try to protect them and make them strong to fight their natural enemies, the same as you protect your human children and endeavor to make them strong. Your care of your bushes will be well repaid.

I do not suppose that conditions similar to those that I have outlined as existing in Montreal will be found in many, if any, localities in America, but my experience shows that many tender roses can be grown successfully, even in a cold climate.

The Second Year of Back-Yard Bloom-Record

By A. P. GREELEY, Washington, D. C.

EDITOR'S NOTE.—In comparison with, and extension of, his record, presented on pages 135-138 of the 1918 Annual, Mr. Greeley writes to bring the information up to date. It is such recording that determines facts. It is interesting, too, that the Washington Mr. Greeley has the same disposition for detail investigation as Mr. Greeley of Williamsport!

THE roses in my back yard, reported on in the 1918 Annual, made a better bloom-record this year than last, in spite of the fact that a considerable number were killed by the hard winter and others were more or less severely injured. The best bloomer which I have, G. Nabonnand, and which has stood seven winters without injury, was killed to the roots but came up well, giving, however, only 144 blooms for the season as against 482 in 1917. Other roses were correspondingly injured.

My roses were practically unprotected when snow fell, the last of November, just in time to prevent my distributing the protecting material which I had ready for use, and it remained on the ground until February. Any rose which, under the circumstances, shows more blooms than in 1917 is entitled to a high rating for hardiness for this latitude, and those that came through at all, even with injury, are certainly fairly hardy.

Of a number of plants set out in November, 1917, just before the snowfall referred to, nearly all did very well this season, though hardly better than some set out in March. All of these, and most of those set out in March, are budded on Multiflora and, of course, were received dormant. Those received later as growing plants on own roots have not done so well, though it is interesting to note how a number of own-root plants set out last year and, giving little or no bloom last season, have shown up this year with a creditable number of blooms.

Of the roses on the accompanying record all seem to me to be good to very good, except Mrs. Andrew Carnegie, Hugo Roller, Dean Hole, Etoile de Lyon and Lady Greenall.

The record of the roses which gave me five or more blooms during the season follows on two succeeding pages:

	Own Roots or Grafted	Date set out	Blooms 1917	Blooms 1918	First bloom 1918	May	June	July	Aug.	Sept.	Oct.	Nov.
Mme. Eugene Marlitt	O. R.	1910	193	200	May 18	133	30	2	15	9	11	2
George Elger	G. R.	Nov. 1917		185	May 18	41	32	39	35	20	16	7
G. Nabonnand	O. R.	1910	482	144	May 15	26	13	32	26	22	11	1
Leonie Lamesch	G. R.	Nov. 1917		131	May 14	19	17	33	28	20	13	
Eugenie Lamesch	O. R.	1916	50	101	May 18	11	13	22	26	15	14	
Lady Ursula	O. R.	1917	24	99	May 15	10	18	25	19	9	14	1
Ecarlate	O. R.	1917	17	87	May 14	8	17	16	21	11	18	
Lucullus	O. O.	1909	120	71	May 9	49	3	14		5	13	3
Mme. Edmee Metz	G.	Nov. 1917		61	May 19	9	14	22	6	3	4	1
Antoine Rivoire	R.	1916	39	50	May 18	3	15	8	11	3	9	3
Winter Gem	O. R.	1909	11	47	May 20	3	11	20	3	8	4	
Melody	G.	Mar. 1918		46	May 25	7	13	13	6	1	6	
General-Superior Arnold Janssen	G.	Nov. 1917		35	May 21	4	8	9	7	2	5	
Mrs. Herbert Stevens	R.	1917	5	30	May 27	4	4	11	9	1	1	
Grus an Teplitz	O. R.	1916	20	30	June 26		7	17	3	2	1	
Mme. Maurice de Luze	G.	Mar. 1918		28	May 26	4	10	8	2	1		
Mrs. Charles Russell	G.	Nov. 1917		27	May 21	3	9	15		2	5	
Lady Pirrie	G.	1917	10	27	May 20	1	7	9	4	3	2	
Gloire Lyonnaise	O. R.	1910	52	25	May 16	4	2	9	2	1	1	
Tip Top	O. R.	1917	11	25	May 22	7	1	9	4	7	2	
Hoosier Beauty	O. R.	1917	4	25	May 13	2	9	13	1	1	1	
Lady Alice Stanley	R.	Apr. 1918		22	June 5		5	5	3	10	5	
Climbing Moella	O. R.	1909	69	19	Mar. 23	5	12	2	2	2		
Mme. Colette Martinet	G.	Nov. 1917		18	May 21	1	9	6		1		
Herzogin Maria Antoinette	G.	Apr. 1918		18	May 28	2	8	5	3	2	4	
Mrs. F. W. Vanderbilt	G.	Nov. 1917		18	May 19	2	10	2	3	1		
President W. H. Taft	G.	Apr. 1918		18	June 4		4	11	3	1		
Friedrichsruh	G.	1917	8	18	May 14	6	8	4		1		
G. Amedee Hammond	R.	1917	3	17	June 3		6	4	4	2	3	
Mrs. B. R. Cant	O. R.	1910	5	17	June 15		1	7	3	1	2	
White Maman Cochet	O. R.	1916	13	17	May 25	3	5	4		2	3	
Harry Kirk	O. R.	1916	12	16	May 20	5	2	6		1	2	
Mme. Edmond Sabiayrolles	R.	Mar. 1918		16	May 31	2	4	7	2	3	2	
Joseph Hill	O. R.	1917	1	15	May 22	1	2	4	3	2	2	
Radiance	G.	1916	9	15	May 20	2	3	3	3	1	1	
Etoile de France	G.	Nov. 1917		15	May 25	2	6	2	2	2	2	
Tipperary	G.	Mar. 1918		14	May 24	5	3	1		2		
Mrs. James Lynas	R.	Mar. 1918		14	May 28	6	4	2	1	1		
Mme. Edouard Herriot	G.	1916	2	14	June 5		5	2	4	2	1	
Panama	O. R.	Apr. 1918		13	June 10		4	3	1	1		
La Tosca	O. R.	1916	16	13	May 13	1	8	1	2	4	4	2
Mrs. Charles E. Pearson	O. R.	1916	8	13	May 30	2	3	3	1	1	1	
Mme. Jules Bouche	R.	Apr. 1918		12	June 20		1	3	1	2		
National Emblem	O. R.	Nov. 1917		12	May 17	1	5	3	3			
Laurent Carle	R.	1916	12	12	May 26	1	6	5	3	2	1	
Konigin Carols	G.	Apr. 1918		11	June 20		6	2	2			
Francis C. Seton	O. R.	1916	20	11	May 27	1	2	4	1	5	3	

	Own Roots or Grafted	Date set out	Blooms 1917	Blooms 1918	First bloom 1918	May	June	July	Aug.	Sept.	Oct.	Nov.
Queens Scarlet	O. R.	1909	26	11	May 22	4	3	3	1	1		
Mrs. S. T. Wright	G.	Mar. 1918		10	May 28	2	2	3	2	2		
Marquise de Querhoent	O. R.	1917	20	10	June 5		5	1	1			
Mrs. Frank Bray	O. R.	1916	10	10	June 7			1	4	1		
Miss Cynthia Forde	G.	Apr. 1918		9	May 27	1	4	6	1			
H. D. M. Barton	G.	Mar. 1918		9	May 18	2	3	1	1			
Marquise de Ganay	G.	May 1918		9	June 11			5				
Paul Neyron		1910	16	9	May 22	9	3	4	3	1	1	
Mme. Caroline Testout	O. R.	1917	14	9	May 21	2	2	4	1	3	1	
Mrs. Aaron Ward	O. R.	1916	12	9	June 5		2	4	1			
Comte G. de Rochemur	O. R.	1917	8	9	May 31	1	2	2	1			
Mrs. A. R. Waddell	O. R.	1917	1	9	June 10		1	3	2		4	
Mrs. Andrew Carnegie	O. R.	1917	1	9	June 10		1	2				
Cleveland	G.	Mar. 1918		8	May 25	1	4	3			2	
Donald MacDonald	G.	Nov. 1917	17	8	May 21	1	4	2	1	1		
Autumn Tinta	G.	1917	12	8	May 13	2	4	1	1	3	1	
George Dickson	O. R.	1916	7	8	May 24	1	4	3	2	1		
Miss Alice de Rothschild	G.	1917	4	8	June 3		2	2	8		1	
Lyon Rose	O. R.	1917	1	8	May 28	1	3	4	1			
Hugo Roller				7	May 21	1	1	3	15	2		
Flame of Fire	G.	Mar. 1918		7	July 1			3	3	2		
Mme. Ravary	G.	May 1918		7	May 23	4		8	1	1	2	
Mrs. Wakefield Christie-Miller	O. R.	1917	23	7	June 12		4	2	2	1		
Mrs. Amy Hammond	G.	1917	12	7	May 18	2	1	2	1	1		
White Killarney	G.	1917	10	7	May 18	1	2	3	2		1	
Senateur Mascurand	O. R.	1917	2	7	May 15	2	2	2	1		2	
Etoile Poitevine	O. R.	1917	2	7	May 16	1	2	3	1	1		
Dean Hole	O. R.	1916	2	7	May 15	1	1	2	1			
Etoile de Lyon	O. R.	1917	0	7	June 13		1	2	2		2	
Earl of Warwick	O. R.	Apr. 1918		6	May 28		1	4	1	1		
Irish Fireflame	G.	Apr. 1918		6	Aug. 9				2	3	1	
Souv. de Gustave Prat	O. R.	Apr. 1918		6	June 30			2	3	1		
Mme. Segond Weber	O. R.	1917	23	6	May 17	2	1	1	1	1		
Gorgeous	O. R.	1916	7	6	May 24	1	2	1	1	1		
Edward Mawley	O. R.	1917	5	6	May 29	1	2	2	1			
Florence Forrester	O. R.	1917	3	6	June 11	2		4	1			
Col. R. S. Williamson	O. R.	1917	0	6	June 16			2	1			
Marie Van Houtte	O. R.	1917	0	6	June 24			1	1	1	1	
My Maryland	O. R.	May 1918		5	May 23		2	2	1		2	1
Duchess of Wellington	O. R.	1917	13	5	June 7		2	1	1	1	1	
Los Angeles	O. R.	1917	12	5	June 8	1	1	2	1			
Lady Plymouth	O. R.	1917	4	5	May 25		1	1	2	1		
George C. Waud	O. R.	1917	2	5	July 6			1	1			
Lady Greenall	O. R.	1917	1	5	July 21			2	3			
Rhea Reid	O. R.	1917	1	5	May 31	1	1	2	1	1	1	
Lieut. Chaure	O. R.	1917	1	5								

More About Crown-Canker

By L. M. MASSEY, Plant Pathologist, Ithaca, N. Y.

EDITOR'S NOTE.—The further study of the crown-canker that sometimes seriously injures greenhouse roses gives added knowledge of its cause and control. It is unfortunate that the American Rose Society was not able to support the continuance of Dr. Massey's capable pathological investigations, and it is hoped that the settled conditions likely to ensue in 1919 will permit the scientific study of rose diseases to be resumed. It is only by such study that rose-growers can be assured of protection against many diseases yet likely to appear as a menace to our favorite flower.

Greenhouse rose-growers are urged to acquaint themselves with the details of this bad disease. To many, there is confusion, because the terms are not understood. In this paper a clear explanation is made to avoid misunderstanding. Neglect may prove most expensive.

THE first report of the disease of greenhouse roses to which the name "crown-canker" was given was made by the writer in December, 1917.* An account of the trouble was given in the American Rose Annual for 1918 (pages 64–67, Plate IV). As stated in this report, the disease manifests itself in the production of brown, dead areas (cankers) on the stems, usually at the crown. Plants of the varieties Hoosier Beauty, Ophelia, Hadley, Mrs. Charles Russell, Sunburst, American Beauty, and many seedlings have been observed to be affected with the disease, and records have been obtained of its occurrence in the states of Missouri, Pennsylvania, Indiana, Michigan, Massachusetts, and New York. Plants are seldom killed outright, but linger on and produce increasingly poor and few blossoms. Such plants do not respond to forcing. Dead plant-parts are conspicuous in affected houses.

Work upon the control of this disease was undertaken in coöperation with Profs. A. V. Osmun and P. J. Anderson, of the Massachusetts Agricultural Experiment Station. A report of the work, in bulletin form, has been made by Professor Anderson.† Much of the information contained in the following paragraphs has been obtained from this report, it seeming to be desirable at this time to furnish readers of the American Rose Annual with a summary of all published facts up to date.

*Massey, L. M. The Crown-canker Disease of Rose. Phytopathology 7: 408–417. 1917.
†Anderson, P. J. Rose-canker and Its Control. Mass. Agr. Exp. Sta. Bul. 183: 10–46. 1918.

PLATE VI. ROSA XANTHINA, as Blooming near Washington, D. C.
(A hardy, clear yellow rose, introduced from China in 1906 by the late Frank N. Meyer. Photograph supplied by Office of Foreign Seed and Plant Introduction, Department of Agriculture. See page 39; also, see Plate VIII.)

IMPORTANT FACTS CONCERNING CAUSE OF CROWN-CANKER

Crown-canker is produced by the growth of a fungus* within the tissues of the plant. Prior to observations, made by the writer, of its occurrence as a parasite on the rose, this fungus was known to exist only as a saprophyte (that is, growing only on decaying vegetable matter), having been found growing on an old pod of the honey locust and on dead papaw leaves. To just what extent the fungus is to be found in nature, growing under saprophytic conditions, is unknown. There is a possibility that it is widely distributed, growing on dead and decaying plant tissue, and, possibly, existing as a natural inhabitant of the soil. Data are at hand to show that the fungus will live in the soil for at least a year, without the presence of the rose plant, and still retain its ability to infect.

Sources of Infection.—It is probable that most diseased plants become infected from being planted in soil infested with the fungus. In contact with a rose plant the mycelium, or vegetative part of the fungus, quickly grows through the bark into the tissues, upon which it lives. Spores are produced on the surface of the cankers of affected plants, especially when growing under very moist conditions. Just what part these spores play in the dissemination of the fungus is unknown. Information is at hand to show that when these spores are placed in contact with the plant under proper conditions of temperature and moisture, infection is readily obtained, so that any agency, such as insects, currents of air, man in cultivating, might carry spores and aid in spreading the disease.

The fungus may be carried from one place to another through the exchange of diseased plants or of plants to which have adhered particles of soil carrying the organism. Such infested soil may remain dry for months without killing the mycelium, or interfering with its power to infect rose plants with which it may come in contact.

Temperature Relations.†—Spores‡ of the fungus germinate at

Cylindrocladium scoparium Morgan.
†Data from Mass. Agr. Exp. Sta. Bul. 183.
‡Spores or reproductive cells of a fungus correspond to the seeds of higher plants. The vegetative part of a fungus (mycelium) consists of numerous threads or hyphæ. The spores of many fungi offer greater resistance to frost and heat than the mycelium, and of most fungi the high and low temperatures at which the spores are killed are different from those required to kill the mycelium.

any temperature between 46° and 97° F., the most favorable temperature for germination, unfortunately, being about the same as that for the growing of roses. This eliminates the possibility of retarding the progress of the disease by maintaining a temperature unfavorable to the development of the fungus. All spores are killed by freezing for thirty-six hours and will fail to germinate after being exposed to a temperature of 120° F. for ten minutes. The spores (not the mycelium) are also killed by drying, fifteen days under dry conditions being sufficiently long to kill them, while in a humid atmosphere they will live several weeks.

It has already been stated that the fungus can live for an indefinite period in the soil without the presence of the host (rose plant). Mycelium probably exists in the soil to a depth of several feet, depending on the character of the soil. The mycelium develops best at a temperature of 79° to 81° F., the minimum temperature for growth being about 47° F. and the maximum between 86° and 90° F. Under favorable conditions the mycelium will grow through a foot of soil in about forty days.

The fungus cannot be destroyed by exposing soil to freezing temperatures. An exposure of the mycelium to a temperature of about 122° F. for ten minutes will kill it. Soil may be thoroughly freed from the fungus by treating it with formalin solution—one pint of commercial formalin to twenty-five gallons of water—at the rate of two gallons per cubic foot. Sterilization by steam is a very efficient manner of killing the organism in the soil. Since the fungus is killed when exposed to a temperature of about 122° F. for ten minutes, there is a possibility of being able to disinfect the soil with hot water; and, when steam is used, the higher temperature and longer periods of time recommended for killing other fungi in the soil are possibly unnecessary. Of course, the higher temperatures give additional assurance. Growers will probably look upon the use of hot water with disfavor, because it leaves the soil in poor condition to be worked, and leaches fertility from it. Steam, however, is not so objectionable.

Recommendations for Control.—It has been pointed out that crown-canker is an important and serious disease of roses under

MORE ABOUT CROWN-CANKER

glass. Once a house is infested with the fungus, the cost and labor involved in eradicating the organism are of no small consequence. Growers should acquaint themselves with the symptoms of the disease and thoroughly inspect their houses to see if any plants are affected. If not, make an effort to keep it out. The suppression of a disease, which, if given no attention may later cause thousands of dollars' worth of damage, may be accomplished at this time. As previously noted, the fungus may be brought into a rose house either in or upon diseased plants, or in particles of soil clinging to plants. Look to the source of the plants and then examine them carefully for signs of disease, rejecting any with questionable dead areas on the bark.

If but a few plants in a house are affected, they should be removed at once and destroyed by fire, together with as much of the surrounding soil as possible. As an additional precaution, drench the soil from which the diseased plants were removed with formalin of the recommended strength. In case the disease is prevalent in the house, the only practical method of procedure is to destroy all plants, remove the old soil, thoroughly disinfect the house with formalin (one pint of the commercial solution in twenty-five gallons of water), and then secure soil known to be free from the fungus in which to set disease-free plants. Infested soil may be sterilized by treating it with formalin at the strength given above, applied at the rate of two gallons per cubic foot, or by steam. When the latter is used, the soil should be thoroughly heated to about 122° F. for at least ten minutes, as determined by thermometers placed in the soil. A higher temperature and longer time make for additional safety.

Cuttings should be taken only from disease-free plants and placed in soil known to be free from the fungus. Strict sanitary measures should be practised throughout the development of the plant. In eradicating the fungus from a house, attention should be given to the possibility of the fungus existing in the soil of the walks between the benches, for if it occurs there it will sooner or later be carried to the benches. This soil should be treated in disinfecting the house, and, as an additional precaution, be kept covered with lime. Care should be taken to see that the fungus is not carried to the sterilized benches in particles of soil clinging to tools, boots, and clothes of the workmen, and the like, and through the use of infested manure. A different set of tools should be used, or those which may have come in contact with infested soil should be thoroughly disinfected by dipping them into boiling water or formalin. All pots used in connection with the culture of diseased plants should be disinfected with hot water or formalin. Once the disease has made its appearance in an establishment, the utmost vigilance of the grower will be demanded to insure the eradication of the fungus.

The writer is planning to continue his investigations on the control of this disease. Much remains to be done. Growers can materially aid the work by sending material and reporting the occurrence of the disease. Assistance in determining whether or not the trouble exists in houses will be gladly furnished, and such help on the control of this and other diseases will be rendered by the writer as his other duties will permit.

Save and Use the Roses

By MRS. ANDREW WRIGHT CRAWFORD, Philadelphia

EDITOR'S NOTE.—It was a casual visit to a hospitable home that brought to the Editor knowledge of the splendid work done with surplus vegetables and flowers by an organization of fine-spirited women in several of the "main-line" communities near Philadelphia. The request of Mrs. Crawford for details brought the following plan for 1919 rose beneficences which is heartily commended to all who have or can get at the flowers and the folks who need them.

DON'T let roses die on the plants unpicked! Put them to work making smiles and bringing cheer to the shut-in sufferers who cannot enjoy them in the open. Have you ever seen the change that one rose brings to a sick-room, the new light and life to the patient's face? Tens of thousands of blooms went unpicked last year; let us all join to prevent such a waste in 1919.

The following method has been used with success for two seasons by the Committee for the Collection and Distribution of Surplus Produce, who, with volunteer workers, six days a week,

SAVE AND USE THE ROSES

picked fruit and vegetables free of cost, and took them into a well-organized scheme of distribution—why not do as well with roses? Think of the pleasure of picking the flowers and the benefit from the outdoor exercise, to say nothing of the real good the blooms will do.

Get in touch with owners of rose-gardens in your vicinity, and obtain permission to bring workers to pick their flowers, keeping the plants cleaned up and full of vigor, and putting the posies to good use.

Get the boys and girls to volunteer for certain hours each week.

Place supervisors who have a thorough knowledge of how to cut roses in charge of each group, making sure that they understand the necessity of so cutting as to improve and not hurt the plants.

Get donations of baskets and scissors, and let each supervisor keep a supply on hand.

Obtain offers of motors, when necessary, to carry workers and flowers with the least delay and to remove drudgery.

To have the roses do their best in this work, pick them early in the morning, before the sun's rays have pulled the moisture from the petals, or in the late afternoon. It is always best to put the roses promptly in water, and if they can be stored for an hour or two in a cool, dark place—a cellar is fine!—they will transport better and keep better. Cut the roses with as long stems as practicable.

When picked, the roses may be delivered to:

1. A hospital or home,
2. A day nursery,
3. A central place where a rose-market may be held, the flowers to be sold for the benefit of some proper relief organization.

Perhaps the workers will pick your rose-bugs into kerosene! And why limit the workers to roses; why not the joy of being at work from the time of the early violet until the last little autumn-colored chrysanthemum is smothered in snow? Put all your surplus flowers to work.

The 1918 Rose Season in England
By HERBERT L. WETTERN, London, England

EDITOR'S NOTE.—Written in the early part of October, 1918, these wartime words of Mr. Wettern show how courageously our English friends have been facing the situation. A hard winter, a blue spring, a summer of breathless suspense until the tide-turn of July 18 started the immediate defeat of the Germans—is it not remarkable that a great exhibition could be managed?

ALTHOUGH the winter of 1917–18 was quite an average one, the spring of 1918 proved to be one of the cruellest our rose plants have experienced for many years past. Ushered in by a spell of warm, sunny weather, which started plants well into growth, there followed several days of midwinter, when not only was a fall in temperature to several degrees of frost recorded, but also bitter easterly winds.

The result was soon apparent in casualties of the heaviest description, both killed and wounded. Many plants died outright. Others were blackened nearly down to the brier-junction, and if such a plant eventually succeeded in throwing up a new shoot, it was generally a poor, weakly thing, and the plant did not, and never will, recover. Newly budded stocks were killed wholesale, to one-half the planting.

In the writer's well-sheltered garden 10 to 15 per cent of rose plants were killed outright, particularly the Teas, whilst of newly budded standards and dwarfs hardly 10 per cent survived. Most of the rose-gardens and nurseries all over England suffered; in fact, the reverses of the spring of 1918 were serious.

Summer started off with heat and drought; in fact one could never remember seeing rose-gardens looking more miserable, owing to gaps in beds where plants had succumbed, and to the struggle for moisture of the thin, weak shoots on those that had survived—moisture delayed till the time of full bloom.

Summer has now passed, and autumn is treating us liberally with rain, but the growths on our roses are far from strong, and a year or two must elapse before the plants will recover their vigor after such a bitter experience.

Of new rose work there is little to record—the war has been keeping our souls and bodies too fully engaged!—but while the advent of the American troops in France and elsewhere has stimulated us nationally, the American Rose Annual of 1918 has encouraged our rose hopes and aspirations.

Our National Rose Society boldly decided to hold its big Annual Show. All credit to them for their wisdom, for it was a brilliant success, honored by the presence of Her Gracious Majesty, Queen Alexandra, the Society's patroness.

The classes had naturally been cut down, with the result that the number of competitors increased; in fact, in one of the smaller amateur classes, a record number of thirteen showed up.

Exhibition blooms were not up to their usual high standard quality, due not only to the unseasonable weather, but also to "No men, no maidens, and no manure."

The blooms were not of the weight one is accustomed to see at this great rose function, and that strong blooms were scarce is evidenced by such varieties as General MacArthur, Lady Hillingdon, and Mme. Leon Pain being found in some of the leading boxes. It shows, however, what can be done, and how garden varieties can help an exhibition box upon occasion.

There were several noteworthy exhibits. A gorgeous display of decorative roses by Frank Cant & Co., of Colchester, was one of the finest ever staged at the National Rose Show, the bunches of Isobel, Sheila Wilson and Silver Moon being perfect. Messrs. Paul, of Cheshunt, and Mr. Elisha J. Hicks, of Twyford, also had good displays, while the baskets of Messrs. Alex. Dickson & Sons, Ltd., were magnificent.

Interest and competition for the Ladies' Dinner-Table Decoration was as keen as ever, although Mrs. Courtney Page's beautiful table decoration of Ophelia with Rubrifolia foliage was preferred by some to that of the winner.

Considering the strenuous times we are passing through, the attendance at this feast of roses was remarkably good, whilst the keen interest our beloved Queen Alexandra showed in the exhibits was encouragement alike to exhibitors and visitors.

It is to be hoped that all societies will decide to hold their rose shows in 1919, if only to provide a little ray of sunshine and give pleasure to a nation of war workers. After our victorious peace is fully established, we shall try to forget all the cares and anxieties of the war in our home rose-gardens.

The Roses of an English Labor Leader
Letters to THE EDITOR

DURING March of 1918 there came to the United States, to help make us realize the seriousness of the war, a great English labor leader, Mr. W. A. Appleton, secretary of the General Federation of Trades Unions, made up of more than a million British union workmen. The word-pictures Mr. Appleton drew, his account of the efforts England was putting forth, did much to speed up our war work.

It was incidental to a conference with him on other affairs that the Editor discovered his fondness for the rose. A copy of the 1917 Annual was mailed to Mr. Appleton's home, and in May came this response:

Thanks for your Rose Annual and all it suggests.

When I reached my own little garden, my rose trees welcomed me. They looked spruce and somewhat attenuated after the March pruning, but there was an appearance of welcome and understanding that comforted me beyond expression.

When I looked at them it seemed as if they smiled, and when I said, "Well roses, what of the situation?" they became articulate, at least to me, and they said, "Why, look up, as we do, to the sun, and you will see that only the sun is permanent—the clouds always pass."

Then I said, "Roses mine, what are we to do during the war? Are we to clothe ourselves in somber garb, or shall we take inspiration from those dear ones who have died for love or duty; shall we wander about disconsolately, or go into the world with smiles on our faces and our best clothes on our bodies?"

"Smiles," said my roses, "indicate faith, and hope, and surety; so smile, that those who have no roses may be encouraged and strengthened. Wear your best clothes also, as we always do, for all these things help to lift men's minds from the unbeautiful."

"And now, my roses," said I, for I was hungry for appreciation, "are you glad to see me back again?"

Instantly they replied, "We are always glad to see those who love us. We live and bloom and die for such!"

"Then, my roses, your beauty and your fragrance are for my friends in America as well as for me?"

At this, Mme. Abel Chatenay and Mme. Melanie Soupert, who, because of their beauty and their standing, claim a little precedence, seemed to rise on their stems and then to bend in the graceful sweep of the old-fashioned curtsy. It was as if they had said, "Certainly!" And all the other roses nodded acquiescence.

To you, my friend, who understand the language, I send the roses' message. Please interpret it to my other friends in America.

After the nerve-racking strain of the war was over, so that even a busy labor leader had an opportunity to relax, and after he had had time to get acquainted with the 1918 Annual, Mr. Appleton wrote:

> I cannot let the old year pass without writing to assure you of the pleasure that I have derived from the perusal of the American Rose Annual.
> Next year I hope to have a still better show because recently I have been guided very largely by the results American growers have achieved. I want to compare my results with the results of friends on the other side.
> During the time of crisis, my roses have been always a source of relaxation and frequently of inspiration. Their cultivation and the spirit this cultivation develops, helps one to maintain mental balance and equilibrium. To deal only with men and with political problems would mean a dull existence, even if it did not also lead to some deterioration of one's better qualities. Association with the roses, contemplation of their beauty and enjoyment of their fragrance help to keep one's own mind and life on less sordid planes.

Mr. Appleton has supplied yet another reason for growing roses in wartime; and surely the days of peace merit the same relaxation and inspiration, so that we may construct again to the best advantage!

The National Rose Society in Wartime
By THE EDITOR

IT WAS Robert Pyle, I think, who did me the favor of pushing me into membership in the National Rose Society of England, some years ago. It was a real favor, and the publications of that great organization, with more recently the correspondence of its officers, have been most valuable. England takes the rose to her heart, as may be realized when it is noted that in the third year of the great war the total membership of the National Rose Society, "after allowing for losses by death and resignation," was 4,795.

The American Rose Society can well emulate its older and stronger sister, not only in membership and in exhibition, but in publications. A very pleasant interchange membership arrangement between the two organizations has been effected, so that publications of both go promptly to the officers of both. There is possibility also of bringing about an international registration compact, to avoid name duplication and to foster the best quality in new roses.

It seems but fair to the readers of the Annual to transcribe here paragraphs from the correspondence with Mr. Courtney Page, Hon. Secretary of the National Rose Society, and Editor of its Annual, whose portrait is presented in Plate VII, facing page 86, also on a basis of interchange. Writing during the wartime August of 1918, Mr. Page said of the 1918 American Rose Annual:

> I need hardly tell you how delighted I was with it. The articles were most interesting and the symposium on "Shall We Grow Roses in Wartime?" most appropriate. I am quite jealous of that; you anticipated me! But I had my revenge by reprinting on the back of our programmes at the Royal Botanic Show Mrs. Edward Biddle's contribution, the finest of the lot.
> It is hard in these times to get matter for the Annual, as we are all so engaged in prosecuting the war. . . . I am one of thousands who nightly thank God for America's intervention. When I meet your sailors or soldiers in the streets—and there are plenty of them—I say to myself, "Now really the end of the war is in sight." . . . All my staff have joined up; and although I am 51 years old, I am to be examined for service. . . . The war is brought very near to us, and the roar of the guns makes my house shake, although I am 100 miles away.

On November 4, 1918, only a week before Germany begged off in time to avoid the just punishment then coming to her, Mr. Page again wrote:

> We here are fully alive to the valuable help you are sending, and it would appear that long before these lines reach you we shall see the fruits. Germany is defeated, and what is more, she knows it.
> I am too old to have been permitted to fight, but I have done my little to help things along. First, a voluntary munitions worker, and then a "policeman," I have been in the thick of every air-raid on London, save the last. . . . I have seen seventeen Zeppelins under gunfire and heard twenty-three, three of which have been brought down in flames—two within a mile of my house. Guns are all around us, and the din and screaming of shells when in action will always be remembered. . . .
> One thing this war will have done is to cement the two great nations together for the common cause of humanity so strongly that no earthly power will be able to separate them. . . .
> What a wonderful photograph of Excelsa! I wish we could grow them in this country to such beauty*.

Every rosarian will join heartily, I am sure, in Mr. Page's opinion as to the accomplished union of purpose in the great English-speaking democracies and their colonies. We shall all be glad, also, to increase our knowledge of and interest in the great rose organization for which he speaks.

*Mr. Page refers here to a photograph of the same plant of Excelsa as that shown as the color frontispiece of the 1916 Annual, but a year older.

Roses in Italy
A Letter, and a Memorial to M. Pierre Guillot

EDITOR'S NOTE.—The Countess Senni's rose observations will delight American rose amateurs, and her kindness in sending us the letter from Madame Guillot will be appreciated. There is added a courteous letter to the Editor from the widow of Pierre Guillot, to whom the whole world is indebted for the rose La France, which he introduced in 1867. Further to his credit are 146 other introductions, of which 26 have been given gold or silver medals, while scores of decorations and recognitions for his rose accomplishments have been bestowed upon this veteran of two generations who died September 27, 1918. It is the Editor's hope next year to present a full account of this greatest rose establishment in the world.

<p align="center">CIAMPINO, POSTA GROTTAFERRATA,
PROVINCIA DI ROMA, ITALY, <i>December 9, 1919.</i></p>

TO THE EDITOR OF THE AMERICAN ROSE ANNUAL:

You have, perhaps, learned of the death of M. Pierre Guillot, one of the great rose-growers of Lyons. I am taking the liberty to send you a copy of a letter from his wife; it will surely interest you as an admirable picture of the best French qualities of mind and character. For several years my best roses came from him, and also many helpful letters. I admired much the way he "carried on" in the face of difficulties; wherefore his death was a sincere sorrow.

May I also thank you for a great deal of pleasure and knowledge given by the last three American Rose Annuals? Each one is more interesting than the last, and, in some respects, they suit our climate better than the English Annual.

I live on a farm outside of Rome. We sometimes have mild and sometimes severe winters, with almost no snow and no severe frosts, but we are liable to three days of "sirocco," which burns tender shoots and turns them black, worse than frost. Our summers are hot, windy, and long, with easily four months of absolute rainlessness. Roses stand the summers better than anything else; they often lose all their leaves and are quite dormant until the time of the equinoctial rains, and then flower all through the autumn, the China hybrids and the single Irish roses keeping on through the winter, if mild.

After several years' struggling for mixed borders, only to see everything burnt to cinders in June, I have put roses everywhere

—Rugosas and Brier hybrids as hedges, Wichuraianas on banks and climbing over olive trees and up cypresses (where they are a beautiful sight, even in winter, with their glossy leaves), and tea and other bush roses in beds and on walls back of orange trees. The double *R. bracteata* and the old but lovely Beauty of Glazenwood are especially luxuriant, even on north walls, and a beautiful red-and-white combination is Bardou Job and Mme. Alfred Carriere. The former is here the truest of red roses, with a velvety black shadow in it like Chateau de Clos Vougeot at its best. One hopes that America will give us a Wichuraiana of the same dark red, with no trace of purple or blue.

In the very comprehensive lists of Mr. (Captain George C.) Thomas and others printed in the Annual there are a few climbing roses missing which might well be better known, among which I may name the following:

Florence H. Veitch is a beautiful, fragrant red, with fine foliage, and on a warm wall is quite vigorous.
Marie Lavalley is a very fine semi-double red rose, quite beautiful when half open.
Ards Rambler is a weak grower, but well worth trying for the blossoms, which are very large, very fragrant, and of a glowing American Beauty rose-color, almost flaming in its intensity.
Setina is a very pretty, almost perpetual pink climber.
Pissardii is old, but fragrant and very pretty.

For those who like Veilchenblau, the Multiflora Donau is good; it is a richer purple, and very fine at the end of blooming, when it is like the Royal Purple sweet pea. It is a strong grower.

Paul's Scarlet Climber and Ghislaine de Feligonde were both fine this year, even though young plants. None of your lists mention Renée Danielle, which is here a very fine Wichuraiana, of glossy, persistent foliage and lovely jonquil-yellow flowers. Neither do I see mention of the fine René André (an orange- or shrimp-pink), Désiré Bergera (coppery rose), or the lovely Léontine Gervais. I should put Francois Juranville almost at the head of the Wichuraiana list for lovely foliage, good-sized individual flowers of a strawberry-pink, and some fragrance; it is never "sick" and grows anywhere. Contrary to Mr. Thomas, we find Sweet Lavender very good, with plenty of bloom and a lovely lilac-pink-cream color.

PLATE VII. Mr. Courtney Page, Hon. Secretary of the
National Rose Society of England
(See page 84)

Lest this climate seem too easy (which it is not, with its winds and droughts) to prove my theory of the rose being every man's flower, let me say that many of these roses are doing equally well in a little house three thousand feet high in the Apennine watershed, where the snow is three to four feet deep in winter, with no warm weather until June. Bardou Job, the yellow Banksia, Lamarque, Mme. Leonine Viennot, and others have come through several winters there, which leads one to think they might be generally grown "north of Washington."

I have quantities of roses there, on the house, in beds, as hedges (Rugosas, Ayrshires, etc.) to keep wandering animals out, and in thickets where they bloom like glorified and more perpetual wild roses. In these thickets are the Rugosas, *R. Moyesii*, *R. Hugonis*, Sheila Wilson, Maharajah, Laurette Messimy and her sisters (of which Mrs. Edward Clayton and Mlle. de la Valette are perhaps the most beautiful), the charming and very fragrant Stanwell Perpetual, Irish Modesty, Irish Engineer, Irish Pride—all the Irish single ones, in fact—and the true and hybrid Briers. Some of these are always in bloom, and the clump of them where two paths meet is always gay. Part of the soil is strong red clay and part almost shale, too poor for vegetables, but the roses thrive and spread; even on a scrubby bank, where only balsam firs grow, they twine among the branches and cover the ground. The Anemone variety of *R. sinica* (*R. lævigata*) is stronger than the parent Cherokee (and its saucer-like flowers, of a striking and rather cold pink, are more than beautiful among purple wisteria here), so I am going to try it in the mountains this year.

No flower gives such constant pleasure, and none, in proportion to what they give, demands less attention. This applies, of course, to the average amateur, and not to the finest rose-gardens. My gardener is a prisoner in Germany, now happily returning, and I have had to depend upon a few days' help now and then for spading, manuring, etc., doing the rest myself. Therefore I write thus from actual and direct knowledge.

Thanking you again for knowledge and pleasure, I am
                    Yours truly,
                        COUNTESS GIULIO SENNI

Letter from Madame Pierre Guillot to the Countess Guilio Senni

LYON-MONPLAISIR, FRANCE, *November 22, 1918.*

. . . My dear husband left me just when victory was bringing us joy. He was so patriotic, so full of faith in the destiny of France, unclouded by a minute's doubt, but he had not the consolation of seeing victory, and it is from on high that he watches our deliverance. He came back from the mountains full of spirit and glad to be home, and two days later he died in my arms, inside of ten minutes, with a ruptured aneurism. I cannot yet realize this terrible loss.

My husband was the best of men, a model husband, and my children may well be proud of such a good father. His life was wholly given over to his family and the growing of the beautiful roses he loved so passionately. He did this as an artist, and not only as a means of livelihood. The only sorrow he ever caused me in our thirty-three years of marriage was in leaving me. . . .

The business will continue, for I was my husband's helper all these years. Unfortunately, I have not his special knowledge of plant hybridization, but I can direct things, and now, with peace, our old employees will come back; and there is my twenty-year-old son. I will try to run things until he can do it alone. Alas, his father would have been such a help to him; but now he must learn by himself.

I hope to have your good will, and that you will recommend me to your friends. It will be two years before things are as they were, for we have been so deprived of the necessary men, the seeds are lacking, and many varieties temporarily gone. But courage and hope! We shall yet win out, as we have won over the terrible Boche. Thank God! he is down, and let us have him so. He will be up again soon enough. *Vive la victoire, nos alliés et vive la paix!*

LOUISE GUILLOT.

From Madame Guillot to the Editor

LYON-MONPLAISIR, FRANCE, *January 29, 1919.*

MR. J. HORACE MCFARLAND, Editor American Rose Annual.

Sir: We have been very much touched by the expression of sympathy which you have been so kind as to address to us on the occasion of the death of M. Pierre Guillot. His death, unexpected and sudden, which occurred on September 27, 1918, has been a very severe blow to all his family; and it is in despondency of heart that we send you brief information concerning his work with roses.

Our establishment was founded at Lyons in 1850, on Rue de la Guillotine, Hirondelles, by J. B. Guillot. After an intervening removal in 1860, and shortly following the death of the founder of the house, my husband, Pierre Guillot, moved in 1895 to the present location.

The nurseries now occupy some thirty acres, intensively devoted to the culture of roses, of which we have more than 2,000 different varieties. The annual production is nearly 300,000 plants, distributed locally and sent to all parts of the world.

Besides the roses raised for commerce, we maintain a complete collection of all new varieties produced anywhere, and also of all available species used in the propagation of new varieties. Thousands of seed-plots are maintained, and, in fact, the larger part of our nursery area is reserved for this purpose. Here the blooms of the artificially pollinated roses are studied, and from them are selected the carefully tested varieties we have the pleasure to introduce.

It is our intention in the third generation to maintain the good name of Guillot. My son, Marc Guillot, will continue, I am convinced, the principles of integrity and good will that have been characteristic of my dear husband.

I beg you to accept, Sir, with my thanks, my distinguished salutations.

LOUISE GUILLOT.

Roses in Bermuda

By MRS. F. ST.G. CAULFEILD, Chelston, Bermuda

EDITOR'S NOTE.—Through the kindness of the Director of the Bermuda Agricultural Station, Mr. E. J. Mortley, American rose-lovers are brought in contact with knowledge of rose-growing in the interesting island about a thousand miles east of the United States. Mrs. Caulfeild evidently finds conditions similar to those in Florida.

ROSE-GROWING in Bermuda, from an English point of view, is a sore tribulation and weariness of the spirit.

Coming from the Thames Valley, where my rose-garden was indeed a riot of color, a wealth and profusion of bloom, a joy and delight to the eye of the beholder, I had visions in this Fairy Island, with a climate that struck me then as nearly perfection, of pergolas and bowers, of arches and pillars—all the hundred and one ways the ardent lover of roses seeks to bestow them, each after its kind to the best advantage.

If hearty and continuous discouragement could have daunted me, I should never have planted, not only roses, but any sort of plant or tree in my present so-called garden. For, alas! I am perched on a hill, swept on every side by every wind that blows, reached by the salt spray from the sea, which is devastating, and, on a really windy day when Bermuda is at its worst, I am blown out of one door and in at the other with a violence that leaves me breathless and indignantly wondering why my husband chose such a spot to plant a really gardening woman! It is true there is a view, so beautiful one never wearies of it; and it is never too hot in summer, or too cold in winter. At first, full of enthusiasm, I started to garden, planted my rose trees, and hopefully waited results.

The aforesaid husband, who has his uses, built me a pergola. Everyone said "It will be utterly ruined by the first strong wind," but he builded wisely and well, and not even the hurricane disturbed a twig of it; but the roses I had chosen with such care, and had fondly hoped to see covering it, a mass of splendor, flourished not at all! Cut off in their prime, they lost heart. The pergola is still naked and unashamed. I shall dress it in oleanders!

Let me say at once that all known methods of pruning may be

discarded here, and you must just prune by the light of common sense and your own local experience, manure heavily, and trust to luck. That I should live to write thus recklessly on this sacred subject! But it is so!

The roses that do well here bloom practically all the year round, though not in profusion all the time, the best season being from January till April. I do not consider that any of the Wichuraianas do really well here, and we have very few successful climbers. The old-fashioned Seven Sisters grows easily and blooms freely. I have tried climbing roses which in England are inconveniently prolific, such as Aimé Vibert, American Pillar, that glorious climber, Carmine Pillar, Lady Gay, Felicite Perpetue, and many others, with small success. They grew at a terrific rate as regards foliage, but not even Blush Rambler, that amazingly free bloomer, bloomed at all. Accordingly, I wrote to B. R. Cant, of Colchester, who advised me to cut back hard. I did cut very hard, but the result was the same—profuse foliage, no flowers. Climbing Niphetos and Climbing Mrs. W. J. Grant both did fairly well. Malmaison is the best of all climbers here and grows easily from slips, and Lamarque is also good. It does not follow that because they do not succeed in my wind-swept garden they should not flower more inland.

I am absolutely of the opinion that all roses here should be grown on their own roots. Those grafted on Briers do not seem to do nearly so well, at any rate, after the first year. I have seen blossoms here of such perfection that they could have been exhibited at the Temple Show in London, certain of receiving a prize; and then, from that same bush, not another bloom worth looking at! Hugh Dickson is one of these. Marquise de Sinety, the first year, on a Brier, was wonderful, both as to bloom and foliage; the second year, medium; this year, a failure. I am now going to try her again on her own roots. Lady Hillingdon, a rose delightful for the bronze foliage which is so charming a contrast to the almost orange-colored flowers, and which in England blooms continuously from April till November, here loses all color as far as foliage goes, while the flowers are a good color but in no abundance.

The best of all roses here is, undoubtedly, Killarney, white and pink. The Shell Rose and the Agrippina grow like weeds, and very easily from cuttings. Other successful ones here are Ben Cant, Marie Van Houtte, Lamarque, Frau Karl Druschki, Cabbage Rose, Mme. Abel Chatenay, Mme. Lambard, Dr. Grill, Irish Elegance. Most of the China roses do well, as also the Rugosas, and I have had success with the dwarf Polyanthas, Jessie, Mrs. W. H. Cutbush, and Eugenie Lamesch. There are, doubtless, hundreds of other roses which might do well here, but the ones I have named I can vouch for.

I do not think that I have ever been in a place where such constant and unremitting care is required to obtain any really good results, and yet again and again I have seen roses which have had no care or attention for years, apparently quite indifferent to the neglect, and flowering on and on.

There is no doubt but that heavy fertilizing,—an expensive item these days,—a sheltered spot away from the salt spray, loving care, and careful selection of the sorts suitable to the island, are necessary to insure success with rose-growing in Bermuda.

This world that we're alivin' in
Is mighty hard to beat.
You get a thorn with every rose,
But ain't the roses sweet?
—FRANK STANTON
Atlanta Constitution

Roses in Australia
By GEORGE W. WALLS, Melbourne, Australia

EDITOR'S NOTE.—Through Capt. George C. Thomas, Jr., the Editor has been brought in contact with an Australian rose friend, from whose letter the pleasant words which follow have been adapted. It is significant to note that, as in all English-speaking countries, the tremendous pressure of the world war did not intermit attention to and love for the rose, but that on the contrary the Queen of Flowers served to rest, and thereby to strengthen, those who were sustaining the hard work of backing up the men at the firing-front.

I HAVE just been reading the symposium in the 1918 American Rose Annual on "Growing Roses in Wartime."

Personally I agree with the various writers on the subject. It would have been a calamity to have given up growing roses in wartime. From my own experience of a busy city life I have long found the great pleasure and restfulness, after a tiring day, of going into my garden among the roses, watching nature's ways of adding to one's delight and pleasure. The people who do not go in for gardening cannot realize the pleasure and contentment they miss, and the objects that both your Society and mine have are for the common good of the community, to broaden the views of the people at large, to get them to come closer to nature, to get them to feel that they will derive pleasure and contentment from their gardens, and to make them realize that life is worth living after all.

That our American friends may realize the strength of our rose-interest in this part of Australia, I am forwarding our official catalogue of roses, reprinted early in 1918. It includes a goodly sprinkling of roses of American origin.

It is indeed a pleasure to get in touch with rose enthusiasts in another part of the universe, and to know that they are by their efforts trying, as we are doing out here, to get people to grow the best of all flowers, the rose.

To American eyes the announcement that our Spring Show will occur on October 30 will seem strange until it is remembered that this is the other side of the globe!

I am glad to extend, on behalf of the National Rose Society of Victoria, our hearty greetings to the American Rose Society. In addition to a common language and common ideals, we have a common love for the most beautiful and widespread of flowers.

Wayside Roses in France

By GEORGE C. THOMAS, Jr., Chestnut Hill, Philadelphia

EDITOR'S NOTE.—Captain Thomas, whose wonderful rose-gardens are perhaps the best testing-place in America for roses, and whose hybridizing work is of great and increasing importance, is again at his home, having been released from his work as adjutant of one of the aërial squadrons in France early in 1919. His story of the station woman's rose ought to teach us more of a lesson than its reference to an old rose friend of the Editor, Gloire de Dijon. Why not such wayside roses in America?

IT is wartime France, and a hot day in May, rendered infinitely hotter because of the rarity of such temperature. The American troop-train stops again, with the usual series of bumps and jerks, groanings and squeakings. It has made an average of five miles an hour for two days, with the said average steadily diminishing as it nears the front.

A score of enterprising men leap off to see what may be discovered. Their first idea is water, because that in their canteens has long since vanished or has been heated beyond the cooling-point; but the officer in charge speedily anticipates and checks their proposed raid on the shallow well of the railroad gate-house at the crossing, as it is against orders for the men to drink from unknown wells. The gate mistress—for women were doing most of such work in France during 1918—seems surprised that the men are not allowed to drink what to her is "perfectly good" water, which she had started to draw for their use. Noting her disappointment, the officer first thanks her and then tells her that he and his men must obey certain regulations.

Lifting his eyes from the ruddy face of this peasant war worker, he notes for the first time her neat little house, with its tiny but well-kept grounds, but, most striking of all, the wonderful Gloire de Dijon rose which luxuriates and rambles all over the south side of the cottage, and is even sending forth enterprising shoots on the roof itself. In his stumbling French he felicitates Madame on her beautiful Gloire de Dijon.

"Ah, *mon Capitaine*, you love the rose; you know my wonderful one by name—it is most strange! Would you care to see my other plants? I have some very beautiful roses, is it not so? None can compare with mine, everyone says it. *Voila mon Capitaine*," as he follows her, "Do you know what this is, and this?" Fortunately for her opinion of him, he does know, and smilingly identifies a fine standard of Lady Ashtown, unmistakably distinct, a Druschki, with wonderful petalage and substance, and several other well-known varieties; but he is unable to name an attractive yellow climber with a bloom almost like Sinety which she calls Nikola, and he forgets the name of a stalwart specimen of Queen of the Belgians.

It is shaded and cool in the little rose-garden, and the perfume brings back memories of other roses and other gardens, for they are all so much the same in many ways; even the never-failing aphis is busy as usual.

The men crowd nearer; another officer enters the little garden, and Madame is overjoyed to see them all, and does the honors unaffectedly, making all welcome in her delightful French way, quite evidently glad to see them and especially pleased that her roses are so appreciated and admired. Bustling here and there, she points out one bud, just opening, "Is not the color quite exceptional, the stem remarkably long, even for one of my roses?" Another plant must be carefully inspected; "It is a new one and has survived its first winter well; it replaced an old bush which died two years ago. Are there any roses like this in America?" She is glad her visitors grow roses in their gardens; of course they realize that before the war she had very many more varieties than now; her husband did the work then, and she had time for her beautiful roses.

The Americans linger, forgetful of time, drinking in the beauties of the cool fragrance seasoned with the woman's gracious hospitality. But it is all interrupted by the warning whistle of the locomotive, given in the usual dwarf squeak of the French production. Everyone but Madame starts for the train; but before they can go she must really insist that the officers accept these few blooms she has cut; she will not miss them. So, thanking her and taking the flowers, they regain the train.

In a moment it starts, and soon the little French rose-garden of the gate-keeper's wife is out of sight. Out of sight, but perhaps its modest glories have given a message to the hearts of the men on the train—the kind of a message that does good. At all events, the three officers talk roses, and forget the tiresome journey in recounting just what varieties they know and deciding what kinds they will grow when they get home.

All have fallen in love with the Dijon. At lunchtime one orderly states that his family in Nantucket have some very wonderful roses. He describes the house and just where the plants are, and it brings up a picture of the quaint island village.

After this experience it was easy to keep a lookout and note the roses grown and the difference between the wayside garden in France and America. Generally speaking, one finds that the French like standards, and such seem to thrive better over there than they usually do with us. But the one rose which stands out is Gloire de Dijon, and this applies from Clermontferrand, in central France, clear to Nancy.

Was it Dean Hole who said that were he placed on an island and allowed only one rose bush he would choose this variety? At all events, Dijon deserves many more owners than it has. Near Philadelphia, if given winter protection and placed in a southern exposure, it will grow by fall to a height of over ten feet, and in November one may count two dozen blooms on one plant of it. Incidentally, it is of larger and finer growth if budded on Multiflora than on Brier, and it should not be grown outside on its own roots where it must withstand much frost. Parsons knew well the value of budded plants and recommended them, and his advice is borne out by the action of Dijon which, however, winters especially well on Multiflora.

There is no other yellow climber which compares with Dijon in hardiness and blooming. Climbing Mme. Melanie Soupert is another rose which, with protection, sometimes does exceptionally well as a yellow climber near Philadelphia, but it gives much less growth and bloom than Dijon.

Somehow it always seems that a hardy climbing or semi-climbing rose, with the form of the Hybrid Tea and more than one period of bloom, is the type most to be desired for the climate of the Middle Atlantic States. The South has the climbing Tea, the cooler North a longer period of bloom for the hardy climbing Perpetual. In France, where Gloire de Dijon is used so successfully, the climate approaches in severity the cold of our middle eastern section, so why not take a hint from the thrifty gate-keeper's wife and grow this variety?

A Great French Rose Nursery
By CHARLES PENNOCK, Philadelphia

EDITOR'S NOTE.—The great war has brought closer those who love roses in many lands. It was quite natural that Mr. Charles Pennock, son of Past-President S. S. Pennock, should, in the interim of his war duties, seek a rose nursery. His account of what he saw there, and his suggestion as to a certain propagating method, will be of interest to rose-lovers.

Mr. Pennock was yet in France at the time the Annual went to press, serving the Friends' Reconstruction work of the civilian Red Cross, operated under the auspices of the Friends' organizations in England and America. This reconstruction work is increasing constantly in importance, and now engages more than 500 men in the field, with more going over constantly. Charles Pennock was below the draft age when he went to France, and he has been working in the horribly desolated Verdun section. Elsewhere will be found a survey of the new French roses, written for us by Monsieur E. Turbat, who has been for several years an interested member of the American Rose Society.

LEAVING Paris for Orleans on the express in the usual drizzling rain, we were soon out in the country and away from the dismal climatic conditions of the big city. Two hours later the city of Joan of Arc was reached, and after some lunch and visits to several of the historically famous places, such as the house where the Maid of Orleans slept, the cathedral, and the town hall, with its beautiful interior, I took the little four-wheel train out the Route d'Olivet to Turbat & Co.'s place.

After a ride of about a mile and a half over perfectly level country and past the places of numerous horticulturists and nurserymen, I saw the house number for which I was looking. I jumped off and went up to the office door, M. Turbat himself meeting me. I told him who I was, and after excusing himself for about ten minutes to show a man some plants, he called me into his very pleasant little office and we had a short talk. The shipping conditions between France and America and the new restrictions on sending plants to the United States, to take effect on and after June 1, 1919, were the main topics of our conversation.

It was fairly well along in the afternoon by this time, and as I had to get back to Paris that night we hastened on to inspect the place. It would probably be well to state here that, owing to the short time I had to spend, we saw only the

A GREAT FRENCH ROSE NURSERY 97

four or five acres nearby, which M. Turbat uses wholly for propagating and temporary planting prior to shipping. His three different places in the immediate vicinity of Orleans comprise about eighty acres of cultivated stock.

But to come back to the part we visited, and to give a short description thereof: As I have said above, this section is used merely for propagating and temporary planting, and consequently contains many varieties of the different species of plant-life. Some very few of the species awaiting shipment are: Peach, plum, quince, strawberry, Douglas fir, berberis, herbaceous plants, spirea, *Rosa canina*, *R. multiflora*, and *R. Manetti*. There are many other species and varieties of the above-mentioned—so many, in fact, that in order to cover as much ground as possible we had to hustle by many of them.

The next thing of interest was the propagation of the roses under the bell-glass. This method was practised by M. Turbat and other Orleans people for the propagation of the general collection and old varieties. It is rather interesting to know that it was not used before the war by M. Turbat for the propagation of novelties, that being done in heated houses; but due to the fact that he couldn't get coal to heat his houses, he was forced to employ the bell-glass, and, rather to his surprise and satisfaction, it turned out just as well as the houses, and at the same time saved the cost of coal. There are, of course, disadvantages, but, in the main, bell-glass propagation may be said to have proved a wartime success, in this case at least.

To return to the roses: The two pieces which are to be grafted are cut on an angle so that they will fit together, and are then bound with raffia, or some similar material. They are then put in the ground—a mixture of dirt and sand—under the glass, and left there until they have taken root and are strong enough to be put out in the open. The particular roses that we saw were nearly all to be set out about April 1. His roses, started in this way and not yet moved after the graft, include, among hundreds of others, Tipperary, Flame of Fire, Titania, Crimson Emblem, Aladdin, Red Cross, Nellie Parker, Mrs. F. W. Vanderbilt, and later novelties, such as Golden Emblem, K. of K., Lillian Moore, Etoile, Baby Lyon, and the like. Among those to be moved in April is all the general collection, some 1,500 varieties, included in which is Her Majesty, the big pink rose largely used for the summer cut-flower trade in Paris.

Other plants propagated by the bell-glass method are ivies, laurel, lilacs, conifers, and many more shrubs.

We went on from the beds to look over the packing- and shipping-house, which is up-to-date in nearly every way, one of the most important points being its freedom from frost without a heating plant. The bottom floor, situated five or six feet below the surface, but with an abundance of light nevertheless, is used for pruning, sorting, and so on; the second is the packing-room, while on the third floor are stored large quantities of the moss and straw employed so extensively in the packing process. This moss, M. Turbat told me, is taken from the surface of the ground under oak trees, and after careful drying is stored and later used, moistened, around the roots of the plants, as it is needed. M. Turbat packs all foreign shipments in straw and then in boxes, while local shipments are merely put up in straw.

Having a few minutes more to spare before going back to catch my train, we took the train on out into the country to the edge of a beautiful little river, the Loire, where we hurriedly looked over another plot where the plants, fully able to stand natural conditions after having been started by graft or cutting, are put in. Most of these were about two years old.

We had only a few minutes or so here, and soon found ourselves back on the train, headed for the city. M. Turbat left me at his house, after I had thanked him for the very profitable and enjoyable afternoon I had spent with him. I returned to the capital city, arriving just too late for dinner, after standing in the corridor during the whole two hours from Orleans to Paris; but, as the French people say, "*C'est la guerre*" (It's the war), which incidentally now has become "*C'est la paix*" (It's the peace), for which none of us are sorry.

The rose looks fair, but fairer it we deem
For that sweet odour which doth in it live.
—SHAKESPEARE.

The New Foreign Roses

BELIEVING American rose-lovers want early and first-hand information of the roses originated abroad, the Editor has, for several years, by persistent effort, sought to establish the proper connections with the great hybridizers of France, England, Scotland, and Ireland. Some have responded courteously, and others curtly; the English growers seem less inclined to "come across" than the identity of language would imply!

The lists which follow are as complete as data received permit, and are accurate in presenting the originators' descriptions, which are by no means guaranteed for the United States!

It is practicable to import new roses for propagation and for testing, despite Quarantine Notice No. 37. Details are given on page 113.

New Roses in France

The noted French rosarian, M. Turbat, writes, "In answer to your courteous demand, and as I had the honor to write you last year, the war which kept to duty all the French men having fifty years of age and under, influenced badly on the raising of new roses, and principally on their distribution. The rose-growers and rose-lovers who remained at home had already too much job to keep alive their collections.

"Owing to these considerations, the list of novelties distributed in the years 1917 and 1918 is very brief.

"At first I have to make an addition to the 1916 list, in which were not enclosed the varieties raised and distributed by Messrs. Barbier & Co., at Orleans, that you will find below:

INTRODUCTIONS OF 1916–17 NOT PREVIOUSLY REPORTED
Hybrid Perpetual

Henri Coupe. (Barbier & Co.) Reine des Neiges × Gruss an Teplitz. Flowers double, 5 to 6 inches across, fragrant, generally solitary on long stems. The color is a fresh salmon and silvery rose, uniform, and very lasting, even in very hot weather, and is retained until the petals fall. Vigorous, floriferous, and hardy.

Dwarf Perpetual Polyanthas

Amarante. (Barbier & Co.) Seedling of an unnamed variety. Flowers of medium size or small, in large, dense corymbs of twenty-five to seventy, dark amaranth in color, sometimes striated white. One of the best dark red sorts, keeping its color well. Dwarf grower; very floriferous.

Magenta. (Barbier & Co.) Seedling of unnamed variety. Flowers semi-double, cup-shaped, of medium size, in long spikes of twenty to forty; violet-red, the middle of petal magenta-violet—a new shade in the dwarf Polyanthas—sometimes turns reddish violet. Dwarf grower; very floriferous.

Climbing Hybrid Tea

Catalunya. (A. Nonin.) A sport from Gruss an Teplitz, with the same qualities, except that it is a very much stronger grower.

Hybrid Wichuraiana

Auguste Gervaise. (Barbier & Co.) Wichuraiana type × Le Progress. The buds are coppery yellow, tinted aurora-apricot, opening to coppery yellow and rosy salmon, passing to creamy white. The enormous flowers measure from 4 to 5 inches across, and are produced in great abundance in clusters of ten to twenty. A very strong grower, and very effective.

INTRODUCTIONS OF 1918

Pernetianas

Mrs. Farmer. (Pernet-Ducher.) Large, half-double flowers of indian-yellow, the reverse of the petals reddish apricot—a charming color. Foliage bronzy green. A strong grower, with numerous branches.

Pax Labor. (Chambard.) Very large bud of orange-gold, bordered with carmine; flowers very large, full, pale golden yellow, slightly shaded coppery carmine when opening, passing to sulphur-yellow when fully open. Foliage deep bronzy green. Hardy and vigorous.

Severine. (Pernet-Ducher.) Medium-sized, half-full flowers of coral-red, passing to shrimp-red when fully expanded—a new color; lovely when bud is opening. Foliage bronze-green. A strong, bushy grower, with erect branches.

Hybrid Teas

Benedicte Seguin. (Pernet-Ducher.) Bud reddish apricot, shaded carmine; flowers large, full, globular, Roman ocher, shaded coppery orange. Foliage reddish, bronzy green. Strong, erect grower.

Elegante. (Pernet-Ducher.) Long sulphur-yellow bud, opening to a large, full flower of creamy yellow. Foliage bright green. A strong grower, with divergent branches; very floriferous.

Franklin. (Pernet-Ducher.) Long, flesh-colored bud and large, full, ovoid flower of salmon, shaded yellowish salmon. Foliage bronzy green. Strong, bushy, erect grower.

Serge Basset. (Pernet-Ducher.) Very full, perfectly formed, medium-sized flowers of brilliant garnet-red. Foliage deep green. Strong grower; dwarf and bushy; erect branches. Always in bloom.

Hybrid Perpetual Bourbon

Jean Rameau. (Darclanne; intro. by E. Turbat & Co.) Sport of Mme. Isaac Periere, and a great improvement over it in color. Long, full bud of tender pink; flower double, the reverse of petals rose Nilson, interior iridescent rose. Very hardy.

Dwarf Perpetual Polyanthas

Beaute d'Automne. (E. Turbat & Co.) A glorified Bordure. The fine red buds open into double, bright rose-pink flowers, which are borne in enormous corymbs of fifty to seventy. Wood and foliage clear green. It is a late-blooming variety, being at its best when other sorts have finished flowering, and in France is unsurpassed outdoors in October and November.

Eblouissant. (E. Turbat & Co.) The best dark red dwarf perpetual Polyantha. Flowers of good size, in bouquets of ten to twenty, in color similar to Cramoisi Superieur and Fabvier, with the advantage that they are produced on a true dwarf perpetual Polyantha. They last a long time without fading or turning violet, and when fully open take a cactus form. Wood and foliage purplish green. Erect grower. Will be used in cut-flower work with George Elger and Cecile Brunner, because of its shapely bud.

Etoile Luisante. (E. Turbat & Co.; intro. in U. S. by Henry F. Michell Co., of Philadelphia.) Long, pointed, vermilion-red buds; flowers in long, pyramidal corymbs of forty to fifty, scarlet-red and bright shrimp-rose, with coppery red reflexes; golden yellow aiglets. Wood and leaves clear green. Dwarf; vigorous grower.

Verdun. (Barbier & Co.) Seedling from an unnamed variety. Flowers are borne in pyramidal trusses of twenty-five to fifty, and are rather large, well-formed, globular, of a splendid carmine-purple, brighter than Crimson Rambler. Do not fade or turn to violet. Dwarf, branching shrub; exceedingly floriferous.

Multiflora (Climbing)

Daisy Brazileir. (E. Turbat & Co.) Single flowers of fire-red and purple-red, with yellow anthers; very showy. Completely covered in autumn and winter with orange-red berries which create a gorgeous effect. Wood and foliage deep green. Vigorous, erect grower.

Wichuraiana Hybrids

Fernand Rabier. (E. Turbat & Co.) The flowers are of good size, double, perfectly formed, pure deep scarlet, and are produced in large, erect corymbs of forty to fifty. Very vigorous and floriferous.

Henri Barruet. (Barbier & Co.) The bud is deep yellow at first, passing, while expanding, to coppery and clear yellow, and finally to white tinted lilaceous rose when fully open. The large flowers are borne in clusters of eight to fifteen, and the varying shades are effective. Strong grower; profuse bloomer.

Maxime Corbon. (Barbier & Co.) Sport of Leonie Lamesch. Deep coppery red buds; flowers deep coppery yellow, washed red, passing to apricot-yellow and white tinted straw-color, borne in panicles of six to twenty. Strong grower.

A New French Rose for 1919

Mons. Marc Guillot, of the great rose-growing firm of Pierre Guillot, Lyons, France, writes, February 5, 1919, as follows:

"We call your attention to a new rose which we will put in commerce in the autumn of 1919, and which every friend of France will desire for his garden. Its name will be:

La France Victorieuse. A very beautiful Hybrid Tea rose with large petals of firm substance. The color approximates the light silvery salmon of my father's rose, Mme. Leon Pain, but the edges of the petals are bright carmine. The flower is very large, and borne upon long and stiff stems. The plant is of vigorous growth, of erect, branching habit.

Other new roses will be introduced during the coming summer and autumn.

New British Roses of 1918

Some of our British friends have lost a year in this report by referring the Editor to their catalogues, not yet issued! We have compiled the following list from catalogues at hand.

Hybrid Teas

Alexander Emslie. (A. Dickson & Sons.) Deep, globular bloom of pure solid ruby on deep, delicate, velvety crimson, with base slightly white; attar-of-rose perfume. Free grower, branching; very floriferous.

Alfred W. Mellersh. (W. Paul & Son.) Salmon-yellow, shaded with rose, amber center. Vigorous branching habit; very free-flowering.

Ariadne. (W. Paul & Son.) Moderately full flowers of bright crimson, center shaded with yellow.

Blushing Bride. (Hugh Dickson.) Flowers large, full, beautifully formed, with high-pointed center, a clear white, with faint blush in middle. Growth free, branching, and compact.

Chameleon. (A. Dickson & Sons.) Pure flame-edged cerise. Foliage cedar-green, delicately perfumed. Very free grower of branching habit. Produces as many as twenty buds at a time.

Christine. (McGredy & Son.) Flowers deepest golden yellow, perfectly shaped, with petals of great substance. Awarded Gold Medal of N. R. S.

Dr. Joseph Drew. (Walter Easlea.) Resembles Mme. Melanie Soupert, but superior in growth, with fine large flowers of salmon-yellow, richly suffused with pink, the latter color predominating as the bloom ages; very sweetly scented. Vigorous grower; free bloomer. Certificate of Merit of N. R. S.

Emma Wright. (McGredy & Son.) Flowers pure orange without shading. An attractive bedding variety of good habit and free-flowering character.

Evelyn. (W. Paul & Son.) Large, full, imbricated flowers of salmon-white, shaded and edged with rose, yellow at base.

Frances Gaunt. (A. Dickson & Sons.) Pure, deep, fawny apricot, toning to silvery flesh. Its lovely shell-shaped petals form a beautiful, globular, cup-shaped bloom on rigid flower-stalk. Strong Persian-rose fragrance. Foliage glossy. Vigorous grower; branching; very floriferous.

Golden Ophelia. (B. R. Cant & Sons.) A seedling from Ophelia, possessing many of its characteristics. Flower of fair size, very compact, opening in perfect symmetrical form, golden yellow in center, paling slightly at outer petals.

Helen Chamberlain. (Walter Easlea.) Flower of exquisite shape, with huge guard petals, giving it a distinctive appearance. The color is rich creamy yellow, shading to orange-gold in center, and paling to almost white on outer petals.

H. P. Pinkerton. (Hugh Dickson.) Long buds; large, full flowers of brilliant scarlet, heavily flamed velvety crimson. Very free-flowering. Mildew-proof.

Irish Afterglow. (A. Dickson & Sons.) A sport of Irish Fireflame, but differing very decidedly in color. The bud is a very deep tangerine, passing to crushed strawberry in the open flowers. Vigorous grower; free bloomer.

Lamia. (Walter Easlea.) Beautiful buds, opening into lovely medium-sized semi-double flowers, without the looseness that characterizes so many of the newer roses. The color is an intense reddish orange. The foliage is of a lovely reddish hue. Vigorous grower. Awarded Gold Medal of N. R. S.

Marchioness of Ormonde. (Hugh Dickson.) Flowers of great size, very full, finely formed, with high-pointed center; clear wheat-straw-color, center deep honey-yellow. Growth vigorous and branching; free bloomer.

Mrs. George Marriott. (McGredy & Son.) Very large flowers, perfectly formed, of a deep cream and pearl, suffused rose and vermilion. Awarded Gold Medal of N. R. S.

Mrs. H. D. Greene. (Walter Easlea.) Reddish bronze flowers, opening to flame and coppery pink; rich fragrance. Foliage beet-root color, plentiful, forming a lovely contrast to the flowers. A vigorous grower, producing a profusion of blooms on fine erect stems.

Mrs. Henry Balfour. (McGredy & Son.) Ivory-white, with primrose shading at base, edge of petals vermilion-rose, like a picotee.

President Wilson. (Walter Easlea.) The flowers are very large, and of a most delightful shade of shrimp-pink, reminding one of Willowmere, but of a clearer, paler, and more refined hue. A vigorous, erect grower.

T. F. Crozier. (Hugh Dickson.) Flowers large, full and globular, with high-pointed center, deep canary-yellow. Strong, vigorous, branching growth.

The Queen Alexandra. (McGredy & Son.) Medium-sized flowers of intense vermilion, deeply shaded old gold on reverse of petals. Foliage mildew-proof. Free bloomer. Awarded Gold Medal of N. R. S.

Ulster Volunteer. (Hugh Dickson.) Large, single flowers, 5 to 6 inches across, brilliant cherry-red, with distinct cone of clear white at the base of the petals. Growth free and branching.

Pernetiana

Sunny Jersey. (Philip le Cornu.) A sport of Mme. Edouard Herriot. Similar to its parent, except in color, which is a lovely combination of bronze, apricot-salmon and orange.

Wichuraiana

Emily Gray. (B. R. Cant & Sons.) A fine yellow climbing rose, with foliage like *Berberis vulgaris*, very glossy and of great substance. The blooms are almost as large as those of Mme. Ravary. Awarded Gold Medal of N. R. S.

Hybrid Bracteata

Mermaid. (W. Paul & Son.) A single climbing rose, with large flowers of sulphur-yellow color, and deep amber stamens, which stand out very prominently. Foliage deep bronzy green. A continuous bloomer from early summer until autumn. Awarded Gold Medal of N. R. S.

Hybrid Moschata

Pax. (J. H. Pemberton.) Semi-single flowers, 3 to 4 inches in diameter; white with golden anthers; buds tinted lemon; real musk fragrance. Foliage dark green, young shoots claret. Blooms produced in corymbs, on long stems.

Thisbe. (J. H. Pemberton.) Chamois-yellow, of rosette shape, borne in large trusses on long upright shoots. A vigorous, bushy grower; perpetual flowering.

Hybrid Noisette

Daybreak. (J. H. Pemberton.) Semi-single, golden yellow flowers, borne several on a stem. Foliage handsome dark green. Vigorous, bushy grower; perpetual bloomer.

The Rose Cut-Flower Situation of 1918

By S. S. PENNOCK, Past-President American Rose Society

EDITOR'S NOTE.—The sharp curtailment of greenhouse rose-growing in the early winter of 1918 enforced by the United States Fuel Administration, has given rise to a most interesting situation, of which Mr. Pennock here gives the essential facts. One thing at least is quite evident—that scarcity and high prices do not prevent the use of the rose as a cut-flower to the limit of its supply.

THE rose-growers of the United States, particularly the eastern part, after the strenuous winter of 1917 and 1918, in making their plans for the winter of 1918 and 1919, with the Government coal embargo reducing their allowance of coal 50 per cent, almost to a man felt that the only proper and the wisest course to pursue was to shape their plans so they would have about one-half the glass of former years to run during the winter months.

The coal situation was not the only serious trouble that was facing them. The labor situation, if anything, was far more serious than the coal situation. Many of those who had been accustomed to working in greenhouses all their lives were going into other lines of work—yielding to the temptation of very much higher salaries. As a consequence, experienced greenhouse men were almost impossible to secure, necessitating the use of "green" help. In some instances, women did the work satisfactorily. Especially was this so with the plantsmen, where, probably, there is more detail work that a woman could do than in the establishments that are devoted exclusively to cut roses.

The season of 1918 and 1919 opened with a good cut for the early months. Then, coming along in October, was the influenza epidemic, which created an unprecedented demand for all kinds of flowers. The rose-growers, not knowing what was coming for the winter months, thought it was better to get what they could then, and, accordingly, cut very hard all through October and early November. Instead of pinching some of the crops, as is usually done for later cropping, these flowers were marketed.

The combination of a short labor-supply, shortage of coal, and the epidemic made roses for the midwinter season scarcer than they have been for years. This was not only with one

PLATE VIII. Terminal Twig of ROSA XANTHINA
(About half natural size. See page 39; also, see Plate VI)

THE ROSE CUT-FLOWER SITUATION

grower but practically every grower in the country; possibly not so much so, though, in the West as in the East.

There was a fair cut of roses for Christmas, but nothing wonderful; probably not more than a third or a quarter of the usual crop, except in isolated cases where the growers had the usual amount, and, in these instances, they did unusually well. As a matter of fact, prices have been better all season than other years—in some cases two or three times as high as they were the corresponding time other years.

Most of the better businessmen of the cut-flower trade felt that the embargo, when it was placed, would be a help rather than a detriment to the business. Their reason for thinking this was mainly on account of the labor situation, and, as it turned out, it was really a blessing to the florists. Everything was so very much higher, particularly labor, that the growers generally were forced to cut down expenses, and probably made out really better than if they had been running their places full capacity. In fact, with the rose-growers who are adjacent to large manufacturing districts, it would have been impossible to run their places full capacity on account of their help leaving their employ to accept better-paying positions.

Socially, there was not nearly as much going on as in other years. The social "four hundred" used less flowers, giving very few functions compared to other seasons.

There has come into the market a newer class of buyers— those who have been getting salaries that they never dreamed of, who have been spending money for luxuries. With them, flowers are considered a luxury, not a necessity, as the wealthier people consider them. So the war conditions have brought about a new field for the florists, which will mean a wider and a better opportunity to sell cut-flowers. I cannot help but feel that the next few years will see the business in good shape, with a more general class of buyers than heretofore.

The roses that have been the best sellers this season, and the favorites, have been Ophelia, Columbia, Russell, American Beauty, Pink and White Killarney, and Hadley.

Ophelia is still the favorite that it has been ever since its introduction. This is a very pleasing rose. It lasts well, has a good stem, and splendid foliage. Seedlings of great value are coming from Ophelia as one of the parents. Columbia is one, and, coming out next year, we have Premier. Both of these roses will probably give Russell a close run, as they are somewhat in the same class. Neither one, however, is as good a rose as Russell, from the standpoint of substance and color, but if they can be grown to produce two or three times as many blooms, they will supersede Russell, particularly where Russell does not do extra well. Well-grown Russell roses are very hard to beat.

The small, or "debutante" roses have not met with the success of former years, yet because roses of all kinds were scarce, they have sold well. In many cases they were used as a makeshift where the larger roses could not be procured, and they have fitted in very nicely. Cecile Brunner is the most popular and probably the best-paying of any of the "debutante" roses.

The rose with all its sterling qualities of beauty, fragrance, durability, and distinctiveness will always remain a favorite with the public. Then, too, it has a wide range of possibilities.

For the amateur there is nothing more fascinating than a rose-garden, whether it be large or small, and anyone becoming interested will continue a rose enthusiast with more interest each succeeding year, as he learns more fully what roses are and what they mean.

Experience and Prophecy

By WALLACE R. PIERSON, Cromwell, Conn.

EDITOR'S NOTE.—Few commercial rose-growers are as well qualified, both by experience and opportunity, to speak of the rose-future as is Past-President Pierson. He conducts a great business and his outlook is world-wide.

THE cut-rose industry during 1918–19 has suffered very seriously, owing to war conditions. These conditions were forced upon the florists of this country as a result of international complications, and have caused a great deal of hardship, of which the florists have been obliged to make the best.

The production of cut-roses has suffered seriously. In the first place, the Fuel Administration restricted the coal-supply 50 per cent, and, while that had some influence in restricting the number of roses grown, yet labor was very scarce during the summer of 1918, and there was very little replanting done. The majority of rose-growers have been cutting, this winter, from plants that should have been discarded a year or two ago. There has been almost as much area used, but in spite of that there has been a very greatly decreased production of cut-flowers.

With regard to the prospect for the future, there has been, this year, the largest call for young roses for replanting purposes that there ever has been in the history of the greenhouse industry. This is due to the fact that the winter of 1918–19 has seen an era of high prices that is almost without precedent in our business, and, as previously stated, to the fact that most of the growers are running sections of worn-out rose plants that must be replaced if they are to continue producing under the conditions that will exist this coming year.

There will be very few roses planted next year in addition to those already benched, so far as numbers are concerned, but the plants themselves will be in better condition. There will be a greatly increased number of young plants put into benches that will be producing this next year more flowers than that same space produced this past year.

But not by any means will the florist business be up to 100 per cent production during 1919–20 because there will not be plants enough to replant all the roses that should be replanted and that have been suffering for lack of replanting during the past two years.

There has been a big change in the varieties grown by the commercial rose-growers. The Killarney family has seen its day. With the exception of Double White Killarney, there is practically no call for any of the Killarney family. The new roses, Columbia and Evelyn, we consider the best of last year's introductions, and Columbia will replace Mrs. George Shawyer. Rose Premier, which is being offered for delivery this season, and of which there has been a very heavy sale, will almost entirely replace Mrs. Charles Russell. The list of varieties grown by commercial growers will be more restricted than in the past, and the quality of the flowers offered to the cut-flower-buying public will be better than ever before, owing to the fact that better varieties are being used for replanting. We feel safe in predicting a very bright future for the cut-flower rose business

Roses Cut and Roses Growing

By CHARLES H. TOTTY, Madison, N. J.

President Society American Florists and Ornamental Horticulturists

EDITOR'S NOTE.—Few men in America can speak upon the rose in commerce with more knowledge than Mr. Totty. He "knows the game" in all its pleasant variations.

Elsewhere a detailed account is given of the quarantine exclusion policy adopted by the Federal Horticultural Board, to which Mr. Totty refers. See article, "Where Are Our Roses Coming From?" on page 111.

THE rose, from a cut-flower standpoint, has had, during the present winter, and still is having, a phenomenal sale. This is due to a variety of causes, but primarily to restricted output because of the drastic regulations of the Fuel Administration which, when first promulgated, meant a cutting down on coal of 50 per cent to the commercial florist. Naturally, this resulted in many old houses being discontinued and a general tightening up in other establishments, because roses need a comparatively high temperature for winter forcing, necessitating the use of a great deal of coal. Firstly, then, we were confronted with a restricted output.

Then, unfortunately, all through October, the influenza epidemic created a tremendous call for cut-flowers, which was very inadequately met. The price of roses naturally, in common with every other flower, began to try for the "altitude record."

Then, in the month of November, the signing of the armistice was a signal for a general letting-down of the bars, for people, having been pent up for the past year or two, now felt they could once more have a little party, make their friends presents, or otherwise comport themselves as they had been accustomed to doing before the days of the war. Christmas was a much truer day of rejoicing this year than we have had for some time.

Since that time business has steadied, and there has been some reduction in prices on cut roses, but they still continue to be quite satisfactory to the grower who was so fortunate as to be able to run 60 to 80 per cent of his capacity.

It is true that, even with the increased prices, the florist will never get into the billionaire class, because labor has doubled in cost, glass has gone 'way up out of sight, and such coal as was available naturally was procured at a greatly enhanced price.

What a relief to the florist January, 1919, seems alongside of January, 1918! Last January the Government had declared us a non-essential, was seriously discussing closing down every greenhouse in the country, and, in fact, would have done so had it not been for the officials of the Society of American Florists, who went to Washington and presented their case before the Fuel Administration. Then, every florist saw ruin staring him in the face; today the skies look very clear, and I think of all branches of the profession the rose-grower has suffered the least.

NEW ROSES

The new rose, Columbia, which was introduced last year, met with instant and splendid appreciation on the part of the public. That the rose warrants it, goes without saying, but it is seldom that a rose will in one season establish itself as did Columbia. Its record is a matter of history in all the large markets of the country. No eulogy is needed from me of its twin sister, Rose Premier,* which is being introduced this winter, and is likely to have an equal amount of popularity, since it is an entirely different shade of color, being the color of a well-grown Russell. Columbia is several shades lighter in color.

What a wonderful thought it was of Mr. Hill to use Ophelia as the mother-parent of these splendid varieties! It is safe to say that today Ophelia is being used by practically every rose hybridist, and we may look for further fine varieties.

The advantages of Rose Premier over Russell are several: Firstly, the growth is just as free as Ophelia, and the crops are produced in much quicker rotation with Rose Premier than they are with Russell. Secondly, the plants are not nearly so prone to black-spot, which is the "bane of the grower's life" who is handling Russell in quantity. We have proved it to be just as lasting as Russell, the flowers of Rose Premier keeping for over fifteen days in good condition in my home, The fragrance is much more pronounced and pleasing than is the case with Russell. When we say a rose is superior to Russell, we are say-

*See colored frontispiece of E. G. Hill Company's Rose Premier.

ing a great deal, and this accounts for the phenomenal sale that has been enjoyed by this new variety.

OUTDOOR ROSES

What shall we say of roses from the garden viewpoint? Undoubtedly, with the pressure of war removed, many people are going to think more of flowers and less of vegetables than they did the past two years, and their thoughts turn naturally to roses. The importation of roses will be very greatly restricted this spring, with the specter of the Federal Horticultural Board looming up, and the spring of 1920 will see absolutely no roses being imported. While the Federal Horticultural Board may have good ground for shutting off some importations, there seems no good reason in the case of roses.

If this "Chinese Wall" policy had been enforced for the past twenty-five years, how lamentably backward would we be in the case of rose-growing, both as to varieties and culture! If this embargo is not removed, what will the next twenty-five years show? While America is very much better able to hold its own now in regard to new roses than it was twenty-five years ago, is it necessary to bar out the fruit of other men's labors, with just the selfish thought of America for Americans and American products? The thing above all else that made America great is the full and free interchange of commerce between the states. The same free interchange of commerce between countries in the future should work out equally as well.

Every rose-lover should protest against this embargo. The only argument heard in its favor is that of the scientist and entomologist, who insist that the importation of these plants is the cause of many diseases being admitted into the country. If everything is to be prevented coming into the country it will not be necessary to have scientists and entomologists! The scientist should be able to cope with the diseases he knows of, and with the embargo on all horticultural stock coming into the country, in a few years he will find himself like Othello, "his occupation gone."

It will be interesting to see if the other countries will be willing to sit back and keep silent under the stigma of sending injurious diseases into America.

Where Are Our Roses Coming From?
By THE EDITOR
(With letter from the Chairman of the Federal Horticultural Board)

AMERICA has a hearty rose appetite, increasing each year. As the universal flower, the rose is universally wanted and universally grown by the garden folks in the cold North, the hot South, the breezy West and the settled East.

But the supply for this hearty rose appetite is by no means as universal, and certain conditions now apparent make it not improbable that we are soon, and unwillingly, to go short on roses, unless our rose nurserymen wake up.

Broadly considered, the United States uses roses in two classes—those grown on their own roots, and those budded or grafted on stocks presumed to impart additional vigor.

The own-root plants may again be divided into those sold in active growth, usually from pots and under a year in actual age, either direct to mail purchasers in the spring or for planting out in some favorable location to grow through the year and be sold as dormant plants; and those sold in the dormant condition, usually after one or two years in the open ground. The first division of this class includes Teas, Hybrid Teas, and practically all of the roses in an extended list, while the second class of own-root dormant roses includes mostly climbers,

The budded or grafted plants are again in several broad divisions. Even during the war there have been imported large quantities of what are known as "finished" roses. (See table on page 114.) Probably 75 per cent of these imported roses, especially the cheaper grades from Holland, are worked on the Dog-rose or Brier stock (*Rosa canina*), most of the remainder being on the better Manetti (*R. chinensis Manetti.*)

By far the larger portion of the roses in American commerce are budded or grafted in this country, on either Multiflora, Manetti or Dog-rose stocks, mostly imported. For example, in the year ended June 30, 1918, there were imported of rose stocks, 3,593,028, of which two-thirds came from England and France, and less than a quarter of a million from Holland.

In the United States are grown comparatively the smaller

quantity of stocks for roses, including, as before noted, Multiflora and certain stocks peculiar to the Far West. It is another story to discuss this whole question of rose stocks.*

California's special climate, considerably resembling that of eastern Europe, permits the growing in that state of large quantities of rose plants, both own-root and "worked" on Manetti, Multiflora, Dog-rose or certain varietal stocks. In some of our southern states favorable conditions also exist for wholesale rose-growing, especially of own-root plants.

In the last month of 1918 the Editor made a careful inquiry into the existing rose situation of the country. One large grower in central New York reported the possession of something like 600,000 budded plants and about 300,000 own-root plants of climbers, together with ownership of about 150,000 "California roses," not mentioned as to whether they were budded or own root. This shrewd merchant said, *"We wish we had about a million more than we have.* We never knew roses to be in such strong demand as they are this season."

Another large disseminator of good dormant rose plants in the East said: "The call for two-year-old roses which we experienced this fall would naturally indicate that people will want roses in the spring. . . . I suppose there will be no surplus of two-year-old budded stock."

Another eastern grower, who believes in the Multiflora stock, reports approximately a half-million so grown, adding, "We expect a big demand for our home-grown, hardy roses."

Still another eastern grower, who has specialized on Multiflora, reports a goodly number on hand, which he says "will be more than taken up by a good margin by our retail trade." Writing, as he did, immediately after the signing of the armistice, this grower added, "I am sure, however, that, regardless of general conditions, there will be in this broad country of ours many thousands of people eager to buy roses."

Another grower, whose largest item is the sale of roses budded on Manetti to florists for greenhouse-growing, surprised the Editor by saying, "We will not import any stock this year. . . . so roses are going to be scarce." It is quite apparent that

*(On page 56 of the 1918 Annual, Dr. Van Fleet gave facts and made suggestions, and on page 47 of the 1917 Annual, Dr. Huey gave details for using the Japanese Multiflora stocks.)

the supply of rose plants for greenhouse growing-on will be short, because, first, of the scarcity abroad of the Manetti stock, and second, because so many florists carried over plants grown for winter bloom which must now be discarded and replaced, and which the high prices received for cut roses will justify replacing, with probably extended planting.

The head of a great nursery west of the Alleghanies, whose acreage of roses is a wonder, writes that his stock "is much smaller than usual." Referring to the reason for this, he says:

> The production of roses in France, England, and Ireland in the past two years has been much smaller than usual. The seasons have all been against them, and prices are about three times as high as they used to be. . . . It has been almost impossible to obtain Manetti stocks in quantity for the past few seasons. . . . With the cutting off of the importation of rose plants after next spring, with the shortage of rose stocks in Europe, I think there can be no possible question but that field-grown roses, outside of hardy climbers that can be grown from cuttings in the South, are going to be scarce and high-priced, for several seasons at least. . . . However, the demand for roses is going to be large for the next few seasons, providing, of course, the country remains prosperous.

From a very live California grower comes the statement that he has on hand "quite a stock of good roses, but the chances are that before next February we will be sold out." He anticipates an increased demand and doubts that foreign roses would be able to compete with the California product "when the virtues of the latter are fully known."

No mention has above been made of the quantities of roses involved in the own-root supply sold in full growth, and broadly covered by the term "Springfield roses," upon which Mr. John M. Good, of Springfield, Ohio, wrote in the 1917 Annual. Of these the product at Springfield alone is counted in millions.

THE JUNE, 1919, FEDERAL EXCLUSION

Now comes the complicating relationship of the Federal Horticultural Board, which in its "Notice of Quarantine No. 37, with Regulations," approved by the Secretary of Agriculture on November 18, 1918, forbids the importation into the United States, after June 1, 1919, of a large class of horticultural items, included in which are finished roses, but excepted from which, under Item 3 of Regulation 3, are "rose stocks for propagation," presumably of any sort. We do not here discuss the wisdom of this exclusion, but accurately present the fact of it, and in fairness state the reason given, which is "to prevent the further introduction into the United States of injurious insect pests and fungous diseases."

Let us see just what this means, by noting the figures for the last six years:

ROSE IMPORTATIONS, FROM RECORDS OF FEDERAL HORTICULTURAL BOARD

Year Ended June 30	From Holland	From France	From Great Britain	All other Countries	Totals
1913	1,632,252	200,283	163,257	184,909	2,180,601
1914	1,439,718	318,625	90,348	55,016	1,903,707
1915	2,502,834	235,080	697,576	80,078	3,515,568
1916	2,375,823	180,461	536,359	30,581	3,123,224
1917	1,648,375	104,995	202,833	486	1,956,689
1918	736,185	165,014	154,904	400	1,056,503
Total	10,335,187	1,204,458	1,845,277	351,470	13,736,292
Percentage	75.2%	8.9%	13.4%	2.5%	100%
Annual Average	1,722,531	200,743	307,546	58,593	2,289,382

Noting that all these sources of roses will be closed after June 1, 1919, and presuming that our American after-war appetite for roses will be at least as vigorous as the pre-war hunger, it will appear that next year, and later, we will be short all of the three millions or more roses Europe has sent us annually. We must either produce them here or do without them.

Now the Editor confesses that he is not able to answer the question which is the title of this article. There will not be three millions of foreign roses possible (because of shortage abroad) to be brought in prior to June 1 of this year, so that none, or practically none, can be "carried over," and next year there will be none at all. Moreover, it is apparent, from the citations given above, that rose stocks themselves which can be imported are scarce in supply and high in price.

There is food for thought in this situation. America can grow all the roses America needs on American stocks if American nurserymen are willing to bestir themselves. The American rose-users are willing to pay the price, it is evident. It is a question of courage, of taking chances, of investigation, of the study of new stocks as well as the cultivation of those well known to be successful. It is, after all, a business proposition; and more than a business proposition, for the rose-supply is more important in its influence on the lives of the people than the money involved.

HOW TO IMPORT NEW ROSES

It is worth while to be able to report that it will be possible, even after the fateful June 1, 1919, to have relatively convenient access to all the new varieties of roses grown abroad. Inquiry at the office of the Federal Horticultural Board brings the following letter from its Chairman:

WASHINGTON, D. C., *March 4, 1919.*
MR. J. HORACE McFARLAND, *Editor American Rose Annual.*

Dear Sir:—You have inquired concerning the application of Quarantine No. 37 to the importation of roses. That quarantine is a part of the determined effort of the Federal Horticultural Board to exclude from the United States, so far as possible, other foreign insect pests and fungous diseases as dangerous and destructive as the brown-tail moth, the alfalfa weevil, the citrus canker and the chestnut-tree blight, among others, have proved to be. (Incidentally, it is believed that the brown-tail moth reached this country, from Holland, on roses.)

While Quarantine No. 37 prevents the importation of commercial quantities of budded or grafted finished roses (fully three-fourths of which have hitherto originated in Holland), it permits continuance of the importation of rose-stocks for propagation. But this needed protective quarantine does not exclude from the United States new varieties of roses, novelties, or other important plant material necessary for propagation here.

Through the courtesy of the Bureau of Plant Industry, there have been developed, in connection with its Office of Foreign Seed and Plant Introduction, adequate facilities for such highly developed quarantine and inspection service as will handle the necessarily limited quantities of new plant material from the moment of its arrival, with full care for its welfare, under the supervision of plant experts.

I should be glad to have you make known to the members of the American Rose Society the simple conditions under which such importation of limited quantities of propagating material can conveniently be made after June 1, 1919, under the general provisions of Regulation 14 of Quarantine No. 37. Requisite details are here briefly summarized:

1. Request to the Federal Horticultural Board in Washington will bring a special blank upon which application may be made for a permit to import. There will be required a statement as to the bona-fide nature of the novelties to be imported, the name and address of the exporter, and the quantity of the material it is desired to bring in. In certain cases it may be necessary to limit importations by bulk, rather than by number.

2. If the permit is issued, the applicant will be furnished shipping instructions and shipping tags to be forwarded with his order to the exporter. The plants will, in consequence, be addressed to the importer in care of the Office of Foreign Seed and Plant Introduction, United States Department of Agriculture, Washington, D. C., and arrangements must be made with some responsible agency in Washington* for the clearance of the plants when received through the Custom House at Georgetown, D. C., together with the payment of all charges involved.

3. Upon clearance through the Georgetown Custom House, the material will be turned over to the Office of Foreign Seed and Plant Introduction by the authorized agent of the importer, and, in the specially equipped inspection houses

*Information as to such Custom House agencies in Washington will be promptly supplied upon application to the Editor of the American Rose Annual, Harrisburg, Pa.—EDITOR.

and under expert care as to the welfare of the plants, be carefully examined by inspectors of the Federal Horticultural Board. If found free from dangerous insects or diseases, the shipment will be immediately and carefully repacked and forwarded by express, charges collect, to the importer.

4. Cleaning and disinfection will occur for slight infestation, but should the material be found to be so infected or infested with either disease or insects that it cannot be so adequately safeguarded, it will either be destroyed or, when possible and desirable, returned to the point of origin. In such cases, complete record will be furnished the importer, to promote proper adjustments with the exporter who may have sent in such dangerously infested material.

It is believed that the really interested rosarians and plant-growers of America will, when they understand the situation, cheerfully assist the Federal Horticultural Board in thus safeguarding the nation against the further admission of destructive pests and diseases such as have done great devastation in the past. Yours truly,

C. L. MARLATT, *Chairman, Federal Horticultural Board.*

The National Rose Test-Garden in 1918

By F. L. MULFORD, Horticulturist, Bureau of Plant Industry, United States Department of Agriculture

THE report of the National Rose Test-Garden at Arlington, Va., covers the two principal groups of cut-flower roses— the Hybrid Perpetuals and the Teas and their hybrids— for the seasons of 1917 and 1918, as far as the different varieties were available for observation during this period.

The tables following show the average number of roses cut per plant for the plants under observation. The other observations recorded also represent an average. For these classes of roses it is believed that the essential items of information for a fair comparison of varieties is included. When similar data is available from all the test-gardens for a series of years, much valuable information about the behavior of roses in the different sections of the country will be at hand, in shape to be utilized by prospective rose-growers. When this is supplemented by a composite description of the rose and bush, compiled from observations in several localities and by different observers in the same locality, rose-variety selection will not be the lottery it now is.

It is felt that much advancement has been made in the garden the past year, but continued progress can only be made by continued coöperation and continued contributions of roses.

HYBRID PERPETUAL ROSES IN THE NATIONAL ROSE TEST-GARDEN

		Height Feet	Habit	Foliage	First Bloom	No. of blooms per plant						Plants Noted
						June	July	Aug.	Sept.	Oct.	Total	
Baron de Bonstetten	1917	4	Med.	Suff.	June 5	26	3				29	3
	1918	4	Med.	Suff.	May 20	84					84	6
Baroness Rothschild	1917	4	Med.	Suff.	June 5	3	4				7	6
	1918	4	Med.	Plent.	May 24	37	6		1		44	6
Black Prince	1917	5	Tall	Suff.								
	1918	5	Tall	Suff.	May 29	37	4	2	1		44	3
Captain Christy	1917	2½	V. low	Suff.	May 25	4	4	3			11	3
	1918	2	V. low	Suff.	May 16	13	2	1	3	1	20	5
Captain Hayward	1917	3	Low	Suff.								
	1918	2½	V. low	Suff.	May 20	63	2	6		1	72	2
Clio	1917	6	Tall	Suff.	May 24	8	7	3		1	19	3
	1918	6	Tall	Suff.	June 5	57		4			61	6
Coquette des Alpes, H. Nois.	1917	4	Med.	Plent.	May 29	14	60	29	6	5	114	3
	1918	4	Med.	Suff.	May 24	40	30	3	14	7	94	6
Coquette des Blanches, H. Nois.	1917	3	Low	Plent.	May 25	2		2			4	3
	1918	3½	Low	Plent.	May 20	76				3	79	6
Countess of Roseberry	1917	3½	Low	Plent.	May 24		6				6	2
	1918	4	Med.	Plent.	June 5	63	6	27	2	6	104	5
Duke of Edinburgh	1917	4	Med.	Suff.	June 5	2					2	2
	1918	5	Tall	Suff.	May 18	25	2	1			28	4
Earl of Dufferin	1917	4	Med.	Suff.	June 5	10	4				14	3
	1918	3½	Med.	Suff.	May 24	24	1	1			26	6
Eugene Furst	1917	4	Med.	Suff.	June 1	70	20	1			91	1
	1918	3½	Med.	Plent.	May 18	70	2	5	3		80	4
Fisher Holmes	1917	3	Low	Suff.	June 1	14					14	2
	1918	3½	Low	Suff.	May 20	50					50	4
Francois Levet	1917	7	Tall	Plent.	May 22	3	7	1			11	3
	1918	5	Tall	Plent.	May 20	66	2	5			73	6
Frau Karl Druschki	1917	6	Tall	Plent.	June 1	22	19	1	1	1	44	3
	1918	7	Tall	Plent.	May 18	24	21	2	5	3	55	6
Gen. Jacqueminot	1917	5	Tall	Suff.	May 29	6	12				18	2
	1918	4	Med.	Suff.	May 20	47		1	1		49	6
Gen. Washington	1917	3	Low	Plent.	June 8	13	8	11	3	2	37	2
	1918	3	Low	Plent.	May 18	41	12	31	8	9	101	5
George Arends	1917	4	Med.	Suff.	June 8	9	20	6		3	38	1
	1918	5	Tall	Suff.	May 24	30	3	6	4	6	49	8
Gloire de Chedane Guinoisseau	1917	3	Low									
	1918	3½	Low	Suff.	May 24	8	1				9	3
Gloire de l'Exposition de Bruxelles	1917	5	Tall	Suff.	June 1	21	6				27	3
	1918	5	Tall	Suff.								
Heinrich Munch	1917	3	Low	Suff.	June 12	1	2				3	1
	1918	6	Tall	Suff.	May 24	19	6			1	26	1
Her Majesty	1917	8	Tall	Plent.	June 8	5	3				8	2
	1918	3	Low	Plent.	May 24	7		1	1	1	10	5
Hugh Dickson	1917	6	Tall	Plent.	May 29	21	15	1			37	2
	1918	6	Tall	Suff.	May 16	12	7				19	6
J. B. Clark	1917	4	Med.	Suff.	June 1	65	6	1	2	2	76	3
	1918	7	Tall	Suff.	May 18	82	1	1			84	6
John Hopper	1917	5	Tall	Suff.	May 29	11	7	2	2		22	1
	1918	5	Tall	Suff.	May 18	29	4				33	1
John Keynes	1917	5	Tall	Suff.	May 29	51	13				64	1
	1918	5	Tall	Plent.	May 20	147				1	148	3
Jubilee	1917	4½	Med.	Suff.	May 29	11	6	2			19	2
	1918	5½	Tall	Suff.	May 18	52	2	3			57	4
Jules Margottin	1917	4	Med.	Suff.	June 5	43	2	3			48	3
	1918	4	Med.	Suff.	May 20	61	1	11		1	74	6
Mabel Morrison	1917	4½	Med.	Suff.	June 5	9	12	2	2	1	26	1
	1918	4½	Med.	Suff.	May 24	63	10	2	2	1	78	3
Mme. Charles Wood	1917	5	Tall	Plent.	June 8	1					1	3
	1918	5½	Tall	Plent.	May 20	60					60	3
Mme. Gabriel Luizet	1917	7	Tall	Plent.	May 29	15					15	1
	1918	3½	Med.	Plent.	May 20	134		4	1	2	141	2
Mme. Masson	1917	2	Low	Suff.	May 18	6	5	3			14	2
	1918	1½	Low	Suff.	June 8	4	2	3	4	6	19	4
Mme. Victor Verdier	1917	2	Low									
	1918	2½	Low	Suff.	May 24	12	3	1	1		17	2

(117)

HYBRID PERPETUAL ROSES IN THE NATIONAL ROSE TEST-GARDEN, continued

	Height Feet	Habit	Foliage	First Bloom	No. of blooms per plant						Plants Noted
					June	July	Aug.	Sept.	Oct.	Total	
Magna Charta	1917	6	Tall	Suff.	June 1	1					1	2
	1918	5	Tall	Suff.	May 24	53		1			54	6
Maharajah	1917	2	V. low	Sparse								3
	1918	3½	Med.	Suff.	May 18	26					26	6
Marchioness of Lorne	1917	6	Tall	Plent.	May 29	13	10				23	1
	1918	6	Tall	Suff.	May 18	65	5	2			72	4
Marchioness of Dufferin	1917	3	Low	Suff.	June 15	1	4		2	2	9	1
	1918	Cut		Suff.	June 12	1	2				3	1
Margaret Dickson	1917	5	Tall	Suff.	June 5		2				2	2
	1918	6	Tall	Suff.	May 29	12	2				14	6
Marie Baumann	1917	1½	Low	Plent.	May 29	16	17	4			37	1
	1918	1½	Low	Suff.	May 24	26	4	6	4		40	2
Marshall P. Wilder	1917	5	Tall	Suff.	May 25	13	6	1		1	21	3
	1918	3½	Low	Suff.	May 18	63		6	1	1	71	6
Mrs. John Laing	1917	4	Med.	Suff.	June 5	4	9	6	2	8	29	3
	1918	4	Med.	Suff.	May 24	26	7	4	9	8	54	6
Mrs. R. G. Sharman-Crawford	1917	3½	Med.	Suff.	May 29	7	21	8	1	2	39	3
	1918	4	Med.	Suff.	May 18	39	3	17	10	7	76	6
Oakmont	1917	6	Tall	Suff.	May 25	51	11	1		1	64	3
	1918	6	Tall	Suff.	May 16	127		4	1		132	6
Paul Neyron	1917	4	Med.	Suff.	June 5	13	5	5	1	3	27	3
	1918	4	Med.	Suff.	May 20	25	3	5	5	3	41	6
Pierre Notting	1917			Suff.	June 1	1					1	2
	1918	4	Med.	Suff.	May 24	14	1	1			16	9
Pius IX	1917	4	Med.	Plent.								
	1918	3½	Med.	Plent.	May 18	101	7	4	8	6	126	3
President Lincoln	1917	3	Low	Suff.	May 29	6	2				8	3
	1918	3	Low	Suff.	May 18	5	1				6	6
Tom Wood	1917	3	Low	Suff.	June 5	11	9	2	1	3	26	3
	1918	4	Med.	Suff.	May 20	64	1	6	3	3	77	6
Ulrich Brunner	1917	7	Tall	Plent.	June 1	14	7				21	3
	1918	5	Tall	Plent.	May 20	15	5	3			23	5
Victor Verdier	1917	7	Tall	Suff.	May 29	71	5	1			77	3
	1918	5½	Tall	Suff.	May 16	142	1	4	1	1	149	6

TWO-YEAR BLOOM RECORD OF HYBRID TEA AND TEA ROSES

The Tea varieties are followed by the initial "T"	Height Feet	Habit	Foliage	First Bloom	No. of blooms per plant						Plants Noted
					May	June	July	Aug.	Sept.	Total	
Alsterufer	1917	1½	V. low	Suff.	May 29	10	25	11	1		47	5
	1918	1½	V. low	Suff.	May 18	29	17	14	9		69	10
Ambrosia	1917		V. low	Suff.	June 8	1	3	1			5	5
	1918	1¼	V. low	Suff.	June 4	2	1	1	3		7	4
Arthur R. Goodwin	1917			Suff.	May 29	5	13	13	3		34	1
	1918											
Balduin	1917	1½	V. low	Suff.	June 29	18	25	5	3		51	2
	1918	2	V. low	Suff.	May 16	14	14	12	21		61	5
Beaute Inconstante, T.	1917			Suff.	June 4	6	9	14	2		31	1
	1918											
Betty	1917	1½	V. low	Suff.	June 4	2	10	4	2		18	6
	1918	1½	V. low	Suff.	May 16	4	13	2	3		22	9
Blumenschmidt, T.	1917	1½	V. low	Suff.	June 1	13	21	11	2		47	5
	1918	2½	V. low	Plent.	May 18	7	15	12	5		39	11
Bridesmaid, T.	1917	1½	V. low	Suff.	May 25	1	6	3			10	5
	1918			Suff.	May 24			1	1		2	3
British Queen	1917	1½	V. low	Sparse	June 8	5	13	5	11		34	3
	1918	1	V. low	Sparse	May 24	5	11	2	2		20	6
Catherine Mermet, T.	1917	1	V. low	Suff.	June 1	4	3	1	1		9	4
	1918	¾	V. low	Sparse	June 1	1	6		1		8	4

Two-Year Bloom Record of Hybrid Tea and Tea Roses, continued

		Height Feet	Habit	Foliage	First Bloom	No. of blooms per plant: May	June	July	Aug.	Sept.	Total	Plants Noted
Champ Weiland	1917											
	1918	¾	V. low	Suff.	May 24		1	7	3	3	14	6
Chateau de Clos Vougeot	1917	1	V. low	Suff.	June 4		7	8	3		18	3
	1918	1½	V. low	Suff.	May 18		10	7	2	2	21	6
Cleveland	1917			Suff.	June 26		1	7	6		14	6
	1918	½	V. low	Suff.	May 20		2	8		1	11	7
Col. R. S. Williamson	1917	2	V. low	Suff.	June 4		4	7	2	1	14	6
	1918	2½	V. low	Suff.	May 18		6	6	3	5	20	12
Countess of Gosford	1917	1¾	V. low	Suff.	May 25		11	9	7	3	20	5
	1918	2	V. low	Suff.	May 16		7	12	5	7	31	10
Dawn	1917											
	1918	3½	Low	Suff.	May 27		4	1			5	3
Defiance	1917			Suff.	June 8		2	21	7	2	32	2
	1918	1½	V. low	Suff								
Dora	1917			Suff.	June 12		1	4		1	6	1
	1918											
Dorothy Page Roberts	1917	2	V. low	Suff.	June 4		9	5	4		18	5
	1918	2½	V. low	Plent.	May 24		10	5	3	4	22	11
Dr. Grill, T.	1917	1½	V. low	Suff.	June 19		5	9	2	3	19	3
	1918	2	V. low	Plent.	May 20	7	13	29	23	9	81	6
Duchesse de Brabant, T.	1917	1½	V. low	Suff.	June 1		6	16	3	4	29	5
	1918	2	V. low	Plent.	May 18		11	21	1	9	42	10
Duchess of Albany, T.	1917	¾	V. low	Suff.	June 8		2	7	2	1	12	5
	1918	1¼	V. low	Suff.	May 20		4	6	2	5	17	10
Duchess of Westminster	1917	¾	V. low	Suff.	June 8		3	6	1		10	2
	1918	1	V. low	Suff.	May 18		4	6	1	2	13	6
Earl of Warwick	1917	1¼	V. low	Suff.	June 8		3	3	4		10	2
	1918											
Etoile de France	1917	¾	V. low	Suff.	May 29		3	2	2	1	8	2
	1918	2	V. low	Suff.	May 18		8	9		5	22	3
Etoile de Lyon, T.	1917	¾	V. low	Suff.	June 18		3	6	1		10	4
	1918	¾	V. low	Plent.	May 24	1	1	2	2	2	8	2
Farbenkönigin	1917	1½	V. low	Suff.	May 25		1	3	2	1	7	4
	1918	1½	V. low	Suff.	May 20		6	5	2	2	15	9
Frances E. Willard, T.	1917	3	Low	Plent.	June 4		2	3	1		6	5
	1918	2½	Low	Plent.	May 24		3	6	1	5		8
Francisca Kruger, T.	1917	1½	V. low	Suff.	June 4		7	10	6	2	25	6
	1918	2	V. low	Plent.	May 20	10	8	15	11	10	54	5
Freiherr von Marschall	1917			Suff.								
	1918			Plent.	May 18	3	1	6	3	4	17	7
General MacArthur	1917	1½	V. low	Suff.	May 20		3	4	4		11	2
	1918	1¾	V. low	Suff.	May 16		9	7	9	5	30	6
General - Superior Arnold	1917	2½	V. low	Suff.	June 4			6	8	1	15	1
Janssen	1918	2½	V. low	Suff.	May 16		17	19	9	17	62	3
George Dickson	1917	4	Med.	Suff.	June 1		2	2			4	2
	1918	5	Tall	Suff.	May 18		21		1		22	4
George C. Waud	1917	1¼	V. low	Suff.	June 8		2	9	3	2	16	2
	1918											
Gloire Lyonnaise	1917	6	Tall	Plent.	May 22		5	2			7	3
(Five blooms in Oct.)	1918	5½	Tall	Plent.	May 16		20	31	1	14	71	
Gorgeous	1917	¾	V. low	Suff.	June 4		1	4	3	1	9	6
	1918	1	V. low	Suff.	May 16	2	1	6	2		11	10
Grace Molyneux	1917	2½	V. low	Suff.	June 1		11	15	8	1	35	6
	1918	2	V. low	Suff.	May 20	9	7	13	4	8	41	11
Grandesse Royale	1917	3	Low	Suff.	June 8		2	3			5	2
	1918	4½	Med.	Plent.	May 24		45	2	8		55	6
Grossherzog Friedrich	1917	1¼	V. low	Suff.	June 1		3	8	2		13	3
	1918	1¼	V. low	Suff.	May 18		11	13	4	12	40	5
Gruss an Teplitz	1917	2½	V. low	Suff.	May 25		33	47	19	4	103	6
	1918	2½	V. low	Suff.	May 16		78	31	34	27	170	11
Gustav Grunerwald	1917	1¾	V. low	Suff.	May 29		12	8	10	2	32	6
	1918	2	V. low	Suff.	May 18		15	15	5	10	45	12
Hadley	1917											
	1918	1½	V. low	Suff.	May 29		1	3	4	4	12	12
Helen Good, T.	1917	¾	V. low	Suff.	June 22		1	1			2	5
	1918	1½	V. low	Suff.	May 29		1		2		3	2

Two-Year Bloom Record of Hybrid Tea and Tea Roses, continued

		Height Feet	Habit	Foliage	First Bloom	May	June	July	Aug.	Sept.	Total	Plants Noted
						No. of blooms per plant						
H. F. Eilers	1917	1	V. low	Suff.	June 12		1	4	3		8	2
	1918	1¾	V. low	Suff.			7	4	1	5	17	4
Henry M. Stanley, T. . .	1917			Suff.	June 8		1		3	2	6	1
	1918											
Highland Mary, T. . . .	1917	½	V. low	Sparse	July 19			1	1		2	2
	1918											
Hoosier Beauty	1917	1¼	V. low	Suff.	Aug. 13				1	2	3	6
	1918	1½	V. low	Suff.	May 16		6	4	2	5	17	10
Irish Brightness	1917	5	Tall	Plent.	May 13		73	5	2		80	3
	1918	4½	Med.	Plent.								
Irish Fireflame	1917			Suff.	May 18	2	5	6	6	5	24	6
	1918	1½	V. low	Suff.	May 25		21	26	16		63	5
Isabella Sprunt, T. . . .	1917	2	V. low	Suff.	May 16	23	10	27	17	27	104	10
	1918	2	V. low	Suff.	May 29		1	5	1		7	6
Jonkheer J. L. Mock . . .	1917	1½	V. low	Suff.	May 20		1	4	1	2	8	7
	1918	1	V. low	Suff.	May 29		5	5	2	1	13	4
Joseph Hill	1917	¾	V. low	Suff.	May 16	2	2	6	2	2	14	8
	1918	1¾	V. low	Suff.	June 4		5	7	4	1	17	5
Kaiserin Augusta Victoria .	1917	2	V. low	Suff.	May 18	5	3	4	3	4	19	10
	1918	3½	V. low	Suff.	June 4		9	8	4	1	22	6
Killarney	1917	2½	V. low	Suff.	May 20		8	8	3	6	25	12
	1918	1¾	V. low	Suff.	June 3		14	6	6	1	27	6
Killarney Queen	1917	1¾	V. low	Suff.	May 20		10	8	6	5	29	12
	1918	2½	V. low	Plent.	June 4		14	9	6	1	30	5
Killarney, White	1917	2	V. low	Suff.	May 18	8	3	18	6	7	42	10
	1918	2½	V. low	Plent.	May 29		5	6	1		12	5
Königin Carola	1917	2¾	Low	Suff.	May 18		10	14		5	29	8
	1918	2	V. low	Suff.	June 4		4	8	2	1	15	4
La France	1917	1½	V. low	Suff.	May 18		11	15	4	4	34	8
	1918	1¾	V. low	Suff.	June 8		4	16	10		30	2
La France, Striped	1917	1¾	V. low	Suff.	May 20		11	15	6	9	41	4
	1918	2	V. low	Suff.	May 29		6	13	4		23	6
La France, White	1917	1½	V. low	Suff.	May 18		14	19	4	8	45	12
	1918	1¾	V. low	Suff.	June 1		18	20	12	3	53	3
La Tosca	1917	2½	V. low	Suff.	May 18		41	26	10	6	83	6
	1918	3	Low	Suff.	May 29		4	7	3	1	15	5
Lady Alice Stanley . . .	1917	1½	V. low	Suff.	May 16		11	12	2	9	34	12
	1918	1½	V. low	Plent.	May 25		12	8	7	1	28	5
Lady Ashtown	1917	1¾	V. low	Suff.	May 16		14	15	4	7	40	10
	1918	2½	V. low	Suff.	June 1		4	5	3	2	14	4
Lady Hillingdon, T. . . .	1917	1½	V. low	Suff.	May 24	2	2	20	3	4	31	3
	1918	2	V. low	Suff.	May 25		12	30	10	3	55	5
Lady Ursula	1917	3	Low	Suff.	May 16		14	14	9	8	45	11
	1918	3½	Low	Suff.	May 25		6	4	3	1	14	5
Laurent Carle	1917	1¾	V. low	Suff.	May 16		17	9	6	8	40	10
	1918	2	V. low	Suff.	June 4		2	3	1	1	7	1
Letty Coles, T.	1917			Suff.								
	1918				May 29		2	13	3	1	19	3
Lieutenant Chaure	1917	1½	V. low	Suff.	May 16		15	18	3	6	42	8
	1918	1½	V. low	Suff.	June 4		2	8	6	5	21	2
Lucien Chaure	1917	1	V. low	Suff.	May 16		7	16	4	6	33	9
	1918	1½	V. low	Suff.	June 8		5	8	10		23	1
Luise Lilia	1917	1½	V. low	Suff.	May 16		9	9	6	3	27	4
	1918	1	V. low	Suff.	June 1		3	7	4	1	15	5
Maman Cochet, T. . . .	1917	2½	V. low	Suff.	June 1		6	32	2	1	41	6
	1918	2	V. low	Suff.	May 25		4	2	3	3	12	9
Maman Cochet, White, T.	1917	1½	V. low	Suff.	June 4		4	5	3	1	13	6
	1918	2	V. low	Suff.	May 20	4	5	6	3	4	22	10
Marie Guillot, T..	1917	½	V. low	Suff.	June 22		1	2	2		5	3
	1918	¾	V. low	Suff.								
Marie Lambert, T.	1917	2	V. low	Plent.	May 25		8	36	31	1	76	2
	1918	2	V. low	Plent.	May 20	8	2	22	1	9	42	4
Marie Van Houtte, T. . .	1917	2	V. low	Plent.	May 25		4	9	5	1	19	5
	1918	1¾	V. low	Plent.	May 16	6	2	11	10	8	37	5
Marquise de Querhoent, T.	1917	1½	V. low	Plent.	June 12		9	13	9	1	32	4
	1918	1¾	V. low	Plent.	May 24	3	5	10	3	5	26	6

PLATE IX. ROSA XANTHINA NORMALIS (the Single-flowered Form), as Growing at the Home of

Two-Year Bloom Record of Hybrid Tea and Tea Roses, continued

		Height Feet	Habit	Foliage	First Bloom	No. of blooms per plant						Plants Noted
						May	June	July	Aug.	Sept.	Total	
Marquise de Sinety	1917	¾	V. low	Suff.	June 8		2	4	3	1	10	2
	1918	½	V. low	Suff.	May 24	2	2	2	2	1	9	5
Mary, Countess of Ilchester	1917	2	V. low	Suff.	June 1		15	19	5	2	41	3
	1918	2½	V. low	Suff.	May 18		34	21	9	13	77	9
Mevrouw Dora van Tets	1917			Suff.	June 8		1	6	2	2	11	1
	1918											
Milady	1917			Suff.	June 8		1	4	3		8	2
	1918											
Miss Cynthia Forde	1917	2	V. low	Suff.	May 29		10	11	1	1	23	1
	1918	2½	V. low	Suff.	May 20		14	7	8	9	41	4
Miss Genevieve Clark	1917	1½	V. low	Suff.	May 25		15	22	13	4	54	5
	1918	1¾	V. low	Suff.	May 16		56	32	19	22	129	11
Mme. Abel Chatenay	1917			Suff.								
	1918											
Mme. Berthe Fontaine	1917	1½	V. low	Plent.	June 8		1	1	3	2	7	3
	1918											
Mme. Camille, T.	1917	2½	V. low	Plent.	June 4		11	21	13	1	46	5
	1918	2	V. low	Plent.	May 24		13	10	8	10	41	10
Mme. Caroline Testout	1917	2½	V. low	Suff.	May 29		4	5	3	1	13	6
	1918	1¾	V. low	Suff.	May 20		7	6	5	5	23	11
Mme. Hector Leuillot	1917	2	V. low	Suff.	May 29		2	11	6	1	20	5
	1918	1½	V. low	Suff.	May 16	1	1	6	1	4	13	8
Mme. Jean Dupuy, T.	1917	1	V. low	Plent.	June 1		12	27	8	3	50	4
	1918	1½	V. low	Plent.	May 16		16	19	14	6	55	10
Mme. Joseph Schwartz, T.	1917	1	V. low	Suff.	June 8		12	19	21	1	53	3
	1918	1	V. low	Plent.	May 24	6	4	11	4	7	32	6
Mme. Jules Gravereaux, Cl. T.	1917	4	Med.	Suff.	June 1		9	13	6	2	30	5
	1918	4½	Med.	Suff.	May 16		8	14	10	17	49	11
Mme. Jules Grolez	1917	1½	V. low	Suff.	May 25		7	13	8	2	30	6
	1918	1¾	V. low	Suff.	May 16		12	12	5	8	37	9
Mme. Leon Pain	1917	1	V. low	Suff.	June 8		5	8	5	2	20	3
	1918	1½	V. low	Suff.	May 20		7	8	1	5	21	7
Mme. Lambard, T.	1917	2½	V. low	Suff.	May 25		8	16	3		27	6
	1918	1¾	V. low	Suff.	May 20		14	12	7	8	41	10
Mme. Maurice de Luze	1917	1½	V. low	Suff.	June 15		2	6	3	1	12	3
	1918	1¾	V. low	Suff.	May 20		10	12	4	6	32	6
Mme. Paul Euler	1917	1¾	V. low	Suff.	June 4		3	3	1		7	1
	1918	¾	V. low	Suff.	May 18		3	7	2	2	14	6
Mme. Segond Weber	1917	1½	V. low	Suff.	June 1		2	4	1		7	2
	1918	1½	V. low	Suff.	May 16		7	8	3	1	19	5
Mme. Welche, T.	1917	½	V. low	Suff.	June 4		4	3	1		8	4
	1918	¾	V. low	Suff.	May 29		2	2	1	1	6	6
Molly Sharman-Crawford, T.	1917			Sparse	June 8		2	9	3	2	16	2
	1918											
Mrs. Aaron Ward	1917	1	V. low	Suff.	June 4		2	5	4		11	2
	1918	1½	V. low	Plent.	May 16	6	4	10	3	10	33	4
Mrs. A. R. Waddell	1917	2½	V. low	Suff.	June 1	3	19	6	2	1	31	5
	1918	2¾	V. low	Suff.	May 16	12	7	27	7	9	62	11
Mrs. B. R. Cant, T.	1917	1½	V. low	Suff.	May 29		3	16	8	1	28	2
	1918	1¾	V. low	Suff.	May 16		4	12	3	9	28	3
Mrs. Bayard Thayer	1917			Suff.	June 29			7	2		9	6
	1918	1½	V. low	Suff.	May 24		2	3	2	1	8	4
Mrs. Charles Russell	1917											
	1918	1	V. low	Suff.	May 20		1	1	1	2	5	5
Mrs. Franklin Dennison	1917	1	V. low	Sparse	June 1		2	2	1		5	3
	1918	1½	V. low	Suff.	May 16		3	3	2	1	9	8
Mrs. George Gordon	1917	1½	V. low	Suff.	June 1		2	3	4		9	6
	1918	1½	V. low	Suff.	May 16		9	16	4	7	36	7
Mrs. Herbert Hawksworth, T.	1917	1	V. low	Suff.	June 12		4	8	2	1	15	2
	1918	1½	V. low	Suff.	May 20		6	8	3	3	20	5
Mrs. Herbert Stevens, T.	1917	2½	V. low	Suff.	May 25		4	2	3	1	10	3
	1918	2	V. low	Suff.	May 16		18	17	4	7	46	6
Mrs. Hubert Taylor, T.	1917			Suff.	June 8		1	2	1		4	1
	1918											
Mrs. Hugh Dickson	1917			Sparse	May 29			1		1	2	1
	1918											

Two-Year Bloom Record of Hybrid Tea and Tea Roses, continued

		Height Feet	Habit	Foliage	First Bloom	No. of blooms per plant: May	June	July	Aug.	Sept.	Total	Plants Noted
Mrs. Myles Kennedy, T.	1917	1	V. low	Suff.	June 1		2	1	3		6	2
	1918	1¾	V. low	Suff.	May 20		2	2	1	3	8	4
Mrs. Wakefield Christie-Miller	1917	2½	V. low	Suff.	May 29		9	10	8	1	28	6
	1918	2	V. low	Plent.	May 18		23	6	15	13	57	12
My Maryland	1917	¾	V. low	Suff.	June 8		1	2	1		4	
	1918				June 18		1	6		1	8	9
Natalie Bottner	1917			Suff.	June 8		1		2	1	4	1
	1918											
Norma	1917	2½	V. low	Suff.	June 19		1	1			2	3
	1918	4	Med.	Suff.	May 20		10	4	8		22	5
Ophelia	1917	1¼	V. low	Suff.	June 4		2	4	1		7	6
	1918	1¾	V. low	Suff.	May 16		4	8	8	3	23	11
Panama	1917			Suff.	June 12		6	8	13	15	42	1
	1918											
Papa Gontier, T.	1917	1¼	V. low	Suff.	May 25		6	7	5	4	22	6
	1918	1	V. low	Suff.	May 16		7	7	5	11	30	6
Perle des Jardins, White, T.	1917			Suff.	May 29		2	3	2		7	3
	1918											
Pharisaer	1917	1¼	V. low	Suff.	June 1		2	5	5		10	5
	1918	1½	V. low	Suff.	May 20		9	12	4	3	28	5
Prima Donna	1917											
	1918	1¾	V. low	Suff.	May 18		4	12	2	6	24	12
Prince de Bulgarie	1917	1	V. low	Suff.	June 4		4	5	2		11	4
	1918	1½	V. low	Suff.	May 16	5	3	13	4	4	29	10
Princess Bonnie	1917	1½	V. low	Suff.	May 29		9	1			10	2
	1918	¾	V. low	Suff.	May 18		15	16	4	8	43	4
Radiance	1917	2½	V. low	Plent.	June 1		2	3	2		7	6
	1918	3	Low	Suff.	May 18		12	14	4	7	37	7
Red Letter Day	1917	2	V. low	Suff.	May 29		4	4	4	2	14	1
	1918	2¼	V. low	Suff.	May 16		7	6	6	13	32	4
Red Radiance	1917	2	V. low	Plent.	June 1		2	11	12	4	29	1
	1918	2½	V. low	Plent.	May 16		14	15	6	10	45	10
Reine Marguerite d'Italie	1917	1½	V. low	Plent.	June 4		14	30	24	6	74	1
	1918	1½	V. low	Plent.	May 16		64	40	17	22	143	3
Richmond	1917	1	V. low	Suff.	May 29		6	9	3	2	20	3
	1918	1¼	V. low	Suff.	May 16		17	10	2	2	31	5
Seabird	1917			Suff.	May 4		6	6	3	3	18	1
	1918											
September Morn	1917	1¼	V. low	Suff.	May 22		1	2	2		5	4
	1918	1½	V. low	Suff.	May 20		5	7	2	2	16	4
Simplicity	1917	1½	V. low	Suff.	June 4		4	5	5	2	16	5
	1918	2¼	V. low	Suff.	May 18	13	6	27	6	10	62	8
Souv. de Gustave Prat	1917	1¼	V. low	Suff.	June 1		4	9	8	1	22	6
	1918	1½	V. low	Plent.	May 16	7	3	8	2	7	27	9
Souv. of Wootton	1917	1	V. low	Suff.	May 29		3	21	7	2	33	1
	1918	1	V. low	Suff.	May 13		14	13	4	3	34	6
Sunburst	1917	1	V. low	Suff.	June 4		1	3	1		5	6
	1918			Suff.	May 24	1	1	3	4	2	11	5
The Queen, T.	1917	1	V. low	Suff.	June 4		3	10	13	4	30	6
	1918											
Virginia R. Coxe	1917	1¼	V. low	Suff.	June 1		6	30	6	1	43	5
	1918	1¾	V. low	Suff.	May 16		42	26	8	7	83	9
Viscountess Folkestone	1917			Suff.	June 8		1	14	6	3	24	1
	1918											
W. E. Lippiatt	1917	2½	V. low	Plent.	June 1		8	1	3		12	2
	1918	2¾	V. low	Plent.	May 20		18	1	1		20	5
Wellesley	1917	2½	V. low	Suff.	June 1		12	10	6		28	
	1918	2	V. low	Suff.	May 18		18	8	6	8	40	11
Wm. R. Smith, T.	1917	2	V. low	Plent.	June 1		1	5	2	1	9	4
	1918	2	V. low	Suff.	May 20	2	1	5	6	4	18	4
Willowmere	1917			Suff.	June 8		14	1	6	1	22	1
	1918											
Winter Gem, T.	1917	1	V. low	Suff.	June 1		1	5	3		9	2
	1918	1¼	V. low	Suff.	May 20		4	8	3	6	21	4

Rose Notes

By THE EDITOR AND OTHERS

Railroad Roses in France.—In an interesting and chatty letter dated Sept. 2, 1918, from Capt. George C. Thomas, Jr., then acting as adjutant at one of the flying-fields in France, he tells of what he saw when he traveled "three days in a troop train to go 220 miles. There was ample opportunity at the stops to note the roses in the little gardens of the women who run the signal and roadgate stations. Each little station had its little garden, well kept, and all had roses as the chief attraction. I saw La Tosca, Reve d'Or, Frau Karl Druschki, La France, Hermosa, Reine Marie Henriette (doing very well), and Gloire de Dijon (very beautiful). There were also hardy climbers of no special merit.

"I have lately seen some very interesting specimens blooming in August, the best being a climbing Tea or Noisette (possibly a cross of these kinds), Creme di Nikola, I think; it was perfect in form and color (a dark yellow with no hint of pink), growing fifteen feet high on a cottage, and from evidences had been giving a steady average of about three blooms a day since the early burst of bloom.

"Blanche Belgique is a favorite, being evidently quite hardy and a continuous bloomer. . . . The climate here is very rainy and is usually cool."

Standing a Hard Winter.—Along Lake Michigan roses are exposed to severe cold and fierce winds. That veteran gardener, Mr. W. C. Egan, writes as follows of the "worst-ever" winter:

"Although the winter of 1917-18 was one of unusual severity, good luck gave Egandale an ample covering of snow. This warm blanket, remaining through the coldest period, overcame any disastrous tendencies generally produced by severe winters.

"Out of 175 Hybrid Tea roses, only one had to be replaced in the spring. It went into winter quarters in a weakened condition.

"The protection afforded them was simply hilling up the soil some eight to ten inches, and a covering of leaves about eighteen inches deep placed over them and held in place by brush.

"All of my climbers were laid down, covered with *dry* oak leaves, and a tight-roofed box placed over them. There was plenty of air-space between the leaves and the box. All came through in fine condition, except one large Dorothy Perkins, which had successfully battled with some ten or more winters and was never previously injured. This year it was killed back to within four feet of the ground because of the faulty construction of the roof. I generally watch this feature when the boxes are put up, but I evidently did not in this case. In ordinary winters, with less snow, the injury might not have occurred.

"My rule is to keep the top of the boxes free of snow, but here, again, I was at fault. They were not cleared, the weight of snow sagged the lapped-board roof, and allowed a thorough soaking of the canes injured. Snow was in some places five and six feet deep, and automobile traffic was suspended for over a month. In the endeavor to clear the walks within the boundaries of Egandale, the rose-boxes were overlooked. The box containing this rose is so large that a nailed-together top would be too unwieldy to handle, so it is covered by lapped boards. My other boxes have a roof of matched boards and cannot leak."

Another John Cook Rose Coming.—A letter from the veteran rosarian of Baltimore, under date of February 4, 1919, says: "I have a seedling rose which will be sent out by A. N. Pierson, Inc., and myself in 1920. The ground-color is white, surfaced with a delicate shade of pink. The bud is long and the open flower perfectly double. It is the result of a cross between Ophelia and two unnamed seedlings, and will prove to be a splendid commercial rose."

Here is another evidence of the potence of Ophelia as parent!

An Experience with Multiflora.—In the 1917 Annual, on page 49, Dr. Robert Huey described a method of producing rose stocks and of budding roses upon them. That energetic rose-grower of Portland, Ore., Mr. Jesse A. Currey, writes as follows in consequence:

"Last fall Dr. Robert Huey, of Philadelphia, sent me a little envelope of seed-pods from the Japanese Multiflora, which he and Capt. George C. Thomas, Jr., have frequently advocated for budding stock, with a request that I try them. The results obtained from these seeds demonstrated that every grower can raise his own stock for budding with little trouble and in little space. Desiring to give the seeds every possible chance, I arranged for three plantings, giving a part of the seeds to the Park Bureau so it could give them the expert care of its gardeners. One planting I arranged in pots, to be cared for in my home, as my place is not equipped with a greenhouse. Then, for the third portion of the seeds, I made a flat box about two feet long, one foot wide, and three inches deep. In it I placed soil of one part loam and two parts sand, in which I planted the Multiflora seeds.

"Having no desirable location for the box, and feeling confident I would get all the stock I needed from the seeds in the pots or from the special planting of the Park Bureau, I placed the box in one corner of the garden and left it there all winter. It was rained upon all winter—and we have plenty of rain in Portland during December, January and February.. It was frozen several times and thawed as many times, and more than once it was covered with snow. The weather conditions were such that I gave up any hopes I might have had of any of the seed developing. Therefore, my surprise was great when, after a week of mild weather, upon taking a glance at what I had regarded as a discarded box I found the ground covered with a green growth and the little rose plants forcing themselves upward. In a few weeks I had seedlings by the hundred from this neglected box! It seemed that they liked the rough treatment, for the results obtained were much better than from the two special plantings.

"When the seedlings had developed three or more leaves, I transplanted them along the edge of one of my rose-beds, and there they have flourished wonderfully, some of them developing, despite a long dry summer, sufficiently so that if I followed indoor budding they could have been used the same season. In the transplanting I also tried two methods, with some striking results. One part of the seedlings I planted just as I took them from the seed-box, and of the others, before planting in the open, I pinched off the longer roots. It is quite noticeable that those which had the longer roots pinched off before transplanting have developed more than the others, not so treated, the wood being larger and the shoots much stronger. I note, also, that the root-system is shorter and much more compact.

"From this little flat box I have secured hundreds of seedlings, convincing me that one can, with but little trouble and expense, raise for his requirements all the budding stock necessary."

Rose Advance in Ohio.—On page 93 of the March, 1918, monthly bulletin of the Ohio Agricultural Experiment Station, at Wooster, Ohio, is an excellent article on climbing roses and their culture. It is notable that the experiment stations, of which that in Ohio is conspicuously efficient, should be considering the rose, inasmuch as these institutions have primarily applied themselves to the purely economic side of horticulture.

Members of the American Rose Society resident in Ohio could readily secure this bulletin on application to the Station. It is Volume III, No. 3.

A Wise Chamber of Commerce.—In Auburn, N. Y., there is a commercial organization which can see over the edge of ordinary commercial trenches and realize, in consequence, the advantage, even in troublous times, of attention to the sweet and simple things of God's creation. Mr. Charles G. Adams, the Secretary of the Auburn Chamber of Commerce, has turned his rose enthusiasm to practical account in the organization of rose effort among his members. He has had a rose meeting addressed by Prof. A. C. Beal, of Cornell University, which stirred up much enthusiasm, and, early in 1918, put rose effort and the new Rose Society on a definite foundation.

Other chambers of commerce might greatly advantage their members and their communities, did they take up rose effort in the fashion that Mr. Adams has done.

Roses as Food.—In these days so near to food conservation, it will be of interest, no doubt, to members of the American Rose Society to know that roses and rose petals have a food-value. In Oregon, where the Sweetbrier flourishes, its seed-hips have for years been regarded by many persons as food. The Indians made various concoctions of them, but few of them would prove palatable to the average citizen. The wife of the pioneer who crossed the plains long before the days of the railroad also preserved the seed-hips of the Sweetbrier, and in some Oregon families this has long been one of the standard preserves for winter consumption.

A standard recipe for preserved rose seed-hips has been given me by Mrs. A. D. Charlton, one of Portland's best-known amateur rosarians, and it is as follows: Take the seeds from the center of the hips, after the hips have fully formed. Soak the hips one hour or more in cold water, then draw off this water and cover with fresh water, after which boil them for fifteen minutes. Pour off and measure the liquid, cup for cup, with sugar and then boil this until it is a thick syrup, after which add the rose-hips, boil again until tender, and then put them in jars the same as would be done with other preserves.

Jelly from the rose petals is a dish with which Mrs. R. W. Shepherd, of Portland, tickles the palates of her friends, and this is the recipe she has furnished me: Color as well as flavor is desirable in rose jelly; therefore I prefer the dark red General Jacqueminot rose, for with it you do not have to use any coloring matter, though jelly can be made with petals of any color. To one cup of rose petals, packed down tight, add one cup of water and two teaspoonfuls of lemon-juice. Boil this down until the petals are of a washed-out pink color. Then measure one tablespoonful of liquid to three-quarters of a spoonful of sugar. Boil until the scum rises to the top. Remove this, and put the jelly to set in cordial glasses. Only fresh roses should be used, and only the dark part of each petal if the color is to be preserved.—JESSE A. CURREY, Portland, Ore.

The Rose, Climbing Souvenir of Wootton.—After a careful reading of Mr. Thomas' article in the American Rose Annual for 1917 entitled "Roses Worth While for Everybody," I thought this a good time to put in a word for Climbing Souvenir of Wootton. I have a plant in my garden which has stood the test of fifteen winters and a very changeable climate without loss of any kind. It is situated in an open spot subject to all the elements except a direct northern wind.

It is a strong, vigorous climber, on an arch eight feet high with a span of four feet, growing way beyond this distance if allowed. The strong canes are produced annually from the base, right through the season, these branching at different distances from the bottom.

The canes bountifully produce fragrant, large, fine looking buds, opening into double, cup-shaped flowers of fair to good form, coming singly and in clusters of two to eight, on stems, some short but most from long to extra long, making them fine for cutting as well as garden decoration. In the spring of 1917 and 1918 the plant showed by actual count over 500 buds and flowers. There is a heavy crop in spring always, and almost as many flowers in the fall (but at this time variable), with a scattering of blooms through the summer. The color ranges from deep pink to a rosy crimson, deeper in cool weather and the fall, the lighter flowers being produced in the shade of the foliage, which is large, luxuriant, healthy and lasting, remaining on the plant till heavy frosts appear.

Climbing Wootton, as it might be called, is a rose which should be more generally planted, especially in the latitude of Washington and farther south.

CHAS. E. F. GERSDORFF.

Dr. Van Fleet's Rose Factory.—It was more than a rose factory that the Editor saw, just before the 1919 Washington's Birthday, when he visited the originator of American Pillar, Silver Moon, and many other worthy roses, at his home and working plant, at Bell Station, on the Washington, Baltimore, and Annapolis interurban trolley line. Loving the rose and studying its possibilities with the mind and the skill of the trained hybridizer, Dr. Van Fleet works enthusiastically with other plant material. A blight-resistant chestnut is nearly accomplished, and there are novel and improved sorts of strawberries, raspberries and iris coming through.

But it is in roses that the effort seems most worth while. The stems of the plants were bare, but the Doctor clothes them with foliage and sets them with flowers as he describes the long and patient processes of combination and improvement. The location was chosen because of its favorable soil and aspect, and the neighborhood of predatory rabbits, moles and field-mice had to be accepted. Against these animals it is necessary to protect by underground wire-screening as well as by overhead frames, and every new stem must have its collar to defy the teeth of the cottontails! "They prefer and always choose the rare things," plaintively remarked the Doctor.

The blooming season of 1919 ought to give to the world some notable new rose combinations and afford opportunity for working out many more. The effort is always toward a definite aim, and as the supply of available species and hybrids increases, the breadth of the work increases.

Dr. Van Fleet now rejoices in the possession of a duplicate set of the unique Vilmorin collection of more than 100 species and subspecies of the genus Rosa, propagated for the Arnold Arboretum by Monsieur L. Chenault, of Orleans, France, and sent by Prof. C. S. Sargent to aid in the hybridizing work going on at Bell Station.

An American Rose Poet.—On page 21 is printed a poem, "On a Sun-Dial Wreathed with Roses," by Frederick F. Rockwell, which will commend itself. As a keen garden critic, as a writer of detail suggestions that have helped, Mr. Rockwell is known to the readers of the garden-promoting magazines. It is a pleasure to have him show his fine quality in verse, and to write, in calling attention to it, of his versatility—with no pun intended. In addition to his achievements above noted, Mr. Rockwell is now doing intensive work for American horticulture in stimulating the taste of our citizens for growing, not only roses but other items of flower and fruit that will make a good land even better.

International Coöperation Increasing?—In a letter advising the Editor of his desire to become a member of the American Rose Society, Mr. George Shawyer, of the eminent English rose-growing firm of Lowe & Shawyer, Limited, writes, "I agree that rose growers everywhere cannot do better than to work together as closely as possible."

The need for coöperation is particularly in evidence in relation to names. Noting that the great English growers, Wm. Paul & Son, had offered a rose under the name of "Evelyn," the Editor wrote that firm of the Ophelia sport registered previously as "Evelyn" by A. N. Pierson, Inc., suggesting the propriety of an arrangement for international registration, bringing out the interesting fact that the English growers were unaware of any American registration.

What's the Use of a Long Name?—The Editor's assistant comes with the query as to whether E. G. Hill's new rose, "Rose Premier," is to be so called, or whether the rose is actually and only "Premier." The answer, of course, is that the rose was registered as "Rose Premier." The fact is that it will be called "Premier," and so the Editor is moved to the question of the title, "What's the Use of a Long Name?"

Of course, Mr. Hill would prefer to have his rose called "Rose Premier," but in the circular describing it he says it is a cross between "Ophelia and Russell." It is easy to find out about "Ophelia," for that is the registered name of a rose, but "Russell" doesn't get us anywhere until we find that it is "Mrs. Charles Russell." Probably the full name is used once in a dozen or a hundred times, but most of the time it may be assumed that, if the rose is worth while and gets into active commerce, its name will be shortened to one word.

The Editor feels that the practice which still continues of complimenting some fine lady by calling a rose after her is not so much of a compliment. It is no particular honor to Mrs. Charles Russell to be called by her surname without other designation. If roses now in the public eye—Mrs. Henry Winnett, Mrs. Belmont Tiffany, Mrs. William R. Hearst, and so on—ever get anywhere, they will certainly be named in the trade only as "Winnett," "Tiffany," and "Hearst." Anyone looking in rose catalogues for them, however, under the ordinary and familiar commercial designation, will not find them until he imagines the rest of the name and looks under the letter "M." Of the roses in the list of American originations there are thirty-six prefixed by "Miss," "Mrs." or "Mme." Again, the Editor must ask, "What's the Use of a Long Name?" A simple single name will stick, and it is both common sense, economy, and respectfulness which prompts the Editor to urge that hereafter new roses be named simply, with a name that will stick.

Los Angeles Takes World Honors.—On July 25, 1918, just a week after the beginning of Marshal Foch's memorable drive, which ended in the defeat of November 11 for the Germans, a news dispatch from Paris gave the pleasing information that the rose Los Angeles had been awarded the gold medal, the highest honor available, at the annual competition of new roses at the famous Bagatelle Rose-Garden in the Bois de Boulogne. Despite the war difficulties, there were in the competition roses from France, England, Holland, and the United States. Los Angeles won purely and only on its superior merit. It was illustrated in color as Plate IV in the 1917 Annual.

A Thomas Tiplady Story.—The Germantown Horticultural Society held a rose meeting June 3, 1918, at which one event was the reading of a paper entitled "Garden Roses for Amateurs," by Mrs. H. S. Prentiss Nichols. It is unfortunate that the limits of the Annual prevent the reprinting of this fine essay. In it Mrs. Nichols quoted an incident related of the Reverend Thomas Tiplady, the famous Field Chaplain of the British forces in Flanders, who had walked into the devastated city of Arras, finding there these conditions: "One house impressed me greatly. It had been badly damaged, but its garden was untouched, and in it were half a dozen rose trees. It was the beginning of spring, and each tree was covered over with sacking to preserve it from the cold and from fragments of shells. The owner did not care sufficiently for his own life to move away, but he cared for the life of his roses."

Protecting Tender Roses.—The winter protection usually recommended for covering the more tender varieties is strawy manure. This is rather a loose term, and the ordinary individual is very apt to take the general run of barnyard manure for this purpose. Such manure, as a rule, contains more or less decayed material that lays closely to the stems of the rose, consequently keeping them wet, and often starting decay or rot of the stems and branches.

The ideal covering for tender varieties is any coarse material that will keep off cold winds and hot sun alike, and yet permit ventilation. Fresh stable manure, where long straw had been used for bedding the horses, would serve, if all of the fine particles were shaken out, using only the coarse material for protecting.

An excellent covering is the salt marsh grass that is so abundant in many parts of our Atlantic coast states. If this can be procured, no better winter protection can be offered. Failing this, the easily grown stems and leaves of the Japanese grasses of the Eulalia family form an excellent protection. As this material is coarse and firm, it does not pack, and therefore gives all the protection that is necessary without holding the moisture around the stems.

Another excellent protecting material is evergreen boughs from pine trees, Norway spruce or balsam firs. These are all ideal for this purpose.

It is not the amount of material that one puts around the rose that does the protecting, but its quality of open shading. It is essential that what is used be light enough or open enough so as to permit a free passage of air. As a rule, it is less the severe frosts that injure our roses than the continual thawing and freezing, the exposure to drying winds and to the hot suns of late winter. In other words, as Mr. McFarland has said, "Roses do not require a blanket for their protection," but something that will allow a free passage of air around them and at the same time protect the stems from the sun's rays.—PETER BISSET, Office of Foreign Seed and Plant Introduction, Washington, D. C.

The Toronto Horticultural Society holds its rose-night the first Friday in February. The program for February 8, 1918, included a most interesting rose-calendar, giving the operations for the whole year. Canada's manful part in the war did not prevent the holding of this rose festival, and in 1919 an even more elaborate occasion was scheduled. The rose associations of the province of Ontario, manifested through the various sections of its provincially controlled horticultural societies, are interesting and important. They are not paralleled anywhere in the United States, at least to the Editor's knowledge.

Flowers Barred from a Hospital.—Under date of July 1, 1918, Secretary E. A. White wrote an indignant letter to the Ithaca *Journal* concerning the sudden exclusion of cut-flowers from the city hospital in Ithaca. There had evidently been an outbreak in the college city of that peculiar form of short-sighted patriotism, more in evidence at the beginning of the war, which assumes that nothing beautiful, nothing pleasant, must be even looked at or smelled during a time of need and sacrifice!

Professor White's letter vigorously called attention to the way in which flowers, and particularly roses, had served a most important and useful purpose in the hospitals back of the firing-line in France. He cited the letter of the chairman of the National League for Woman's Service in the city of New York, who had gone to especial effort to secure for the unfortunates in hospitals just the benefit and pleasure being shut out from them in Ithaca. It was no wonder that after this letter saner counsels prevailed, and the Board of Trustees of the hospital promptly rescinded the absurd restriction. More flowers in more hospitals to do their good work, should be the rule.

Hard Rose-Luck in Luxemburg.—Mr. Robert Pyle, President of the Conard & Jones Company, permits the Editor to print the following letter from the well-known firm of Ketten Frères, whose great establishment in the Grand Duchy of Luxemburg has long specialized in roses.

"The possibility being given to correspond again with your place, we take this our first opportunity to congratulate you of the good end of this terrible war, to assure you of our sincerest sympathy and to express our highest esteem for your dear country and its glorious army and navy.

"As you might have learned by the papers, our small country has not been preserved from troubles and privations during the war; occupied by the bandit Boches on August 1, 1914, it has only been delivered from them November 24, 1918, by the American and French soldiers.

"Personally, we had to suffer very much. During the invasion our business was quite paralyzed; this was due to the impossibility to enter into relations with nine-tenths of our customers. Also, it was with the utmost exertion we have been able to keep up our collection of roses with but a few exceptions, nearly eight hectares [about twenty acres] of our cultures having been entirely destroyed by the German brutes in August, 1914.

"We are at present enjoying happiness again and are looking forward that business will revive next autumn. Our stock of roses for the season 1919–20 will be of about half of our stock before the war.

"Hoping to hear from you by the next mail, and thanking in anticipation, we beg to remain, with kindest personal regards to Mr. Pyle, and our best wishes for a Happy New Year."   KETTEN FRERES.

Dr. Van Fleet Does Not Swear!—But he would be justified, possibly, in "cussing out" both printer and Editor because of the really stupid error on page 60 of the 1918 Annual, which makes Rugosa a "Tea rose stock," when the author proposed it as a "Tree rose stock." We like to have the Annual taken seriously, and it has been; for Dr. Van Fleet tells us that he has had much bothersome correspondence by reason of this mistake, for which due apology is now made.

Turning Roses into Red Cross Cash.—From the enterprising town of Kamloops, B. C. (Canada), a member of the American Rose Society, Mrs. M. S. Wade, sends this fine story: "In the 1918 Rose Annual there was an article entitled, 'Shall We Grow Roses in Wartime?' It has occurred to me that what has been done in this small community, a town of less than 5,000 population, may serve to show that the growing of flowers, and particularly roses, can be and has been turned to a most useful and patriotic purpose. There are many flower-gardens in Kamloops. Most of them possess at least one or two rose bushes, while a fewer number of these amateur gardeners devote the greater part of their flower-beds to the Queen of Flowers.

"Last year (1917), a few ladies got together and formed what they called a 'Garden Club,' the object being to obtain money from the sale of flowers and devote the proceeds to whatever fund or funds they deemed advisable. The members gave freely of their time in collecting from the amateur floriculturists such blooms as they cared to donate, and, equipped with baskets and trays in which the floral offerings were daintily displayed, offered them for sale at the two railway stations to travelers on the passing trains.

"The season of 1917 proved so encouraging that the work was resumed in 1918, and, beginning with lilacs in the spring and going through the various changes down to chrysanthemums in October (when the influenza epidemic cut short the labors of the Club), these floral contributions, culled from practically every garden plot in the city, yielded no less a sum than $1,960, which was devoted to Red Cross and Soldiers' Comforts funds. All rose-growers gave generously, my own contributions during the summer including 2,278 roses; and when one considers that the average price paid for a single rose bloom was 25 cents, and many generous-hearted souls gave as much as $1 for a lone rose—the purchaser in every case fixing the price—it is readily seen that it was decidedly worth while to 'grow roses in wartime.' There were no expenses, everything was donated, even the use of motors; and thus every cent realized found its way into the channels for which the money was raised."

To the Editor's inquiring for working details—because he believes this fine impulse will be felt and used elsewhere—Mrs. Wade responded cheerfully as follows:

"At the beginning three ladies got their heads together and began the work of collecting and selling flowers for the benefit of the soldiers. Others soon joined them, and they gave their little society the name of the Garden Club. All were volunteer workers. So great was the success achieved that it was felt that with better organization and preparedness still greater success would result. Accordingly, early in 1918, the local branches of the Daughters of the Empire and the Red Cross Guild assumed the duties of the Garden Club. A meeting was held at which a committee of eight ladies was appointed to carry out the work. The committee appointed one of their number as Convenor, whose duty it was to keep the ball rolling, remind the ladies of the committee of the work devolving upon them, and, in a general way, act as manager of the effort.

"Each member of the committee was required to devote a specified number of days to the task of soliciting and collecting donations of flowers and acting as sellers at the railway stations. Two members were on duty together, and they selected their own assistants, for the most part young ladies, many of them high-school girls. These assistants helped in collecting as well as in selling.

"As one of the railway stations is some distance from the town, the Convenor had to arrange for gratuitous transportation of the committee ladies and their assistants—and the baskets of flowers—to and fro. As I said before, all the workers gave their services voluntarily and there were absolutely no expenses of any kind—nothing but clear profit. The better organization of 1918 proved worthy the trouble taken, and with more workers and their services being regulated by the Convenor, the machinery ran smoothly."

This admirable achievement ought to be considered in connection with Mrs. Crawford's "Save and Use the Roses" on another page of this Annual.

What Are Leaves Good For?—About the middle of September, 1918, one of my roses produced a blossom of improved color, fullness, size, durability and fragrance. After waiting nine days for the flower to fade, I determined to try for new plants with the hope of obtaining a true sport.

First, I prepared my cutting-bed in half shade, out-of-doors, of half white sand and half garden loam, six inches deep, tramped firmly. Out of the wood I obtained four cuttings of two or three eyes each, and fearing my chances of success very slim with such a few, I decided on an experiment. In making the wood cuttings, all leaves but the upper were removed. I gathered these leaves, removed all the leaflets but the end one, and inserted them in the prepared bed in the same way as I did the wood cuttings.

On hand were a large number of leaflets, and since I was in an experimental mood that day, I conceived the notion to test out these leaflets as cuttings. If leaf cuttings will grow, why not leaflets? In planting the leaflets, some were put in whole, while others were put in with their bases removed, leaving about one-half above ground. All the cuttings were well watered and covered with glass jars, and up to freezing weather the bed was carefully tended and not allowed to dry out.

Early one November day, some mischievous boys gained a bit of pleasure by throwing stones at the jars covering my cuttings. Several were broken; so it was up to me to provide new cover jars in a hurry, if I did not wish to lose my cuttings. At this point I investigated the cuttings to note their progress. But two normal wood cuttings were left. These were fairly well calloused. The leaf cuttings were still full of life, but I did not disturb them further.

Of the leaflet cuttings, all with their bases removed had blackened. Those, however, planted whole were fine and green. Since there were plenty on hand, I investigated further, and found on removal of one from the soil that it not only was well calloused, but had several strong white roots, two of which were one and one-half inches long.

Will this leaflet produce wood? Will the wood bloom like the parent plant or like the sport? Since I am writing on January 7, 1919, and these questions remain to be answered, I may still ask "What are leaves good for?"

CHAS. E. F. GERSDORFF.

[The Editor might reply that at least leaves are good for a very interesting experiment! He saw those unbelievable leaf and leaflet cuttings on New Year's Day, and joins Mr. Gersdorff in awaiting the eventual outcome.]

The Revival of Rose Interest.—From Mrs. Francis King, wintering at Coronado Beach, comes a clipping dated February 6, 1919, entitled "Portland Looks at the Rosy Side of Things," and settling the holding of the usual June rose festival in Portland, Ore. This had been intermitted in 1918, but now goes on again as usual.

Sir Walter Raleigh is to be the name of a new rose to be sent out in the autumn of 1919 by Philip le Cornu, of Highview, Queen's Road, Jersey (England). Mr. le Cornu adds to the name of the rose "Governor of Jersey," but six words is too much name for any rose. It is "a cross between Melanie Soupert and Louise Catherine Breslau, with mildew-proof Pernetiana foliage," which sounds interesting and hopeful.

The Climbing Rose, Zephirine Drouhin.—The pleasing picture, which appears as Plate X, facing page 137, is of an unusual climber that bears fine, deep cerise-colored flowers, freely produced throughout most of the season, and finely perfumed. Zephirine Drouhin is classed as a Hybrid Bourbon rose, which accounts for the further interesting and important fact that it is as spineless as Tausendschön, being as good a grower, also, as that excellent variety. The photograph in question is available to the readers of the Annual through the courtesy of Mr. Peter Bisset, of the Office of Foreign Seed and Plant Introduction, Department of Agriculture, Washington, D. C.

Climbing Roses Doing Double Duty.—In late September of 1918, Mr. Charles W. Hartwick, a capable and enthusiastic worker in roses, whose daily duty was to superintend an asphalt street-repair gang, brought to the Editor several magnificent Hybrid Tea blooms, including La Tosca, Pharisaer, and Lady Ashtown, with the information that they had been grown on his Dr. W. Van Fleet climbing rose. Inquiry developed the interesting fact that, after the climber had done its beautiful bloom-duty, Mr. Hartwick had budded upon several of the strong shoots from the ground then available, his favorite Hybrid Tea varieties. This he did late in June. The buds united and grew, when the shoots above the point of budding were cut off, throwing all their strength into the growing buds of the Hybrid Teas.

These shoots made a strong growth and developed fine buds of the selected varieties on long stems. Mr. Hartwick pinched out the ends of the shoots when they were nearly two feet high, and, in turn, removed all flower-buds, but one, on each shoot. The resulting blooms were unusually large and fine, and the experiment was a gratifying success. It is sad to have to say that this fine-spirited amateur died suddenly, of influenza, in November.

The budding method, which any experimenter might use in trying out for himself this double-duty plan, was described and illustrated in Dr. Huey's article, on page 49 of the 1917 Annual. Budding can, of course, be much more easily and conveniently done upon the young canes of any strong-growing climber than upon the "crown" of the Multiflora stock. The climbers usually send up many more shoots from the roots than are needed, wherefore this interesting diversion need not at all interfere with the framework for the climber bloom of the next season. The Editor will welcome information as to what has happened in consequence of similar trials by rose-lovers.

Cut-Roses in Great Demand in France.—Elsewhere in the Annual Past-President Pennock tells of the tremendous demand for roses in the United States during the fall of 1918. A letter received under date of February 6, 1919, from the veteran rose-grower of Orleans, France, Mons. E. Turbat, includes the following paragraph: "The cut-flower trade of roses has been largely employed during all the war, and actually the supply is very much too short for the demand."

California Is "Different."—Mr. W. B. Clarke, of the Cottage Gardens Nurseries, San José, Calif., writes, in reference to the notable article in the 1918 Annual by Capt. George C. Thomas, Jr., "Roses Retained and Discarded," the following interesting comment: "I couldn't help but be impressed in going through his list with the old, old fact that California is 'different' and eastern experience is oftentimes deceiving. To make my point clear, I will cite two examples: On page 115, 'Duchesse de Brabant. Small growth; shy blooming qualities.' This rose is known the length and breadth of California simply as 'Duchesse,' and I think it is no exaggeration to say that it is beyond comparison the freest bloomer in our state. It is usually loaded with flowers nearly the entire year. Again, on page 120, 'Fortune's Yellow. Small grower; needs winter protection.' You, of course, know what kind of a grower it is here. Often it grows up into trees, 40, 50 and even 60 feet high, and turning into a perfect mass of bloom. They are in full flower as I write, and many specimens of the sizes mentioned can be found around San José."

Harison's Yellow Rose Sets Some Seeds.—In an interesting letter from Mr. G. A. Stevens, of Mineral City, Ohio, received last August, were included a number of seed-heps of the fine old yellow rose mentioned. As has been repeatedly said in these pages, this rose is very shy in setting seed. Dr. Van Fleet has reported his failure to get it to provide seeds, from the showing of which he hoped to be able to trace its parentage.

When Mr. Stevens wrote the Editor, he had just been accepted by the Army, and his hybridizing work in roses, undertaken in consequence of the suggestions in the American Rose Annual, was temporarily terminated. In order to see that the best possible care was given to his precious seeds, they were divided between Dr. Van Fleet and the well-managed rose-garden of Capt. George C. Thomas, Jr., from which two sources later will doubtless come a report.

Mr. Stevens writes very interestingly concerning the assumed laws governing heredity in roses. "What, for instance, determines the color of the seedling—the seed parent or the pollen parent? Which parent determines the growth, which the blooming habit, which the fragrance?"

The inquirer himself anticipates the negative answer any scientist would have to give by saying that even in his relatively limited experience there had appeared to be no law governing these matters. Doubtless the law exists, but man has not yet determined it.

The Roses We Need.—Prof. C. S. Sargent, of the Arnold Arboretum, writes thus: "We badly need in this country, especially in the North, races of roses which are better suited to the climate than any we now have."

A Partial List of Roses Introduced in America

Compiled by CHARLES E. F. GERSDORFF

(Corrected in this Fourth Edition to March 10, 1919)

In the 1916 American Rose Annual there was presented "A Partial List of American Hybridized Roses, with Parentage and Date of Introduction so far as Ascertainable." The roses thus listed were in every case admitted only upon information obtained from the hybridizer or introducer, or from a reliable source. Only hybridized sorts, and not "sports," were listed, and no claim of completeness was made. The listing was under headings for each hybridizer.

At much expenditure of time and patience, and through much correspondence, Mr. Gersdorff has now covered the whole field of American introductions, both as to seedlings and sports. The Editor has added the roses recorded by the American Rose Society, and others of his cognizance. Certain rose species recently introduced from the Orient are included as matters of record, though not native to America.

While it is believed that the result is more complete than any previously published, no claim for entire accuracy is made. It is insisted that the list has been most carefully compiled, and that there is in consequence here presented the beginning, at least, of an accurate name and origin list.

The carelessness of growers and introducers in relation to names, origin, etc., has been—and is—painfully apparent. Unfortunate duplications appear, even in roses introduced within the present century.

It is expected that this list will serve to prevent further duplications or name similarities, and protest will be made against the registration by the American Rose Society hereafter of any rose under a name already used, or of a rose for which no parentage is given.

Following the list of Abbreviations and the List of Works Consulted are the References used, the numbers preceding which are found following names in the list of varieties, as authorities.

The Editor urges that any omissions or errors be called to his attention, and that makers of trade catalogues adopt the spelling and classification here presented.

ABBREVIATIONS

The abbreviations used are: B. (Bourbon), B.-C. (Bourbon-China), Bengal-C. (Bengal-China), C. (China), Cl.B. (Climbing Bourbon), Cl.H.T. (Climbing Hybrid Tea), Cl.T. (Climbing Tea), D. (Damask), H.Cl. (Hardy Climber), H.D. (Hybrid Damask), H.Mult. (Hybrid Multiflora), H.N. (Hybrid Noisette), H.P. (Hybrid Perpetual), H. Ramb. (Hybrid Rambler), H. Ru. (Hybrid Rugosa), H.T. (Hybrid Tea), H.W. (Hybrid Wichuraiana), H.W.-Ru. (Hybrid Wichuraiana-Rugosa), Lœv. (Lœvigata), Mult. (Multiflora), N. (Noisette), Per. (Pernetiana), Poly. (Polyantha), Ramb. (Rambler), Semp. (Semperflorens), Set. (Setigera), T. (Tea), W. (Wichuraiana), A. R. S. (American Rose Society).

LIST OF WORKS CONSULTED

A B C of Rose Culture, The, by Edward Mawley. 1897.
Amateurs' Rose Book, The, by Shirley Hibberd.
American Rose Culturist, The, by C. M. Saxton.
Beauties of the Rose, etc., by H.Curtis.1853.
Beautiful Roses, etc., by John Weathers.
Book about Roses, A, by S. R. Hole.
Book of Roses, The, by Francis Parkman. 1866.
Book of Roses, The, by Louis Durand.
Book of the Rose, The, by Foster-Melliar; edited by Page-Roberts & Molyneux.
Catalogue de la roseraie de Bagatelle pour l'année 1913.

LIST OF AMERICAN ROSES

Commercial Rose Culture, by Eber Holmes.
Concours international de roses, etc. 1908.
Cultivated Roses, etc., by T. W. Sanders. 1899.
Cultural Directions for the Rose, etc., by John Cranston. 6th ed.; rev. 1877.
Cultur, etc., der rosen, by C. Nickels. 1845.
Die rose, etc., by T. Nietner. 1880.
England's National Flower, by George Bunyard.
Histoire naturelle de la rose, etc., by J. L. M. Guillemeau. 1800.
La rose, etc., by J. L. A. Loiseleur-Deslongchamps, 1844.
La rose, etc., by Jules Bel. 1892.
La rose, etc., by L. P. F. A. Chesnel de la Charbouclais. 2d ed. 1838.
Le livre d'or des roses, by Paul Herriot. 1903.
Les roses, by H. Jamain. 2d ed. 1873.
Les roses de l'imperatrice, etc., by Jules Gravereaux.
Les roses, etc., by Shirley Hibberd. 1882.
Les Rosiers, etc., by P. C. M. Cochet. 3d ed. 1909.
List of Roses, etc., by Brougham & Vaux. 1898.
New Roses (supplement), by Rose G. Kingsley. 1913.
Nomenclature of the Rose, etc., by Leon Simon. 1st ed., 1899; 2d ed., 1906.
Observations sur la nomenclature . . . roses, by J. Vibert. 1824.
Parsons on the Rose, by S. B. Parsons. 1869. New and rev. ed. 1910.
Podrome de la monographie . . . . roses, etc., by C. A. Thory.

Rosarum monographia, by John Lindley. Rev. ed. 1830.
Rose Amateurs' Guide, The, by Thomas Rivers. 11th ed. 1877.
Rose Book (translation into English), by Julius Hoffman. 1905.
Rose Book, The, by H. H. Thomas. Reprint of 1st ed., 1914.
Rose Garden, The, by William Paul. 10th ed. 1903.
Rose Growing, etc., by J. G. Lockley. 2d ed.
Rose Growing Made Easy, by E. T. Cook.
Rose Manual, The, by Robert Buist. 4th ed. 1854.
Roseraie de l'Hay, Guide, etc. 1910; Nomenclature, etc. 1902.
Roses and How to Grow Them, by Leonard Barron.
Roses and Rose Culture, by T. B. Jenkins.
Roses and Rose Gardens, by W. P. Wright. 1912.
Roses and Rose-Growing, by Rose G. Kingsley. 1908.
Roses and Their Culture, by W. D. Prior. 3d ed. 1892.
Roses, by H. C. Andrews.
Roses, by H. Darlington. 1911.
Roses, by Gemen and Bourg of Grand Duchy of Luxemburg.
Roses, by J. H. Pemberton.
Roses, by Rafinesque-Schmaltz.
Rose, The, by H. B. Ellwanger.
Rose, The, by Henry Shaw.
Société Nationale d'Horticulture de France, Section des Roses, etc. 1912.
Tea Roses, etc., by F. R. Burnside. 1893.

REFERENCES

The number at the end of each description on the following pages refers to the sources considered in the list below. When two numbers follow, the rose has been described in each of the sources cited.

1. Nomenclature de tous les noms de roses, by Leon Simon and P. Cochet. 1899.
2. Beautiful Roses, by John Weathers. 1903.
3. Roses and Rose-Growing, by Rose G. Kingsley. 1908.
4. New Roses, by Rose G. Kingsley. 1913.
5. Société Nationale d'Horticulture de France, Section des Roses, Les plus belles roses au debut du XX siecle. 1912.
6. Les roses, etc., by Shirley Hibberd. 1882.
7. Parsons on the Rose, by S. B. Parsons. 1869 and 1910.
8. The Book of Roses, by Francis Parkman. 1866.
9. The Amateur Gardeners' Rose Book, by Dr. Julius Hoffman; translation by John Weathers. 1905.
10. The Rose Manual, by Robert Buist. 1854.
11. List of Roses, by Brougham and Vaux. 1898.
12. Concours international de roses nouvelles a Bagatelle. 25 juin, 1908.
13. Catalogue de la roseraie de Bagatelle. 1913.
14. Roses and Their Culture, by W. D. Pryor. 1892.
15. Information obtained from various sources, such as American and foreign catalogues, from American growers by correspondence. From catalogues of California Rose Company, Hugh Dickson, Walsh, Alex. Dickson & Sons, Conard & Jones, Good & Reese, Dreer, Fancher Creek Nurseries, Glen Saint Mary Nurseries, J. T. Lovett, Vaughan's Seed Store, Jackson & Perkins Co., Elliott Nursery, Leedle Floral Co., Howard Rose Co., E. G. Hill Co., The Luther Burbank Co., and Hoopes, Bro. and Thomas Co. By correspondence from Walsh, Dingee & Conard, Conard & Jones, Farr, Totty, Biltmore Nurseries, Heller Brothers, A. N. Pierson, Inc., McGregor Brothers Co., Hugh Dickson, the Editor of *The Garden*, London, England, John Lewis Childs, Inc., Gude Bros., and R. Witterstaetter and others.

16. Roses and How to Grow Them, by Leonard Barron. 1905.
17. The Rose, by H. B. Ellwanger. Ed. 1892.
18. Catalogue of W. R. Gray, Oakton, Fairfax Co., Va. 1916.
19. Pract. Beschr. Rozennaamlijst . . . Boom-en Plantenbeurs te Boskoop. 1909
20. The Amateur's Rose Book, by Shirley Hibberd. 1894.
21. On the Culture of the Rose, by Robert Buist. 1844.
22. On the Rose, by Robert Buist. 1851.
23. National Rose Society Official Catalogue of Roses. 1914.
24. The American Florist, Sept. 22, 1917.
25. Catalogue of Roses, Peter Lambert, Trier, Germany. 1911-12.
26. Catalogue of Roses, Hobbies, Ltd., England. 1917.
27. Bulletin of American Rose Society, 1910.
28. Bulletin of American Rose Society, 1914.
29 American Rose Society Annual for 1916.
30 Mr. C. S. Pomeroy, Box 586, Riverside, Calif.
31. Eastern Nurseries, Inc., Holliston, Mass., 1918.

ABUNDANCE, Poly. (Henderson, 1910.) Clotilde Soupert × Souv. du President Carnot. 25.
ADMIRAL DEWEY, H.T. (Taylor, 1899.) Sport from Mme. Caroline Testout. 15, 19.
ADMIRAL EVANS, H.T. (E. G. Hill Co., 1907; not formally introduced.) 5, 13. Liberty × unnamed seedling. 12.
ADMIRAL SCHLEY, H.T. (Cook, 1901.) Colonel Joffe × General Jacqueminot. Received Bronze Medal at Pan-American Exposition. 19.
AGNES EMILY CARMAN, H. Ru. (Carman, 189-.) *R. rugosa* × Harison's Yellow. 29.
ALBA RUBRIFOLIA, H.W. (Van Fleet, 1898; intro. by Conard & Jones Co.) Wichuraiana hybrid.
ALICE ALDRICH, H.Ru. (J. T. Lovett, 1899.) 15. *R. rugosa* × unknown Tea or Hybrid Tea.
ALICE LEMON, H.T. (E. G. Hill Co., 1911.) Mme. Philippe Rivoire × Paul Neyron. 25.
ALIDA LOVETT, H.W. (Van Fleet, 1905; intro, by J. T. Lovett, 1917). *H. Wichuraiana* × Souv. du President Carnot. 15.
AMERICA, H.Cl. (Walsh, 1915.) 29.
AMERICA, N. (Page, 1859.) Large, fine flower of creamy white. 8, 16.
AMERICA, H.Ru. (Garden, Harvard University, 1894.) 5.
AMERICAN BANNER, T. (Cartwright, 1879.) 1, 17. Sport of Bon Silene. 16.
AMERICAN BEAUTY, H.P. (Bancroft, 1886.) Syn., Mme. Ferd. Jamain, as which it seems to have been introduced in France by Ledéchaux, 1873. 3, 17, 19. (Field Brothers.) 16.
AMERICAN BELLE, H.P. (J. Burton, 1893.) Sport from American Beauty. 19.
AMERICAN PILLAR, H.W. (Van Fleet, 1902; intro. by Conard & Jones Co.) *R. Wichuraiana* × *R. setigera*. 19.
AMŒNA, Læv. (Hockbridge, 1909.) 15.
ANNA MARIA, Set. (Feast, 1843.) 1, 13, 19. Syn., Anna Marie. 15.
ANNIE COOK. T. (Cook, 1888.) 1. Seedling from Bon Silene. 17.
APPLE BLOSSOM, H.Cl. (Dawson 189-; not formally introduced.) 29. Dawson × *R. Multiflora*, 31.
APPLE BLOSSOM, Poly. (Schultheis, 1908.) 26.
ARCADIA, H.W. (Walsh, 1913.) 15.
ARNOLDIANA, H.Ru. (Dawson, 1914.) *R. rugosa* × General Jacqueminot, Syns., Arnold; Dawson's Hybrid Rugosa.
ATLAS, H.T. (E. G. Hill Co., 1903.) 19.
AUGUSTA, N. (1853.) Sulphur. 1. Seedling from Solfaterre. 8.
AUGUSTINE GUINOISSEAU, JR., H.T. (California Rose Co., 1911.) Sport of Augustine Guinoisseau. 15, 30.

PLATE X. Climbing Rose, ZEPHIRINE DROUHIN, an unusual, thornless climber
(Photograph supplied by Peter Bisset, Washington, D. C.) (See page 132)

AUNT HARRIET, H. W. (Van Fleet, ——; intro. by *Farm Journal* of Philadelphia, 1918.) Appoline × *R. Wichuraiana*. 15.
BABETTE, H.Cl. (Walsh, 1908.) 15, 19.
BALTIMORE BELLE, Set. (Feast, 1843.) 10, 19.
BEAUTY OF GREENMONT, H. Set. (Pentland of Baltimore, 1854.) 16.
BEAUTY OF GREENWOOD. N. 17.
BEAUTY OF ROSEMAWR, B. (Conard & Jones Co., 1903.) 15, 19.
BEAUTY OF THE PRAIRIES, Set. (Feast, 1843.) 13, 19. Syns., Queen of the Prairies, Prairie Queen, 10; Feast's No. 1, Mme. Caradori Allan, 22.
BEDFORD BELLE, H.T. (Bedford Flower Co., registered 1916.) 15.
BELLE AMERICAINE, H.P. (D. Boll, 1837.) 1, 16, 17.
BELLE PORTUGAISE, Hybrid (?). (California——.) *R. Brunonii* × *R. gigantea*. 29.
BESS LOVETT, H. W. (Van Fleet, 1905; intro. by J. T. Lovett, 1917.) 15.
BIRDIE BLYE, H.Cl. (Van Fleet, 1904; intro. by Conard & Jones Co.) Helene × Bon Silene. 19.
BLUSH MARYLAND, H.T. (Totty, 1912.) Sport. 15.
BLUSH O'DAWN, H.T. (Walsh, 1902.) 13.
BONNIE BELLE, H.Cl. (Walsh.)
BONNIE PRINCE, H. W. (Thomas N. Cook, 191-.) Tausendschön × unnamed seedling.
BOSTON, H.T. (Montgomery Co., reg. A. R. S., 1917.) Mrs. Geo. Shawyer × Montgomery seedling. 15.
BRIDE, T. (May, 1885.) 15, 19. Sport from Catherine Mermet. 16. Syn., The Bride. 15.
BRIDESMAID, T. (Moore, 1892.) 15, 19. Sport from Catherine Mermet. Probably identical with The Hughes. 16.
BRIGHTON BEAUTY, T. (Originated by Bragg; sent out by May, 1891.) 16, 17.
BURBANK, Bengal. (Burbank, 1900.) 5. Armosa (Hermosa) × seedling of Bon Silene. 15, 19.
BUTTERCUP, Cl.T. (California Rose Co., 1908.) 15. Seedling of unknown parentage. 30.
CALIFORNIA, H.T. (Howard & Smith, 1916; reg. A. R. S.)
CAPTAIN HUDSON, Per. (Kersbargen Brothers, 1911.) 15.
CARDINAL, H.T. (Cook, 1904.) Liberty × unnamed red seedling. 19.
CARISSIMA, H.W. (Walsh, 1905.) 15. Seedling of Wichuraiana. 19.
CAROLINE COOK, T. (Cook, 1871.) Seedling of Safrano. 17.
CATHERINE BELL, H.P. 20. (Bell & Son, 1877.) 17.
CHAMPION OF THE WORLD, Bengal. (Woodhouse, 1894.) 1.
CHAMPNEY'S PINK CLUSTER, N. Supposed hybrid of *R. chinensis* × *R. moschata* raised about 1816 by John Champney, of Charleston, S. C. About 1817 Philip Noisette, of the same city, grew from it a rose which his brother, Louis Noisette, of Paris, distributed as Blush Noisette. 2, 16.
CHAMP WEILAND, H.T. (Weiland and Risch, 1916; reg. A. R. S.) Sport from Killarney. 15.
CHARLES GETZ, B. (Cook, 1871.) 17.
CHARLES WAGNER, H.P. (Van Fleet, 1904; intro. by Conard & Jones Co.) Jean Liabaud × Victor Hugo.
CHILDS' JEWEL, H.T. (Childs, 1902.) Sport from Killarney. 15.
CHRISTINE WRIGHT, H.W. (Hoopes, Bro. & Thomas Co., 1909.) Unnamed seedling × Mme. Caroline Testout.
CINDERELLA, H.W. (Walsh, 1909.) 15, 19.
CLARA BARTON. (Van Fleet, 1898.) Clotilde Soupert × American Beauty. 16.

CLIMBING AMERICAN BEAUTY, H.W. (Hoopes, Bro. & Thomas Co., 1909.) American Beauty × Marion Dingee × Wichuraiana. 15. Silver Medal A. R. S., 1915.
CLIMBING BRIDESMAID, T. (Dingee & Conard, ——.) Sport. 15.
CLIMBING CECILE BRUNNER, Poly. (Sport at Riverside, Calif., 1901.) 15.
CLIMBING CLOTILDE SOUPERT, Poly. (Dingee & Conard, 1902.) Sport. 19.
CLIMBING COL. R. S. WILLIAMSON, H.T. (Dingee & Conard, ——.) Sport. 15.
CLIMBING COMTESSE EVA STARHEMBERG, T. (Glen Saint Mary Nurseries, 1917.) Sport. 15.
CLIMBING ETOILE DE FRANCE, H.T. (Howard Rose Co., 1915.) Sport. 15.
CLIMBING FRAU KARL DRUSCHKI, H.P. (Lawrenson, 1906.) Sport. 15, 19.
CLIMBING GRUSS AN TEPLITZ. H.T. (Storrs & Harrison, 1911.) Sport. 15.
CLIMBING HELENE CAMBIER, H.T. (California Rose Co., 1911.) Sport. Syn., Climbing Helene Gambier. 15.
CLIMBING HELEN GOULD, H.T. (Good & Reese, 1912.) Sport from Balduin (Helen Gould). 15.
CLIMBING HUGH DICKSON, H.P. (California Rose Co., 1914.) Sport. 15.
CLIMBING KILLARNEY, H.T. (Reinberg, 1908.) Sport. 15.
CLIMBING LA FRANCE, H.T. (Henderson, 1893.) Sport. 1, 3, 19.
CLIMBING LIBERTY, H.T. (May, 1908.) Sport. 23, 26.
CLIMBING MARIE GUILLOT, T. (Good & Reese, 1897.) Sport. Syns., President Cleveland; Frances Willard. 15.
CLIMBING METEOR, H.T. Sport. 3.
CLIMBING MME. JULES GROLEZ, H.T. (Dingee & Conard, ——.) Sport. 15.
CLIMBING MME. WELCHE, T. (Mellen, 1911.) Sport. 15.
CLIMBING MOSELLA, Poly. (Conard & Jones Co., 1909.) Sport. 15, 19, 25.
CLIMBING MRS. W. J. GRANT, H.T. (E. G. Hill Co., 1899.) Sport from Mrs. W. J. Grant (Belle Siebrecht). Syn., Climbing Belle Siebrecht (W. Paul & Son, 1899). 15, 23.
CLIMBING MY MARYLAND, H.T. (Dingee & Conard, 1915.) Sport. 15.
CLIMBING ORIENTAL, C. (U. S. Department of Agriculture, 1914.) Seedling. 15.
CLIMBING PAPA GONTIER, Cl.T. (Chase & Co., 1905.) Sport. 15, 30.
CLIMBING PERLE DES JARDINS, T. (J. Henderson, 1891.) Sport, 2, 3, 13, 17, 19.
CLIMBING PINK AMERICAN BEAUTY, H.T. (U. S. Nur. Co., reg. 1914.) 15.
CLIMBING PINK MAMAN COCHET, T. (Conard & Jones Co., 1915.) Sport. Syns., Climbing Maman Cochet; Climbing Pink Cochet. 15.
CLIMBING RAINBOW, T. (California Rose Co., 1914.) Sport. 15.
CLIMBING RHEA REID, H.T. (California Rose Co., 1914.) Sport. 15.
CLIMBING ROSEMARY, H.T. (Dingee & Conard, ——.) Sport. 15.
CLIMBING SUNBURST, H.T. (Howard Rose Co., 1915.) Sport. 15.
CLIMBING WHITE KILLARNEY, H.T. (Conard & Jones, ——.) Sport. 15.
CLIMBING WINNIE DAVIS, T. (California Rose Co., 1913.) Sport. 15.
CLIMBING WOOTTON, H.T. (Thos. Butler, 1899.) Sport of Souv. of Wootton. 15.
COLUMBIA, H.W. (Hoopes, Bro. & Thomas Co., 1903.) Unnamed seedling × Mme. Caroline Testout.
COLUMBIA, H.T. (E. G. Hill Co., reg. A. R. S., 1917.) Ophelia × Mrs. George Shawyer.
COQUINA, H.W. (Walsh, 1909.) 15, 19.
CORA L. BARTON, N. (Buist, 1850.) Seedling from Lamarque. 21.
CORNELIA COOK, T. (Cook, 1855.) 15, 19. Sometimes given as Cornelia Koch. (A. Koch, 1855.) Seedling from Devoniensis. 17.
CORONA, H.Ramb. (Burbank, 1913.) 15.
CORONET, H.T. (Dingee & Conard, 1897.) Carmine, 1; white, yellow, 13.
CRIMSON CHAMPION, H.T. (Cook, 1916.) 15.

LIST OF AMERICAN ROSES

CRIMSON QUEEN, H.T. (Montgomery, 1912.) Liberty × Richmond × General MacArthur.
CRIMSON ROAMER, H.W. (Manda, 1901.) Bardou Job × Jersey Beauty.
CUMBERLAND BELLE, Moss. (Dreer, 1900.) Sport from Princess Adelaide. 19.
DARK PINK KILLARNEY, H.T. (A. N. Pierson, Inc., 1910.) Sport. 27.
DARK PINK RUSSELL, H.T. (Montgomery, 1916.) Sport. 15.
DAVID HARUM, H.T. (E. G. Hill Co., 1904.) 3, 19.
DAWSON, H.Mult. (Dawson, 1888; intro. by Wm. C. Strong, 1890.) *R. multiflora* × General Jacqueminot twice. 19.
DAWSONIANA, Mult. (Ellwanger, 1901.) 13.
DAYBREAK, H.W. (Dawson, 1909.) *R. Wichuraiana* × *R. indica carnea*.
DAYDAWN, H.T. (Heller Brothers, 1909.) 15.
DEBUTANTE, W. (Walsh, 1902.) *R. Wichuraiana* × Baroness Rothschild. 15, 16, 19.
DEFIANCE, H.T. (E. G. Hill Co., 1907.) Lady Battersea × Gruss an Teplitz. 19.
DEFIANCE, H.T. (Kress, registered 1914.) Gruss an Teplitz × Etoile de France.
DELIGHT, H.Cl. (Walsh, 1904.) A. R. S. Cert. of Merit. 15, 19.
DINSMORE, H.P. (Henderson, 1888.) 1.
DOROTHY PERKINS, H.W. (Jackson & Perkins, 1902.) *R. Wichuraiana* × Mme. Gabriel Luizet. 9. (1901.) 15.
DOUBLE LÆVIGATA, Læv. (California, 1900.) Syns., Double Cherokee; *R. lævigata flore-pleno*. 15.
DOUBLE OPHELIA, H.T. (E. G. Hill Co., reg. A. R. S., 1917.) Ophelia×unnamed seedling.
DOUBLE PINK KILLARNEY, H.T. (Robert Scott & Son, 1910.) Sport. 15.
DOUBLE WHITE KILLARNEY, H.T. (Budlong, 1913.) Sport. 15.
DOUBLE WHITE KILLARNEY, H.T. (Totty, 1914.) Sport. 15.
DR. KANE, N. (Pentland, 1856.) 16, 17.
DR. W. VAN FLEET, H.W. (Van Fleet, 1910.) *R. Wichuraiana* × Souv. du President Carnot. Syns., Dr. Van Fleet; Van Fleet Rose. 15.
EASTERN GEM, T. (Conard & Jones Co., 1905.) 19.
EDWARD VII, Poly. (Schultheis, 1910.) 26.
EDWIN LONSDALE, H.W. (Hoopes, Bro. & Thomas Co., 1903.) *R. Wichuraiana* × Safrano. 19.
ELEGANS, Set. (Feast, about 1843.) Syn., Chillicothe Multiflora. 10.
ELIZABETH ZEIGLER, H.W. (A. N. Pierson, reg. 1917.) Sport of Dor. Perkins.
ELLA CHATIN, H.T. (E. G. Hill Co., 1909.) 13.
ELLA MAY, T. (May, 1890.) 5.
EMPRESS OF CHINA, Bengal. (Jackson & Perkins, 1896.) 5, 15, 19. Syn.. Apple Blossom. 15.
ENCHANTER, H.T. (Cook, 1903.) Mme. Caroline Testout × Furon. 19.
ERSKINE PARK BELLE, W. (Edw. J. Norman.) Sport from *R. Wichuraiana*. 15.
ETOILE DE FRANCE, JR., H.T. (California Rose Co., 1911.) Sport. 15.
EVA CORINNE, Set. (Pierce, of Washington, D. C., 185–.) 10.
EVANGELINE, H.W.(Walsh, 1906.) 15, 19. *R. Wichuraiana*×Crimson Rambler. 12.
EVELYN, H.T. (A. N. Pierson, Inc., reg. A. R. S., 1918.) Sport of Ophelia. 15.
EVERGREEN GEM, H.W. (Manda, 1889.) *R. Wichuraiana* × Mme. Hoste. 19.
EXCELSA, H.Cl. (Walsh, 1908.) Syns., Red Dorothy Perkins. 15. Hubbard Gold Medal, A. R. S., 1914
FARQUHAR, H.W. (Dawson, 1903; intro. by R. and J. Farquhar). 31. *R. Wichuraiana* × Crimson Rambler. 15, 16, 19. Syn., The Farquhar. 15.

FLAG OF THE UNION, T. (Hallock & Thorpe.) Sport from Bon Silene. 17.
FLORENCE CHENOWETH, Aus. Brier. (Chenoweth, reg. A. R. S., 1918.) Sport of Mme. Edouard Herriot. 15.
FLOWER OF FAIRFIELD, Mult. (Schultheis, 1909.) 13. (1908.) 15. (Ludorf, 1908.) 19. Syn., Everblooming Crimson Rambler. 15.
*FLUSH O'DAWN, H.T. (Walsh, 1902.) Margaret Dickson × Sombreuil. 19.
FRANCIS SCOTT KEY, H.T. (Cook, 1913.) Radiance × No. 411 (an unnamed crimson seedling).
F. R. M. UNDRITZ, H. W. (F. R. M. Undritz, reg. A. R. S., 1917; intro. by Reinhold Undritz.) Dr. W. Van Fleet × Mrs. W. J. Grant (Belle Siebrecht). 15.
FREEDOM, H. W. (F. R. M. Undritz, reg. A. R. S. 1918; intro. by Reinhold Undritz, 1918.) Silver Moon × Kaiserin Augusta Victoria. Syn., Climbing White American Beauty.
GAINSBOROUGH, Cl.H.T. (Good & Reese, 1903.) Sport from Viscountess Folkestone. Syns., Climbing Viscountess Folkestone; Gainesboro. 15.
GALAXY, W. (Walsh, 1906.) 26.
GARDENIA, H.W. (Manda, 1899.) *R. Wichuraiana* × Perle des Jardins. 19. Syn., Hardy Marechal Niel. 15.
GARNET CLIMBER, H.W. (Van Fleet, 1907.)
GEM OF THE PRAIRIE, Set. (Burgesse, 1868.) Beauty of the Prairies × Mme. Laffay. 7.
GENERAL MACARTHUR, H.T. (E. G. Hill Co., 1904.) 19.
GENERAL ROBERT E. LEE, T. (Good & Reese, 1896.) 15.
GENERAL VON MOLTKE, H.P. (Bell & Son, 1873.) Seedling from Charles Lefebvre. Inferior. 17.
GEORGE PEABODY, B. (Pentland, 1857.) 16. Seedling from Paul Joseph. 17.
GOLDEN GATE, T. (Dingee & Conard, 1892.) 9, 19. Safrano × Cornelia Cook. 5, 9. (Jones of New Orleans, about 1888.) 16.
GOLDEN GEM, H.T. (Towill, reg. A. R. S., 1917.) Lady Hillingdon × Harry Kirk.
GOLDEN RULE, H.T. (E. G. Hill Co., 1918.) Ophelia seedling × Sunburst.
GOLDEN TROPHY, Cl. T. (California Rose Co., 1914.) 15. Sport from Duchesse de Auerstadt. 30.
GREVILLE, Mult. (America, 1900.) Syns., Grevillea and Seven Sisters. 15.
HADLEY, H.T. (Montgomery, 1914.) (Liberty × Richmond) seedling × General MacArthur. Awarded Gold Medal A. R. S., 1914.
HANSEN, H. Ru. (Prof. Budd, 189–). Syn., Hansa. 15.
HARISON'S YELLOW, Brier. (Harison, of New York.) 10, 19. (1830.) 15. Syns., *R. Harisonii*; Hogg's Yellow; Yellow Sweetbrier. 21.
HELEN GOOD, T. (Good & Reese, 1906.) Sport from Maman Cochet. 15, 19. Syn., Golden Cochet. 15.,
HELEN MILLS, H.T. (Dingee & Conard, 1910.) 25.
HELEN TAFT, H.T. (U. S. Department of Agriculture, 1913.) Syn., Miss Helen Taft. 15.
HENRY IRVING, H.P. (Conard & Jones, 1907.) 19.
HENRY M. STANLEY, T. (Dingee & Conard, 1879.) 15.
HIAWATHA, H.Cl. (Walsh, 1904.) A. R. S. First Prize. 15, 16. Crimson Rambler × Carmine Pillar. 19.
HIBBERTIA, C. (Buist, about 1830.) 21.
HIGHLAND MARY, T. (Dingee & Conard, 1908.) 19.
HOOSIER BEAUTY, H.T. (F. Dorner & Sons Co., 1915.) Syn., Liberty Beauty.
IDA, H.Cl. (Dawson 189–; not formally introduced.) Dawson × *R. multiflora*. 29.

*Probably identical with Blush o'Dawn, H.T. (Walsh, 1902.) 13.

LIST OF AMERICAN ROSES 141

IDEAL, H.T. (Jacob Becker, 1900.) 15, 19.
IMPROVED RAINBOW, T. (Burbank, ——.) 15.
INDIANA, H.T. (E. G. Hill Co., 1907.) 13. Rosalind Orr English × Frau Karl Druschki. 12.
INTENSITY, H.T. (Dingee & Conard, 1908.) 19, 25.
ISABELLA GRAY, N. (Gray, 1855.) Seedling from Cloth of Gold or Chromatella. 8, 17.
ISABELLA SPRUNT, T. (Sprunt, 1866.) 15. Sport from Safrano. 17.
IVORY, T. (American Rose Co., 1902.) Sport from Golden Gate. 3, 19. Syn., White Golden Gate. 15.

JACKSONIA, C. (Buist, about 1830.) Syn., Hundred-leaved Daily. 21.
JAMES SPRUNT, Cl. Bengal. (Sprunt, 1856.) 6, 9. Sport from Agrippina. 17.
JANE, Set. (Pierce, about 1850.) 1, 10.
JERSEY BEAUTY, H.W. (Manda, 1899.) *R. Wichuraiana* × Perle des Jardins. 19.
JESSICA, H.W. (Walsh, 1909.) 25.
JOHN BURTON, W. (Hoopes, Bro. & Thomas Co., 1903.) *R. Wichuraiana* × Safrano. 19.
J. S. FAY, H.P. (Walsh, 1908.) 15, 19.
JUBILEE, H.P. (Henderson, 1898.) 1, 19. (1897.) 15. (Walsh, 1897.) Victor Hugo × Prince Camille de Rohan. 16.

KALMIA, H.W. (Walsh, 1913.) 15.
KEYSTONE, Mult. (Dingee & Conard, 1904.) 15, 19.
KILLARNEY QUEEN, H.T. (J. A. Budlong & Son Co., 1909.) Sport. 15.
KING DAVID, H.T. (California Rose Co., 1910.) 15. Sport from Vick's Caprice. 30.
KING OF THE PRAIRIES, Setigera type. (Feast, 1843.) 1, 10.

LA DETROIT, H.T. (Hopp, 1904.) 15. Mme. Caroline Testout × Bridesmaid. 19. (P. Breitmeyer's Sons, 1903.) 16, 25.
LADY ANN BORODELL, H.T. (S. J. Reuter & Son, Inc., reg, A. R. S. 1914.) Sport from My Maryland. 28.
LADY BLANCHE, H.W. (Walsh, 1913.) 15.
LADY CROMWELL, H.T. (A. N. Pierson, Inc., 1912.) Sport of My Maryland. 15.
LADY DOROTHEA, T. (Dunlop, 1898.) 16.
LADY DUNCAN, H.W. (Dawson, 1909.) *R. Wichuraiana* × *R. rugosa*.
LADY GAY, W. (Walsh, 1905.) 15, 19. *R. Wichuraiana* × Bardou Job. 5, 16.
LADY MARS, Cl. T. (California Rose Co., 1909.) 15. Sport from Gloire de Dijon. 30.
LA FIAMMA, H.W. (Walsh, 1909.) 15, 19. Syn., La Flamme. 15.
LANDRETH'S CARMINE, N. (D. & C. Landreth, 1824.) Syn., Carmine Cluster. 10.
LANSDOWNE, H.T. (Leonard, registered 1914.) 15.
LE VESUVE, Bengal-C. (Sprunt, 1858.) 3.
LITTLE SUNSHINE, Poly. (Alexander R. Cumming, Jr., reg A. R. S., 1915, A. N. Pierson, Inc.) *R. multiflora nana* × Soleil d'Or.
LITTLE WHITE PET, Poly. (Henderson, 1879.) 1, 13, 19.
LOS ANGELES, H.T. (Howard, registered A. R. S., 1916.) Mme. Segond Weber × Lyon Rose. 15.
LUCILE, H.W. (Walsh, 1913.) 15.
LUTEA, N. (Buist, ——.) Syn., *R. Smithii*. 21.

MADISON, T. (Hentz, 1912.) 15.
MADONNA, H.T. (Cook, 1908.) 19. Lady Mary Fitzwilliam × ——. 12. Sport from White Lady. 19
MAGNAFRANO, H.T. (Van Fleet, 1905; intro. by Conard & Jones Co.) Magna Charta × Safrano. 19.

MAID MARION, H.W. (Walsh, 1909.) 15.
MAID OF HONOR, T. (Hoffmeister, 1899.) Sport of Catherine Mermet. 16, 19.
MANDA'S TRIUMPH, W. (Manda, 1897.) 3. *R. Wichuraiana* × a Hybrid Perpetual. 19.
MARION BRUNELL, C.T. (F. H. Brunell, Alabama, 1917.) Sport of Reine Marie Henriette. 15.
MARION DINGEE, H.T. (Cook, 1889.) Caserta × General Jacqueminot × Marechal Niel × (Pierre Notting × Safrano). 19.
MARK TWAIN, H.T. (E. G. Hill Co., reg. A. R. S., 1902.) 5, 13, 19, 25.
MARSHALL P. WILDER, H.P. (Ellwanger & Barry, 1885.) 15, 16, 17.
MARY HILL, H. T. (E. G. Hill Co., 1917.) Ophelia × Sunburst.
MARY LOVETT, H. W. (Van Fleet, 1915; intro. by J. T. Lovett, 1915.) *R. Wichuraiana* × Kaiserin Augusta Victoria.
MARY WASHINGTON, Mult. Said to have been planted by George Washington on his estate at Mount Vernon and named by him in honor of his mother. 18. Syn., Martha Washington. 15.
MASTER BURKE (*R. Lawrenciana*), Species. (Feast, ——.) 21.
MAUD LITTLE, T. (Dingee & Conard, 1891.) 1.
MAYFLOWER, T. (E. G. Hill Co., 1910.)
MAY MARTIN, H.T. (Martin & Forbes, 1918.) Sport of Ophelia.
MAY MILLER, H.T. (E. G. Hill Co., 1910.) Unnamed seedling × Paul Neyron. 5.
MAY QUEEN, H.W. (Van Fleet, 1898; intro. by Conard & Jones Co.) 19. *R. Wichuraiana* × Mrs. de Graw. 16.
MILADY, H.T. (Towill, 1913.) Richmond × J. B. Clark.
MILKY WAY, H.W. (Walsh, 1909.) 15.
MINNEHAHA, H.W. (Walsh, 1905.) 15. *R. Wichuraiana* × Paul Neyron. 5. 16, 19.
MINNIE DAWSON, H.Cl. (Dawson 189—; intro. by Ellwanger & Barry.) *R. Multiflora* × Dawson. 29, 31.
MINNIE FRANCIS, T. (America,——.) 15.
MISS BELL, T. (Intro. and date unknown.) 10.
MISS KATE MOULTON, H.T. (Monson, 1906.) 15. Mme. Caroline Testout × La France × Mrs. W. J. Grant (Belle Siebrecht). 15, 19.
MISS MAUDY SHUBROOK, H.T. (California Rose Co., 1914.) Sport from Mrs. Aaron Ward. 15.
MISS RUBY DENT, H.P. (California Rose Co., 1916.) Sport from Mrs. John Laing; also classed as a Hybrid Tea. 15.
MISS SARAH NESBITT, H.T. (B. Dorrance, 1910.) 27.
MISS SARGENT, T. (Mackenzie, of Philadelphia, about 185–.) 10.
MLLE. MARTHE HYRIGOYEN, H. C. (E. G. Hill Co., 1902.) 25.
MME. BOLL, H.P. (Boll, 1859.) 5, 6, 16, 17.
MME. BUTTERFLY, H.T. (E. G. Hill Co., 1918.) Sport of Ophelia.
MME. BYRNE, N. (Buist, 1850.) 10. Seedling of Lamarque. 21.
MME. TRUDEAUX, H.P. (Boll, 1850.) 1, 17.
MME. TRUDEAUX, D. (Boll.——.) 10.
MONTARIOSA, Hybrid. (California,——.) *R. Brunonii* × *R. gigantea*. 29.
MONTECITO, Hybrid. (California,——.) *R. Brunonii* × *R. gigantea*. 29.
MONTROSE, H.T. (Cook, 1916.) 15.
MRS. BAYARD THAYER, H.T. (Waban Rose Cons., reg. A. R. S., 1916.) 15.
MRS. BELMONT TIFFANY, H.T. (Budlong, reg. A. R. S., 1917; and intro. by A. N. Pierson, Inc., 1918.) Sport of Sunburst.
MRS. CHARLES BELL, H.T. (A. N. Pierson, reg. A. R. S., 1917.) Sport of Radiance.

Mrs. Charles Russell, H.T. (Montgomery, 1913.) "Mme. Abel Chatenay, Marquise Litta de Breteuil, Mme. Caroline Testout, Mrs. W. J. Grant (Belle Siebrecht), General MacArthur, and three seedlings resulting from these crosses are all combined to produce Mrs. Charles Russell." 15.
Mrs. Chas. Dingee, H.T. (Dingee & Conard, ———.) 15.
Mrs. Chas. Gersdorff, Cl.H.T. (Gersdorff, reg. A. R. S., 1916.) White climbing rose × Killarney.
Mrs. Cleveland, H.P. (Gill, 1897.) 1, 13, 19.
Mrs. de Graw, B. (Burgess, 1885.) 16.
Mrs. E. T. Stotesbury, H.T. (Edward Towill, reg. A. R. S., 1918.) Seedling (Joseph Hill × My Maryland) × Milady.
Mrs. F. F. Thompson, H.T. (Totty, 1915.) Sport of Mrs. George Shawyer. 15.
Mrs. Henry Winnett, H.T. (Dunlop, reg. A. R. S., 1917.) Mrs. Charles Russell × Mrs. George Shawyer. 15.
Mrs. J. C. Ainsworth, H.T. (Clarke Bros., 1918.) Sport of Mrs. Charles Russell.
Mrs. J. Pierpont Morgan, T. (May, 1895.) 15, 16. Sport from Mme. Cusin. Syn., Mrs. Pierpont Morgan. 15.
*Mrs. Lovett, H.W. (Dr. Van Fleet, ———.) 15.
Mrs. M. H. Walsh, H.Cl. (Walsh, 1911.) Syn., Mrs. Walsh. 15. Gold Medal of A. R. S., 1911.
Mrs. Moorfield Storey, H.T. (Waban Rose Conservatories, reg. A. R. S., 1915.) General MacArthur × Joseph Hill.
Mrs. Oliver Ames, H.T. (May, 1902.) 15, 19. Sport from Mme. Cusin. 16.
Mrs. Opie, T. (Bell & Son, 1877.) 17.
Mrs. Pierce, Set. (Pierce, about 1850.) 10, 17. Syn., Mrs. Hovey. 22.
Mrs. Potter Palmer, H.T. (Breitmeyer, 1909.) 19, 25.
Mrs. R. B. Mellon, H. Spin. (Elliott Nursery, 1917.) Seedling. 15.
Mrs. Robert Garrett, H.T. (Cook, 1900.) Caserta × F. E. Verdier.
Mrs. Robert Peary, Cl.H.T. (Dingee & Conard, 1898.) Sport from Kaiserin Augusta Victoria. 15.
Mrs. Sarah Yeats, H.T. (Originated and reg. by Yeats, 1916; intro. by A. L. Randall Co., 1917.) 15.
Mrs. Theodore Roosevelt, H.T. (E. G. Hill Co., 1904.) Sport of La France. 19.
Mrs. W. C. Whitney, H.T. (May, 1894.) 11, 16.
Mrs. Wm. R. Hearst, H.T. (A. N. Pierson, Inc., reg. A. R. S., 1916.) Sport of My Maryland. 15.
Muriel Moore, H.T. (Moore, 1916.) Sport of My Maryland.
My Maryland, H.T. (Cook, 1908.) Madonna × Enchanter.

Nevia, Set. (Feast, 1843.) 10.
New Century, H.Ru. (Van Fleet, 1900; intro. by Conard & Jones Co.) *R. rugosa* × Clotilde Soupert.
Newport Fairy, H.W. (Gardner; intro. by Roehrs, 1908.) 12, 19.
Niles Cochet, T. (California, ———.) 15.
Nokomis, Wich. (M. H. Walsh, 1918.) *R. Wichuraiana* × Comte de Raimbaud.
Norma, H.T. (Dingee & Conard, 1904.) 4, 19, 25.
Northern Light, H.W. (Van Fleet, 1898; intro. by Conard & Jones Co.) Wichuraiana hybrid. 19.

Oakmont, H.P. (May, 1893.) 15, 19.
Old Blush, N. (Noisette, 1817.) 2.

*Probably identical with Mary Lovett, H.W.

OLIVIA, H.T. (E. G. Hill Co., 1907.) 15, 19. Syn., Oliva. 15.
OPHELIA SUPREME, H.T. (Dailledouze Bros.; reg. Soc. American Florists, 1917.) Sport. 24.
ORIOLE, H.T. (California Rose Co., 1910.) 15.
PALLIDA, Set. (Feast, 1843.) 10, 17, 20.
PANAMA, H. P. (E. G. Hill Co., 1908.) Paul Neyron × seedling of Joseph Hill. 5.
PANAMA, H.T. (Cook, 1913.) Dreuschia × unnamed pink seedling. Awarded Silver Medal, A. R. S., 1915.
PAN-AMERICA, H.T. (Henderson, 1902.) American Beauty × Mme. Caroline Testout. 19.
PARADISE, H.W. (Walsh, 1907.) 15, 19.
PAUL DE LONGPRE, H.T. (E. G. Hill Co., 1906.) 19.
PAULINE DAWSON, H. Cl. (Dawson, 1916.) 31.
PEARL QUEEN, W. *R. Wichuraiana* × Mrs. de Graw. 16.
PEARL RIVERS, T. (Dingee & Conard, 1890.) 1, 16.
PERPETUAL MICHIGAN, Set. (Feast, about 1843.) 10. Everblooming Prairie Queen may be a synonym.
PHILADELPHIA, Ramb. Crimson Rambler × Victor Hugo. 16, 19. Probably the same as Philadelphia, H.Mult. (Van Fleet, 1904; intro. by Conard & Jones Co.) Syn., Philadelphia Crimson Rambler. 15.
PILLAR OF GOLD, T. (Conard & Jones, 1909.) 19.
PINK CECILE BRUNNER, Poly. (Western Rose Co., 1918.) Sport. 15.
PINK CHEROKEE, Læv. (California, 1887.) *R. lævigata* × *R. indica.* 15.
PINK FRAU KARL DRUSCHKI, H.P. (California Rose Co., 1910.) Sport. 15.
PINK OPHELIA, H.T. (Howard & Smith, 1916.) Sport from Ophelia.
PINK PEARL, H.W. (Manda, 1901.) *R. Wichuraiana* × Meteor.
PINK ROAMER, H.W. (Manda, 1898.) 19. Syn., Pink Rover. 15.
PINK SOUPERT, Poly. (Dingee & Conard, 1896.) 1. Sport from Clotilde Soupert. 15.
POM POM, H.Cl. (U S. Department of Agriculture, 1910.) 25. Crimson Rambler × *R. Wichuraiana.* 15.
PRESIDENT TAFT, H.T. (McCullough, 1908.) Syns., President W. H. Taft; Taft Rose; Wm. H. Taft. 15.
PRETTY AMERICAN (*R. Lawrenciana*). (Boll, 183– or 185–.) 10.
PRIDE OF THE SOUTH, Set. (America, ———.) 15.
PRIDE OF WASHINGTON, Set. (Pierce, about 185—.) 7, 10, 19.
PRIMROSE, T. (Dingee & Conard, 1908.) 19.
PRINCESS BONNIE, T. (Dingee & Conard, 1897.) 1. Bon Silene × Wm. F. Bennett. 19.
PRINCESS ENA, Poly. (H. B. May, 1907.) Sport of Baby Crimson Rambler. 26.
PRISCILLA, H.T. (Henderson, 1910.) Kaiserin Augusta Victoria × Frau Karl Druschki. 5, 25.
PROF. C. S. SARGENT, H.W. (Hoopes, Bro. & Thomas Co., 1903.) *R. Wichuraiana* × Souv. d'Auguste Metral. (Not the same as Sargent.) 19.
PURITY, H.W. (Hoopes, Bro. & Thomas Co., 1917.) Unnamed seedling × Mme. Caroline Testout. Silver Medal of A. R. S., 1915.
QUEEN BEATRICE, H.T. (Credited to Kramer, 1907, by Good & Reese Co.) 15. (Dingee & Conard, 1906.) 15.
QUEEN OF EDGELY, H.P. (Floral Exchange, 1902.) 19. (Floral Exchange, 1897.) Sport from American Beauty. Syn., Pink American Beauty. 15.
QUEENS SCARLET, Bengal. (Hallock & Thorpe, 1880.) 15, 17. Syn., Red Hermosa. 15.

RADIANCE, H.T. (Cook, 1908.) Enchanter × Cardinal. Awarded Silver Medal of A. R. S., 1914. 19.
RAINBOW, T. (Sievers, 1891.) Sport from Papa Gontier. 3, 19. (Dingee & Conard, 1891.) 2. Sievers was probably the originator.
RAMONA, Læv. (Dietrich & Turner, 1913.) Sport from Pink Cherokee. Syn., Red Cherokee. 15.
RED RADIANCE, H.T. (A. N. Pierson, Inc., 1916.) Sport. 15.
RED RADIANCE, H.T. (Gude Bros., 1916.) Sport. Darker than Pierson's. 15.
REGINA, H.Ramb. (Walsh, 1916.) 15.
RELIANCE, H.T. (E. G. Hill Co., 1910.) 4, 19. Etoile de France × Chateau de Clos Vougeot. 15.
RENA ROBBINS, H.T. (E. G. Hill Co., 1911.) Paul Neyron × Mme. Jenny Gillemot.
RHEA REID, H.T. (E. G. Hill Co., 1908.) American Beauty × red seedling. 12, 19.
RICHMOND, H.T. (E. G. Hill Co., 1905.) Lady Battersea × Liberty. 19. Syn., Everblooming Jack Rose. 15.
ROBERT CRAIG, H.W. (Hoopes, Bro. & Thomas Co., 1903.) *R. Wichuraiana* × Beaute Inconstante. 19.
ROBERT HELLER, T. (E. G. Hill Co., 1911.)
ROBERT SCOTT, H.T. (Robert Scott & Son, 1901.) 15. Merveille de Lyon × Mrs. W. J. Grant (Belle Siebrecht). 19.
ROBIN HOOD, H.T. (E. G. Hill Co., 1912.)
ROSALIE, T. (Ellwanger & Barry, 1884.) Seedling from Marie Van Houtte. 17.
ROSALIND, H.T. (F. R. Pierson Co., reg. A. R. S., 1918.) Sport of Ophelia 15.
ROSALIND ORR ENGLISH, H.T. (E. G. Hill Co., 1905.) 3, 15. Mme. Abel Chatenay × Papa Gontier. 19.
ROSA ACICULARIS. (Lindley, 1820.) 25.
ROSA HELENÆ, Species. (Rehder and Wilson, from Central China, 1907.) 29.
ROSA JACKII, Species. (Jack, from China, 1905.) 29.
ROSA JACKSONII, Hybrid. (Willmott, ——.) *R. rugosa* × *R. Wichuraiana*. 29.
ROSA MICROPHYLLA. (Lindley, 1820.) 25.
ROSA MULTIFLORA CARTHAGENSIS, Species. (Purdom, from North Central China, 1910.) 29.
ROSA SERICEA. (Lindley, 1820.) 25.
ROSA SPINOSISSIMA HYBRIDA. (Elliott Nursery, ——.) 15.
ROSA WICHURAIANA VARIEGATA. (Conard & Jones Co., ——.) 15.
ROSA WILLMOTTIAE, Species. (E. H. Wilson, from China, ——.) 15.
ROSA XANTHINA. (Lindley, 1820.) 25.
ROSEMARY, H.T. (E. G. Hill Co., 1907.) 15, 19.
ROSE PREMIER, H.T. (E. G. Hill Co., reg. A. R. S., 1917.) Ophelia seedling × Mrs. Charles Russell.
ROSE QUEEN, H.T. (E. G. Hill Co., 1911.)
ROSERIE, H.Ramb. (R. Witterstætter, 1917.) Sport from Tausendschön. 15. Syn., Rosary. 15.
ROYAL CLUSTER, Ramb. (Conard & Jones Co., 1899.) Armosa (Hermosa) × Dawson. 19, 25.
RUBY GOLD, T. (O'Connor, 1892.) Sport from a graft of Catherine Mermet on Marechal Niel. 16.
RUBY QUEEN, H.W. (Van Fleet, 1899; intro. by Conard & Jones Co.) *R. Wichuraiana* × Queens Scarlet. 16.

RUGOSA MAGNIFICA, H.Ru. (Van Fleet, 1905; intro. by Conard & Jones Co.)
  R. rugosa × Ards Rover.
RUSSELIANA, Set. 21. (Russel, 1900.) 25. Syns., Russell's Cottage; Russel's
  Cottage. 15. Syns., Scarlet Grevillea; Cottage Rose. 21.
RUTH VESTAL, Cl.T. (Vestal & Sons, 1908.) Sport from Bride. 30. Syn.,
  Climbing Bride. 15.
SANTA ROSA, Bengal. (Burbank, 1900.) 13, 19.
SARAH ISABELLE GILL, T. (Gill, 1897.) 19.
SARGENT, H.W. (Dawson, 1912.) R. Wichuraiana × Crimson Rambler ×
  Baroness Rothschild. 31.
SATISFACTION, N. (California Rose Co., 1915.) 15. Sport from Reve d'Or. 30.
SEASHELL, H.Cl. (Dawson, 1916.) 31.
SEPTEMBER MORN, H.T. (Turner, 1915.) Sport from Mme. Paul Euler. 15.
SETIGERA HYBRID, Hybrid. (Dawson,——) R. setigera × R. Wichuraiana. 31.
SETINA, Cl.B. (Henderson, 1879.) Sport of Armosa (Hermosa). Syns., Climb-
  ing Hermosa; Cetina. 9, 15, 17, 19.
SHEPHERD'S ORIOLE, N. (T. B. Shepherd Co., 1905.) 15.
SILVER MOON, H.W. (Van Fleet, 1910.) R. Wichuraiana × R. lævigata
  (Cherokee Rose). 15.
SILVIA, H.T. (F. R. Pierson Co., reg. A. R. S., 1918.) Sport of Ophelia. 15.
SIR THOMAS LIPTON, H.Ru. (Van Fleet, 1900; intro. by Conard & Jones Co.)
  R. rugosa × Clotilde Soupert. 19.
SNOWBALL, Poly. (Walsh, 1901.) 19, 25.
SNOWDRIFT, H.Cl. (Walsh.)
SNOWDRIFT, W. (Smith, 1914.) 15.
SNOWFLAKE, T. (Strauss & Co., Washington, D. C., 1890.) 15, 17.
SOUTH ORANGE PERFECTION, W. (Manda, 1899.) 3. R. Wichuraiana ×
  Mme. Hoste. 19.
SOUV. DE HENRY CLAY, Scotch hybrid. (Boll, 1854.) 17.
SOUV. OF WOOTTON, H.T. (Cook, 1888.) Bon Silene × Louis Van Houtte.
  Said to be the first Hybrid Tea rose raised in the United States. 19. Syns.,
  Souv. de la Wootton; Souv. de Wootton. 15.
SPECTACULAR, H.T. (Elliott, 1912.) Syn., Striped Killarney. 15.
SUMMER JOY, H.Cl. (Walsh, 1911.) 15.
SUNBEAM, T. (California Rose Co., 1908.) 15. Sport from Golden Gate. 30.
SUNSET, T. (Henderson, 1884,) 2, 9. Sport from Perle des Jardins. 9. (1883.)
  16, 19.
SUPERBA, Setigera type. (Feast, 1843.) 10, 16, 17, 20.
SWEETHEART, H.W. (Walsh, 1903.) R. Wichuraiana × Bridesmaid. 15, 16, 19.
SWEET MARIE, H.T. (California Rose Co., 1915.) Sport from Mrs. G. W.
  Kershaw. 15.
TENNESSEE BELLE, H.Cl. (America, ——.) 15.
THE OREGON, H.T. (E. G. Hill Co., never formally introduced.) Liberty ×
  unnamed seedling. 12.
THORA, H.T. (Burton, 1914.) 15.
TRIUMPH, H.T. (E. G. Hill Co., 1906 or 1907.) 3, 13. Gruss an Teplitz ×
  General MacArthur. 25.
TRIUMPHANT, Setigera type. (Pierce, 1850.) 1, 10, 16.
TROUBADOUR, H.W. (Walsh, 1911.) 15.
UNCLE JOHN, T. (Thorpe, 1904.) 15, 19. Sport from Golden Gate. 30.
UNIVERSAL FAVORITE, W. (Manda, 1899.) 3. R. Wichuraiana × American
  Beauty. 19.
URANIA, H.Cl. (Walsh, 1902.) A. R. S. Special Newbold Fund Prize.

URANIA, H.P. (Walsh, 1906.) 3. (1905.) Seedling from American Beauty. 16. American Beauty (Mme. Ferd. Jamain) × Susanne Marie Rodocanachi. (Mme. Rodocanachi.) 19.
VAUGHAN'S WHITE BABY RAMBLER, Poly. (Vaughan, 1916.) 15.
VICK'S CAPRICE, H.P. (Vick, 1893.) 1. (1889.) 15. Sport from Archduchesse Elizabeth d'Austriche. 15, 16. 19.
VICTOR, H.T. (E. G. Hill Co., 1918.) Ophelia Seedling × Killarney Brilliant.
VICTORY, H. W. (F. R. M. Undritz, reg., A. R. S., 1918; intro. by Reinhold Undritz, 1918.) Dr. W. Van Fleet × Mme. Jules Grolez.
VIRGINIA, T. (Dingee & Conard, 1894.) 1.
VIRIDIFLORA, Bengal. (Originated in Baltimore, Md., about 1850.) 10. 19, (Harrison, of Baltimore, Md., 1856.) 1. (Rambridge and Harrison, 1856.) 15. Syn., Green Rose. 15.
WABAN, T. (E. M. Wood & Co., 1891.) Sport of Catherine Mermet. 16, 19.
WASHINGTON, Bengal. (D. & C. Landreth, about 1824.) 10.
WASHINGTON, N. (Stewart, of Philadelphia, Pa., about 185–.) 10, 17.
WEDDING BELLS, Ramb. (Walsh, 1906.) 19. Seedling from Crimson Rambler. 16.
WELLESLEY, H.T. (Montgomery, 1904.) Liberty × Bridesmaid. 16.
WEST GROVE, H.T. (Dingee & Conard, registered 1914.) Liberty × Kaiserin Augusta Victoria.
WHITE DAWSON, H.Mult. (Ellwanger, 1901.) 19.
WHITE KILLARNEY, H.T. (Waban Rose Conservatories, 1909.) Sport. 15, 19.
WHITE MAMAN COCHET, T. (Cook, 1896.) Sport. 16, 19.
WHITE SHAWYER, H.T. (Totty, 1915.) Sport. 15.
WHITE STAR, H.W. (Manda, 1901.) Jersey Beauty × Manda's Triumph.
WHITE TAUSENDSCHÖN, H.Cl. (J. Roehrs Co., probably in 1918.) Sport. 15.
WINONA, H.Ramb. (Walsh, 1913.) 15.
WINTER GEM, T. (Childs, 1898.) 15.
WM. C. EGAN, H.W. (Dawson, 1900; intro. by Hoopes, Bro. & Thomas Co.) *R. Wichuraiana* × General Jacqueminot. 15.
WM. R. SMITH, T. (Smith, 1908; intro. by Peter Henderson & Co., 1908.) Maman Cochet × Kaiserin Augusta Victoria. Syns., Jeannette Heller; Chas. Dingee; Maiden's Blush; President Wm. R. Smith. 4, 15, 19.
WM. K. HARRIS, W. (Hoopes, Bro. & Thomas Co., 1903.) 15, 19.
WOODLAND MARGUERITE, N. (Pentland, 1859.) 17.
W. T. DREER, W. (Hoopes, Bro. & Thomas Co., 1903.) 4, 19.
YELLOW PRESIDENT CARNOT, H.T. (California Rose Company, 1910.) 15. Sport. 30.

The Editor particularly requests information or corrections to aid in making this list accurate. In sending such, correspondents are requested to give exact details, so far as possible.

A catalogue of roses in American commerce has been compiled, and is in process of careful revision and verification. It will include name, origin if ascertainable, class, color, fragrance, form, petalage, bloom habit, plant habit, disease liability. Accurate information for this work is desired.

The 1918 Work of the American Rose Society

As Reported by the Secretary

The American Rose Society has come through the period of the war in excellent condition, demonstrating conclusively the fallacy of the opinion of many that roses are unessential in wartimes. All through the trying period, flowers have lent their cheering influence in inspiring the American people to increased courage and a stronger faith.

Now, that the war is over, we can again return to our peaceful pursuits, and we can again take up the culture of the flowers which mean so much in the lives of the American people.

Membership in the Society did not diminish in any appreciable degree because of the war. The membership on January 1, 1919, was approximately 1,500, as against 2,000 on January 1, 1918. However, the new memberships now being received in the Secretary's office indicate that the number of members for 1919 will far exceed that of other years. Membership in the American Rose Society should be extended to thousands of homes in the United States, and the immediate future should bring the number up to at least 10,000. To get and retain these members, the Society must give full value for the membership fee. This it already does, in a large measure, through the American Rose Annual and tickets to the exhibitions held under the auspices of the Society. However, that is not enough to satisfy and draw many members. The exhibitions are, of necessity, local affairs, and a large number of members cannot attend. The Society should increase its publications, and especially assist in the organization of local rose exhibitions.

The Society has lost by death one of its most enthusiastic members. The death of Admiral Aaron Ward, at his home in Roslyn, L. I., on July 5, 1918, was indeed a sad loss to the Society he had served so faithfully as a member of the Executive Committee. As a slight tribute to his memory, the Executive Committee have inscribed on their minutes the following resolutions:

WHEREAS, Since the last session of the Executive Committee of the American Rose Society our friend and counselor, Admiral Aaron Ward, has passed into the "Great Beyond," and

WHEREAS, We feel keenly the loss of his wise counsel in the work of the Society where his great love of roses and his thorough knowledge of their culture, both in this country and abroad, made his membership in this Committee and in the Society of inestimable value, therefore, be it

Resolved, That we express to Mrs. Ward and family our sense of loss, our deep sympathy for them in their bereavement, and our appreciation of the rare quality of the character of Admiral Ward; and, be it further

Resolved, That a copy of these resolutions be sent Mrs. Ward, a copy spread on the minutes of the Society, and copies inserted in the horticultural press.

The Nineteenth Annual Meeting

On March 15, 1918, at 3 P.M., the annual meeting of the Society was held in Grand Central Palace, New York City.

The following officers were elected for the ensuing year: President, Benjamin Hammond, Beacon, N. Y.; Vice-President, W. J. Keimel, Elmhurst, Ill.; Secretary, E. A. White, Ithaca, N. Y.; Treasurer, Harry O. May, Summit, N. J. Honorary Vice-Presidents: E. M. Mills, D.D., Syracuse, N. Y.; J. Horace

McFarland, Harrisburg, Pa.; Dr. Robert Huey, Philadelphia, Pa.; W. G. McKendrick, Toronto, Can. Executive Committee for three years: Robert Simpson, Clifton, N. J.; W. R. Pierson, Cromwell, Conn.; John H. Dunlop, Richmond Hill, Ont. To succeed Capt. George C. Thomas, Jr., resigned: S. S. Pennock, Philadelphia, Pa. To succeed W. J. Keimel: George H. Peterson, Fairlawn, N. J. The Executive Committee in full is as follows: E. Allan Pierce, Waltham, Mass. (term expires in 1919); Robert Pyle, West Grove, Pa. (term expires in 1919); George H. Peterson, Fairlawn, N. J. (term expires in 1919); L. J. Reuter, Waltham, Mass. (term expires in 1920); J. A. Currey, Portland, Ore. (term expires in 1920); S. S. Pennock, Philadelphia, Pa. (term expires in 1920); W. R. Pierson, Cromwell, Conn. (term expires in 1921); Robert Simpson, Clifton, N. J. (term expires in 1921); John H. Dunlop, Richmond Hill, Ont. (term expires in 1921); J. Horace McFarland, Editor The American Rose Annual, Harrisburg, Pa.; O. P. Beckley, Advertising Agent The American Rose Annual, Harrisburg, Pa.; President, Vice-President, Secretary, and Treasurer.

The report of the officers follows:

PRESIDENT'S REPORT, MARCH, 1918

To the Members of the American Rose Society:

The past twelve months have been a period of most uncommon conditions that have upset the ordinary routine of affairs generally, and no one has felt this any more than commercial flower-growers. The American Rose Society has a membership which extends from ocean to ocean, coming in touch with hundreds of homes, and, from the interest manifested by our amateur membership, it is evident that the rose is a flower which, through all the trouble of the day, holds its own in the hearts of the people. It is a general service, this bringing together of communities large and small to a flower show, because with all the demand upon time and purse for war duties and sacrifices that are now paramount, the appreciation and sentiment in favor of nice things is the difference between barbarism and Americanism.

The past year, to meet the increased cost of this Society, it was deemed advisable to make a change in the rates of membership dues and thereby change the original form from active and amateur members at two distinct rates to one common sum of $2 instead of the $3 and $1 rate. This action was ratified at the fall meeting of 1917, held in the city of Cleveland during the flower show last November, and has been received with general favor from the amateur and commercial membership.

The incentive to which has been largely due the increased amateur membership is the American Rose Annual, a book of record and dissertation pertaining to growth and culture of roses, national in extent and admirably illustrated, a copy of which goes to each member of the Society. We have issued the book for two years past, and the edition covering the last year is about ready to be mailed, making three years of notable record.

At the last annual meeting the Executive Committee was formally increased in size from six to nine members, so as to afford a fitting representative of amature memberships. This Committee now is able to have representatives from the United States and Canada, from ocean to ocean.

The test-gardens which began in Elizabeth Park, at Hartford, Conn., have become a most interesting adjunct to rose-growing. The test-gardens under recognition of the American Rose Society are Hartford, Conn., Washington, D. C., Ithaca, N. Y., Minneapolis, Minn., and Portland, Ore. In each of these the effect of climate on rose bushes is carefully watched, to determine the ability of varieties to stand the weather, and notes are made of their growth in the section in which the garden is situated. These rose-gardens are proving of great public interest. Application has been made from Texas and from Bellingham and Tacoma, Wash., but the Society could not go too fast in authorizing new gardens because of the necessity of securing, without charge, a goodly number of plants from home and foreign growers.

An important piece of work has been done in setting forth the correct and plain naming of roses so as to have a definite plan and system of acknowledged accuracy in nomenclature. Furthermore, much work has been done toward bringing to completion a list of all roses originated in the United States or Canada.

There is one thing that I would like to impress upon all firms who are commercial rose-plant growers. That is, that one and all of this class of men should become life members of the American Rose Society.

Regarding the registration of new roses: Heretofore there have been some registered with the Society of American Florists, and as the American Rose Society has grown in importance more have come direct to us for official registration. At the meeting of the directors of the Society of American Florists and Ornamental Horticulturists held in January last at St. Louis, a resolution was passed directing that hereafter *all* new roses should be registered for record with the American Rose Society, thus securing a permanent record of authoritative value.

The National Rose Society of England has been an inspiring example to the American Rose Society, and has extended to us much courtesy. Such action tends to hasten the coming day of "peace on earth and good will to men."

This June we expect to have an open-air show of more than ordinary interest in the Rose-Garden at Elizabeth Park, Hartford. The Park Department and others have planned carefully for this public exhibition.

The detail working of the Society will be more fully shown in the reports of our Secretary and Treasurer, and the American Rose Society, with its large and growing membership, stands for Americanism, which is Fidelity, Patience, Industry, and Fearlessness first, last and all the time, and "a rose for every home, a bush for every garden."   BENJAMIN HAMMOND, *President.*

REPORT OF THE SECRETARY

As your Secretary has been in office but nine months, a report of the period must of necessity be brief. In the seventeenth report of the annual meeting of the Society, two years ago, Secretary Hammond reported a paid-up membership of 194 active and 51 associate members. At the Cleveland meeting in November, 1917, the Society voted to so change the Constitution and By-laws as to establish a uniform membership fee of $2 a year, and since that date, 1,114 paid memberships have been received, with 895 memberships paid in 1917 yet to be heard from. The life memberships now number 58, two new members having been added since July 1, 1917: F. R. Pierson, Tarrytown, N. Y., and Mrs. Charles Frederick Hoffman, President of the International Garden Club, New York City.

This wonderful growth has been due in no small measure to the active interest in the work of the organization taken by the editor of the American Rose Annual, Mr. J. Horace McFarland, of Harrisburg, Pa. Through his love of roses, his wide acquaintance as President of the American Civic Association, and his keen interest in the success of the American Rose Annual, he has brought the rose indeed near to many a home and garden.

But in this period of the Society's success we must not forget that there have been years of adversity, and a complete history of the American Rose

Society would show that but for the self-sacrifice of a few men who had an insight into the value which the organization might become, the American Rose Society probably would not now be in existence. Among the early workers to whom much credit should be given, no name stands out more prominently than does that of our President, Benjamin Hammond. He has served the Society faithfully for many years, gave both his time and money to support the organization, and he is now entitled to all the honors the Society can bestow. To the earnest efforts, also, of Messrs. Pennock, Pierson, Farenwald, and the other eight ex-presidents, the success of the Society today may be directly attributed. The rose may well be taken as a symbol of health and longevity, as but two of the former presidents have died during the nineteen years of the Society's history.

The funds of the Society are now on a firm basis, but it must not be forgotten that its running expenses have increased manyfold in the last two years. Financing the Annual is not as simple a matter as it was, and with an increased cost along all lines of publication and a decrease in advertising because of the war conditions, the increase in membership dues does not insure a wide margin of profit for the Society. Again, the postage on Annuals, notices of memberships due and receipts for the same, amounts to no small item.

"Progress and service" has been the watchword of the Society during the year passed. We must look forward to greater service in the year to come. The Society must do more than furnish tickets for exhibitions and the Rose Annual, if it is to satisfy its members, especially the amateurs. In 1917 arrangements were made with Cornell University to frank copies of Dr. A. C. Beal's Reading Course Bulletin on the "Culture of Garden Roses" to all members, and plans are now made with the Bureau of Plant Industry, Washington, D. C., to frank a similar bulletin written by Mr. F. L. Mulford. It ought to be possible for the Society to publish a "Manual of Rose Culture," which should go to every member. The editor of the Rose Annual and Mr. C. E. F. Gersdorff of Washington, D. C., are preparing a catalogue of roses in American commerce which the Society should soon publish for the benefit of its members.

One or two events of progress stand out prominently during the year. Our English friends have drawn into closer relationship with us by an exchange of honorary memberships. In December, 1917, Mr. Courtney Page, Hon. Secretary of the National Rose Society of England, wrote, offering honorary membership in the National Rose Society of England to the President, Secretary, and Treasurer of the American Rose Society, and to the Editor of the American Rose Annual, in exchange for honorary membership in the American Rose Society for the President, Vice-President, Secretary, and Treasurer of the National Rose Society of England. The Executive Committee felt justified in accepting the proposal and extended to our ally the appreciation of the Society for the honors.

It is to be regretted that, because of the lack of funds due to war conditions, the rose-disease work had to be given up. Dr. L. M. Massey had but just begun to get results along the line of a valuable piece of work. It is hoped that as soon as the war is over the Bureau of Plant Industry at Washington, D. C., will find it possible to take up the investigation in coöperation with the American Rose Society. The scope of the work is too broad to be financed by private individuals, and it should be a part of governmental research.

In the year before us, two important meetings are scheduled. The first will be in Hartford, Conn., during the last of June, at a date yet to be definitely decided upon. This event should be an important one in the history of the Society, for Hartford was a pioneer in rose test-garden work, and the results of the added years of experience should bring much of value to every rosarian. There should be a large attendance.

An invitation has been accepted by the Executive Committee for the Society to hold its fall meeting with the Pittsburgh Florists' and Gardeners' Association, in connection with their flower show. The Society has not been to Pittsburgh for a number of years, and this should bring a large number of members together. Pittsburgh is noted for its hospitality.

The last year has been one of progress, but it is hoped that the coming year may witness even better things for the American Rose Society. The Society desires to be of service to its members in every way possible, and one of the greatest aims at the present time should be to strengthen and cheer our American people in this period of national stress. Can anything make us more physically fit than the beauty and freshness of a rose? There must be periods of recreation; and let us keep ourselves physically fit among the natural pleasures and beauties God has intended for us. E. A. WHITE, *Secretary*.

TREASURER'S REPORT
For Year Ending March 14, 1918
RECEIPTS

Cash on hand	$1,854 70
From Secretary and other sources	6,314 52
Interest on mortgage certificates	150 00
Interest on permanent fund	18 89
Interest on general account	29 52
	$8,367 63

DISBURSEMENTS

Rose Annual and printing	$2,366 33	
General expenses	4,217 45	
Deposit permanent fund	50 00	
		6,633 78
To balance		1,733 85
		$8,367 63

PERMANENT FUND

Westchester and Bronx Title and Mortgage Guaranty Co.	
Three mortgage certificates	$3,000 00
Summit Trust Company	
Permanent Fund	300 00
Hubbard Medal Fund	250 00

HARRY O. MAY, *Treasurer*.

Reports of progress in the various rose test-gardens were made by Mr. Robert Pyle for the Washington, D. C., and the Portland, Ore., gardens; Dr. A. C. Beal for the Cornell Garden at Ithaca, N. Y.; and Mr. W. R. Pierson for the Hartford, Conn., garden. Detailed reports of the work of these gardens will be printed in the American Rose Annual which is soon to be issued. Mr. J. Horace McFarland, of Harrisburg, made a strong plea for coördination in the annual report of the test-gardens, and the opinion was expressed that the chairman of each garden should constitute the personnel of the Central Rose Test-Garden Committee. It was moved and carried that the President nominate members of the various rose test-garden committees and that this list be submitted to the Executive Committee for adoption.

Dr. A. C. Beal, chairman of the committee appointed to draw up rules and eguat ons or the exhibition of garden roses, read a detailed report which was

PLATE XI. E. G. Hill's New Hybrid Tea Rose, MADAME BUTTERFLY,
a sport of Ophelia
(Registered with American Rose Society, 1918)

referred to the Executive Committee with power. Mr. Robert Pyle, for the Committee on Registration, reported favorably on the registration of the following: Mrs. Edward T. Stotesbury, proposed by Edward Towill, Roslyn, Pa.; Victory, and Freedom by Reinhold Undritz, West New Brighton, N. Y.

A committee consisting of F. L. Atkins, Rutherford, N. J.; Robert Chase, Chase, Ala.; and John H. Dayton, Painesville, Ohio, was appointed to increase the interest in the work of the American Rose Society and to solicit memberships among nurserymen.

Executive Committee Meetings

Four meetings of the Executive Committee have been held since the publication of the 1918 American Rose Annual, with an average attendance of six members.

Hotel Collingwood, New York City, March 14, 1918.

Plans for the outdoor meeting to be held at the Hartford Rose Test-Garden, June 20, 1918, were discussed. W. R. Pierson reported that enough plants had been donated to fill the Convention Garden, and that he anticipated a good exhibition of garden varieties.

Letters were read from Maj. Spencer S. Sullinger, of Tacoma, Wash., regarding a rose test-garden for that city, and the Secretary was instructed to write Major Sullinger that when enough members of the American Rose Society had been secured in that section to strongly back the movement and to solicit roses from that vicinity for the garden, the American Rose Society would be glad to coöperate.

After a discussion of the report of the committee appointed June 22, 1916, to arrange a set of rules and a tentative set of prizes for amateur shows, the meeting adjourned.

Office of the Pennsylvania Horticultural Society, Finance Building, Philadelphia, Pa., May 10, 1918.

A request was received from the Flower Show Association of the Main Line, Philadelphia, for one silver and two bronze medals from the American Rose Society for their amateur rose show. The organization did not affiliate with the American Rose Society for 1918. The following action was taken:

Resolved, That in cases where there are not less than five annual members of the American Rose Society included in the membership of a local organization, the Secretary may supply a set of one silver and two bronze medals for use at a rose show, provided that the judging at the show is conducted according to the rules of the American Rose Society, and provided, also, that $20 is paid in advance for such medals and for their engraving.

Mr. J. Horace McFarland presented a financial statement regarding the cost of publishing the 1918 American Rose Annual. A comparison was made with the cost of previous editions. Considering the increased expense of all printing material over that of 1916 and 1917, the total expense to the Society was very satisfactory. The Committee expressed their appreciation of the splendid work Mr. McFarland has done for the Society, both in publishing the Annual and in advancing the scope of the work, especially with amateur members. Mr. McFarland suggested that the Society should, in the immediate future, prepare a rose catalogue which should include all roses in commerce, and that the Society should also send to its members a manual of rose cultivation.

The following exchange of membership was voted: "That the American Rose Society extend to the International Garden Club honorary memberships for the President, Vice-President, and Editor, in exchange for honorary memberships in the International Garden Club for the President and Secretary of the American Rose Society and for the Editor of the American Rose Annual."

It was suggested that there should be a definite campaign to get members for the American Rose Society, particularly among nurserymen and florists, and it was voted that J. Horace McFarland should present at the Convention of the American Association of Nurserymen at Chicago, June 26 and 27, a paper on "A Greater Interest by Nurserymen and Florists in the American Rose Society and Its Work."

The Secretary stated that the membership to date was 1,256, and the Treasurer reported a balance on hand of $1,800.

Pond House, Elizabeth Park, Hartford, Conn., June 20, 1918.

Mr. J. Horace McFarland was elected editor of the publications of the American Rose Society, and definite arrangements were made with the J. Horace McFarland Co. for the publication of the 1919 American Rose Annual.

The question of the publication of a catalogue of roses and also a manual on the cultivation of roses was discussed, and it was the opinion of the Committee that these publications should be delayed until after the period of the war.

President Hammond nominated the following members of the committee governing rose test-gardens:

Central Committee: Robert Pyle, West Grove, Pa.; J. F. Huss, Hartford, Conn.; A. C. Beal, Ithaca, N. Y.; Theodore Wirth, Minneapolis, Minn.; J. A. Currey, Portland, Ore.

It was the understanding of the Executive Committee that the Central Committee would elect its own chairman. A postal vote mailed later from the Secretary's office elected Robert Pyle, West Grove, Pa., chairman.

The following were appointed to the other committees:

The Arlington Garden, Washington, D. C.: Robert Pyle, West Grove, Pa.; William F. Gude, Washington, D. C.; Dr. D. W. Shoemaker, Tacoma Park, D. C.; Charles E. F. Gersdorff, Washington, D. C.; F. L. Mulford, United States Department of Agriculture, Washington, D. C.; Joseph Ralph, Washington, D. C.

Hartford Test-Garden: J. F. Huss, Hartford, Conn.; Alexander Cumming, Jr., Cromwell, Conn.; Wallace R. Pierson, Cromwell, Conn.

Cornell Test-Garden: Prof. A. C. Beal, Ithaca, N. Y.; Dr. Edmund M. Mills, Syracuse, N. Y.; Prof. E. A. White, Ithaca, N. Y.

Minneapolis Rose Test-Garden: Theodore Wirth, Superintendent of Parks, Minneapolis, Minn.; Olaf J. Olson, St. Paul, Minn.; Hugh Will, St. Paul, Minn.

Portland Test-Garden: J. A. Currey, Portland, Ore.; A. J. Clark, Portland, Ore.; Alfred Tucker, Portland, Ore.

A letter to President Hammond from Theodore Wirth, Superintendent of Parks, Minneapolis, Minn., was read. Superintendent Wirth urged that the American Rose Society take a more active interest in the support of the Minneapolis Rose Test-Garden, and requested that an effort be made to secure larger contributions to it.

At the last meeting of the Executive Committee it was voted that Mr. McFarland should urge the nurserymen at their coming convention in Chicago to take a keener interest in the work of the American Rose Society, especially as it affected their business so vitally. Because of the illness of Mr. McFarland, it was understood that Mr. O. P. Beckley, advertising agent of the Rose Annual, would take Mr. McFarland's place on the program; and it was the opinion of the Committee that he should request the nurserymen, especially those of the Central States, to contribute material for trial at the Minneapolis Rose Test-

Garden. The Secretary was instructed to write Mr. McFarland to this effect, and also to write Mr. Wirth.

The Executive Committee authorized the Secretary in his next communication to the members of the American Rose Society to state that the Department of Floriculture, at Cornell University, Ithaca, N. Y., is prepared to make zinc labels of varieties of roses, and that they would supply these to local rose societies or individuals at a cost of $1.25 per hundred. Similar labels have already been furnished members of the Syracuse Rose Society and the Auburn Rose Society.

Office of the Secretary of the Society of American Florists and Ornamental Horticulturists, 1170 Broadway, New York City, October 24, 1918.

Mr. E. G. Hill, of Richmond, Ind., was present and was voted the full privileges of membership in the Committee for the meeting.

Mr. Pyle gave a brief report of the convention of the American Nurserymen held in Chicago, July 26, 1918. At a previous meeting it was voted that Mr. McFarland should at this meeting urge a keener interest of the nurserymen in the work of the American Rose Society, inasmuch as it affected their business vitally. Mr. McFarland was prevented by illness from being present at the meeting, therefore Mr. Pyle took the opportunity of speaking in the interests of the work of the American Rose Society and urged the nurserymen to take a more active interest in the work of the rose test-gardens being conducted under the direction of the American Rose Society. He also urged that there be a larger registration of members of the Nurserymen's Association in the membership of the American Rose Society.

A letter was read from Mr. J. Horace McFarland, telling of his work on the Commission on Living Conditions of War Workers at Washington, D. C., and also discussing the rose test-garden at Arlington.

It was proposed that a little later in the year the Executive Committee express to the Washington officials their confidence in the work of the garden and to ask that every effort be made to keep the garden in the best state of cultivation, and that it be put under the direction of an experienced rose-grower.

The time and place of the Society's annual meeting and the exhibitions which the Society would hold during the coming year were discussed. Because of the uncertainty caused by war conditions, it was voted to lay these topics on the table for consideration at a later meeting. The opinion was expressed that if no exhibition was held by the Society in March, 1919, it would be well to postpone the annual meeting until a June outdoor meeting would be held at some rose-garden.

A letter from Mr. Wilfred Rolker, of New York City, in regard to the attitude which the Executive Committee would take on the proposed exclusion of foreign plants from importation, was read and discussed, but no definite action was taken.

A letter from Mr. N. R. Diemond, of Vaughan's Nursery, in regard to the registration of the Hybrid Wichuraiana rose, Columbia, by the Hoopes, Bro. & Thomas Company in 1906, and the duplication of the name for the Hybrid Tea registered by the E. G. Hill Company in 1917, was also read. It was the opinion that if there were objections to the registration of the Columbia rose by the E. G. Hill Company, they should have been made at the time the registration was published in the trade papers. All roses registered by the American Rose Society are published through the trade journals with the statement that, if objections are not received within three weeks from the date of publication, the registration will stand. The opinion was expressed in the Committee that those in charge of the registration should make every possible effort to prevent the duplication of names, and especially should they keep closely in touch with the varieties registered by European rose societies so there would be no duplication of names in the American lists.

A resolution was read from Mrs. H. A. Vivian, Vice-president of the Park Garden Club of Flushing, L. I., asking the American Rose Society to adopt some method to change the names of varieties of roses bearing German or Teutonic names. The Secretary was instructed to write Mrs. Vivian that, in the opinion of the Executive Committee, such an action would not be practical at the present time, as it would create great confusion in the trade and would have a tendency to discriminate against individuals who have originated varieties of roses which now bear German names. The Committee confirmed the opinion expressed by the American Gladiolus Society "that there is a natural disinclination on the part of the general public to buy varieties with German names, and that in the natural course of things these varieties will be gradually dropped, if not already supplanted by other varieties of superior merit bearing unobjectionable names."

The Secretary was instructed to ask the Editor of the American Rose Annual to arrange, if possible, with all nurserymen dealing with varieties of roses to insert membership coupons in their 1919 catalogues, as it was felt that this was one of the best possible means of securing new members.

Fourth Annual Field Day, Washington, D. C., May 27, 1918

A larger number of commercial florists than usual met in Washington on this date because of the combined Field Day at the Rose Test-Garden in Arlington and the hearing before the Fuel Administration regarding the coal situation for the coming winter. After the delegates had been cordially welcomed by the Florists' Club of Washington, they were taken in automobiles to the rose-gardens. The date was somewhat late for the best display, but many attractive varieties were in flower. The judges for the day were Messrs. Leonard Barron, Julius Roehrs, and Charles E. F. Gersdorff. Their report was as follows:

Climbers having special merit: Flower of Fairfield, Pearl Queen, Silver Moon, Oriole, American Pillar, Queen Alexandra, Rubin, Wartburg, Mrs. F. W. Flight, Dr. W. Van Fleet, Graf Zeppelin, Goldfinch, Andreas Hofer, Climbing American Beauty, Countess M. H. Chotek, Bess Lovett, and Dazzling Red.

Teas and Hybrid Teas of special merit: Laurent Carle, Gruss an Teplitz, Mary, Countess of Ilchester, Mme. Paul Euler, Mrs. George W. Kershaw, Cook's Seedling 512, Mme. Leon Pain, Lady Ashtown, Mme. Maurice de Luze, Pink Killarney, Lady Alice Stanley, Kaiserin Augusta Victoria, British Queen, Mrs. Wakefield Christie-Miller, La Tosca, Lady Ursula, Colonel R. S. Williamson, Climbing Teplitz, White Killarney, and Mrs. A. R. Waddell.

Reëntering the automobiles, the party returned to the city where a luncheon was held at the Ebbitt House. After luncheon the committee appointed earlier in the day to appear before the Fuel Administrator made a report. Prof. L. C. Corbett, representing the Department of Agriculture, spoke of the work at the rose test-gardens and extended an invitation to all rose-growers to call upon the Department for assistance when facing problems which they had difficulty in solving. Wallace R. Pierson extended an invitation for all present to come to Hartford, Conn., for the outdoor meeting in Elizabeth Park, June 20.

A hearty vote of thanks was extended to the florists of Washington for their cordial hospitality.

Again the automobiles were taken for a visit to the rose-garden at Twin Oaks, the home of Mrs. J. C. Bell. Mrs. Bell is the daughter of the late Mrs. Gardner Hubbard, who donated the Hubbard Medal for new roses of meritorious qualities. The party was personally greeted by Mrs. Bell, who left other pressing engagements to welcome the rosarians. Refreshments were served, after which the party was shown through the gardens by G. E. Anderson.

The return to the city was made through Rock Creek Park, one of the most beautiful of natural parks. The afternoon was spent at the National Botanic Gardens as the guests of George Wesley Hess, the superintendent.

The Garden Exhibit at Elizabeth Park Rose Test-Gardens, Hartford, Conn., June 20, 1918

Cloudless skies, a brisk, clear atmosphere, and most cordial hospitality greeted the members of the American Rose Society at Hartford on Thursday, June 20.

The local committee, consisting of Messrs. Pierson, Huss, and Cumming, had been most thoughtful in anticipating every detail of a plan to make the day an eventfu lone in the annals of the Society. The Executive Committee of the Society held a session in Pond House, Elizabeth Park, at 10 o'clock, after which the Committee and other guests were entertained at luncheon at Hotel Bond by W. R. Pierson, of Cromwell, Conn.

After luncheon the party was conveyed to the famous rose-gardens at Elizabeth Park. The attendance was disappointing, for notices of the meeting had been quite widely distributed, but those in attendance felt well repaid for the trip. The Hybrid Perpetual, Tea and Hybrid Tea roses were at their best, but the climbers were not yet in their full beauty.

In the older part of the garden, beds of Radiance, Killarney Queen, Miss Cynthia Forde, Frau Karl Druschki, Laurent Carle and George Arends were especially good, while the climbers—American Pillar, Christine Wright, Purity, Leuchstern and Excelsa—were full of bloom and much admired.

In the newer part of the garden there were forty-two beds, each filled with a variety donated by some individual or firm which, in the opinion of the donor, was the most desirable of available varieties. The single Hybrid Tea, Isobel, donated by A. N. Pierson, Inc., Rosalind and Silvia, by F. R. Pierson Co., Mme. Leon Pain and Miss Cynthia Forde, by H. A. Dreer, Inc., were among those especially noted.

In the rose test-garden, the judges, consisting of Prof. Frank A. Waugh, Amherst, Mass.; S. S. Pennock, Philadelphia, Pa.; and Robert Pyle, West Grove, Pa., scored the Hybrid Teas as follows: John Cook's seedling No. 512, 86 points, which, therefore, received the silver medal of the American Rose Society; John Cook's seedling No. 561, 82 points, thereby awarding it a certificate of merit; Bertram J. Walker, 74 points; Mrs. George Gordon, 73 points.

Eighty-two points and a certificate of merit were awarded the climbing rose, Aunt Harriet, introduced by The Conard & Jones Co., West Grove, Pa.; 72 points to Wartburg, introduced by the same firm, by a committee consisting of Prof. Frank A. Waugh, S. S. Pennock, and W. R. Pierson.

After the judging the party was piloted in automobiles through Hartford's splendid park system by George A. Parker, Superintendent of Parks; Mr. Turner, Superintendent of Connecticut State Parks; Thomas Snell Weaver, Park Commissioner; and George Hollister, Superintendent of Keney Park. Leaving Elizabeth Park with its somewhat formal style of gardening, Keney Park was first visited. This comprises about 660 acres of natural landscape, with open meadows where grazed herds of sheep, tended in a picturesque way by shepherds and dogs. Here broad vistas were also striking, and the winding drives through deep wooded areas, carpeted with rank growths of ferns, were most restful. Passing through the city by the Keney Memorial and South Green, Colt Park was next visited. Here the spirit of play was most in evidence, and the park was filled with hundreds of boys and girls, young men and women engaged in all sorts of recreation. Goodwin Park, another area of natural landscape, was interesting because it was used largely as municipal golf-links. At Overlook the party stopped and were treated to soft drinks by the genial Superintendent of Parks. Pope Park, a recreation park with ideal playgrounds, in a section of the city where most of the homes were of the poorer class, was motored through on the return to Elizabeth Park.

At 6 o'clock the party was entertained at a delightful dinner in Pond House given by the Hartford Park Department. After the dinner Thomas Snell Weaver and George A. Parker, of the Park Department, expressed in a few well-chosen words the welcome of this department to the American Rose Society. Benjamin Hammond, President, responded, voicing the appreciation of the American Rose Society for the most generous hospitality extended to its members by the flower-lovers of Hartford.

At 7.30 P.M. the guests and citizens of Hartford listened to a delightful lecture in the Municipal Building on "Outdoor Roses," by Robert Pyle, of West Grove, Pa. Mr. Pyle showed many beautifully colored slides of rose-gardens in America and abroad, and also the various types and varieties of roses. The lecturer's personal acquaintance with many of the most noted rosarians abroad made his talk full of interest. Following Mr. Pyle's lecture, Professor Waugh, of the Massachusetts Agricultural College, gave an interesting and instructive illustrated lecture on "Civic Improvement."

Rules for Registration of New Roses

Any member of the American Rose Society who is an originator of a new rose may register the variety with the American Rose Society without charge for registration. The name of the rose must be given (a number is not sufficient), together with a full description and pedigree of such rose, and this registration shall be considered by the American Rose Society's Executive Committee. It shall then be published in one or more of the trade papers. If no objection to such registration is filed with the Secretary of the Society within three weeks after such publication, the registration shall become permanent. In the event of objection to registration, the decision will rest with the Executive Committee. No description of any variety shall be published by the American Rose Society without the sanction of the Executive Committee. Any person not a member of the American Rose Society may register a new rose upon payment of $3 for each variety so registered.

Adopted at Executive Committee meeting of November 10, 1913, held in New York City.

Registration of New Roses in 1918

From Frederick R. M. Undritz, West New Brighton, Staten Island, N. Y., April 6, 1918:

Victory. H.W. Dr. W. Van Fleet × Mme. Jules Grolez. In color darker than Dr. W. Van Fleet, more double, and with stiffer petals; has better keeping qualities. More vigorous in its habit of growth than Mme. Jules Grolez, and has longer stems, making it more valuable for cut-flowers. It is free from disease, retaining its glossy foliage all summer.

Freedom (Climbing White American Beauty). H.W. Silver Moon × Kaiserin Augusta Victoria. A hardy disease-resistant variety, similar to Kaiserin Augusta Victoria, but of more vigorous growth and greater freedom of bloom. It is much more double than Silver Moon, with but a single flower to a stem. Has excellent keeping qualities.

From Edward Towill, Roslyn, Pa., April 6, 1918:

Mrs. E. T. Stotesbury. H.T. A seedling of Joseph Hill and My Maryland × Milady. A free-flowering variety, light pink in color, shaded to darker pink. The flower is heavier, and the foliage better than Mrs. George Shawyer, which it resembles. It has excellent keeping qualities.

From Thomas N. Cook, Boston, Mass., June 15, 1918:

Bonnie Prince. W. Tausendschön × unnamed seedling. A free-flowering white variety, similar to Mme. Alfred Carriere, but having larger and fuller flowers, and a more prolific habit of bloom. Period of bloom long.

From Martin & Forbes, Portland, Ore., June 15, 1918:

May Martin. H.T. Sport of Ophelia. Similar to Ophelia in general character, but having a mustard-yellow color. A free-flowering variety with excellent keeping qualities.

From The Conard & Jones Company, West Grove, Pa., August 10, 1918:

Aunt Harriet. H.W. Appoline × *Rosa Wichuraiana.* This variety is quite distinct from others of the type, and superior because of the intense brilliancy of coloring, its hardiness, fine foliage, and ease of culture. The color is a rich crimson with a white eye; it is semi-double and very free-flowering.

From Clarke Brothers, Portland, Ore., September 7, 1918:

Mrs. John C. Ainsworth. H.T. Sport of Mrs. Charles Russell. The bloom is a light rose-pink color, very full and fragrant. It has remarkable keeping qualities and is more vigorous and more easily propagated than Mrs. Charles Russell. (See Plate III, facing page 24.)

From M. H. Walsh, Woods Hole, Mass., November 30, 1918:

Nokomis. W. *R. Wichuraiana* × Comte de Raimbaud. A dark rose-pink variety with larger flowers than Lady Gay or Dorothy Perkins, borne in clusters of twenty-five to thirty. Flower double and very fragrant. Superior to other varieties because of its hardiness, perfect foliage, and size of bloom.

From the E. G. Hill Company, Richmond, Ind., November 30, 1918:

Victor. H.T. Ophelia × Killarney Brilliant. Flowers large, deep rose or often red in color, semi-double. The bud is extremely long and has a strong fragrance; has full petals and is a good keeper. The variety is similar to Killarney Brilliant, but shows improvement in size.

Golden Rule. H.T. Ophelia × Sunburst. This variety is similar to Ophelia in all characteristics but is clear yellow in color. It is a stronger grower than Sunburst.

Madame Butterfly. H.T. Ophelia sport. Similar to Ophelia in all characteristics, except that the color is greatly intensified. (See Plate XI, facing page 152.)

American Rose Society Medals and Certificates for Novelties

A Gold Medal is offered for the best new rose not yet disseminated, whether of domestic or foreign origin. Exhibits are to be judged upon the official scale of the Society, and no Gold Medal is to be awarded to any rose scoring less than 95 points.

A Silver Medal is offered at the same time, and under the same conditions, for a novelty scoring not less than 85 points.

A Certificate of Merit is to be awarded to all novelties scoring 80 points.

It is further ordered that the complete scores of all the entries in the competition be filed with the Secretary of the American Rose Society before the award of any medal is confirmed. No duplicate medal will be awarded. It is understood that though the award of the Gold or Silver Medal or Certificate may be made to the same variety from one exhibitor, exhibited in different centers, only one medal will be delivered to the exhibitor.

The Executive Committee of the American Rose Society reserves to itself the right of selection of the judges who shall pass upon the exhibits in the competition for these medals.

Medals Awarded in 1918

Silver Medals—
John Cook, Baltimore, Md.: Seedling No. 550; score 88 points. International Flower Show, New York City, March 14–21.
John Cook, Baltimore, Md.: Seedling No. 512; score 86 points. Exhibit of Garden Roses, Elizabeth Park, Hartford, Conn., June 20.
The E. G. Hill Company, Richmond, Ind.: Columbia; score 86 points. International Flower Show, New York City, March 14–21.
J. A. Frank Neal, Syracuse, N. Y.: Best collection of garden roses, Syracuse Rose Society, June 13.
Mrs. Horatio Gales Lloyd: Best collection Hybrid Tea roses. Exhibit of Flower Show Association of the Main Line, Haverford, Pa., June 12.
Syracuse Rose Society: Best Exhibit Garden Roses at New York State Fair, Syracuse, N. Y., September.

Bronze Medals—
Mrs. E. B. Van Wagenen: Exhibit of garden roses, Syracuse Rose Society, June 13.
James M. Gilbert: Exhibit of garden roses, Syracuse Rose Society, June 13.
J. L. Eysman: Best six blooms of garden roses, Flower Show Association of the Main Line, Haverford, Pa., June 12.
Robert C. Wright: Best five named varieties Tea roses, Flower Show Association of the Main Line, Haverford, Pa., June 12.

Certificates—
F. R. Pierson Co., Tarrytown, N. Y.: Silvia; score 80 points. International Flower Show, New York City, March 14–21.
F. R. Pierson Co., Tarrytown, N. Y.: Rosalind; score 81 points. International Flower Show, New York City, March 14–21.
John Cook, Baltimore, Md.: Seedling No. 561; score 82 points. Exhibit of garden roses, Elizabeth Park, Hartford, Conn., June 20.
The Conard & Jones Co., West Grove, Pa.: Aunt Harriet; score 82 points. Exhibit of garden roses, Elizabeth Park, Hartford, Conn., June 20.

Special Prizes Awarded in 1918

Given by Mrs. Hobart Warren: Fifty dollars for the best red rose not disseminated. Awarded to A. N. Pierson, Inc., for Mrs. Henry Winnett. International Flower Show, New York City, March 14–21.

Special Prizes Available for 1919

The Mrs. Gertrude M. Hubbard Gold Medal to be awarded every five years to the raiser or originator of the best American rose within the five years previous to the award. The medal was awarded in 1914 to M. H. Walsh, Woods Hole, Mass., for Excelsa.

Two Silver Medals from the Toronto Horticultural Society to be awarded as the Executive Committee of the American Rose Society shall direct.

Regulations and Scale of Points for Judging Blooms and Plants

The official scale of 100 points for judging roses is as follows: Floriferousness, 20; vigor, 20; color, 15; size, 15; form, 10; substance, 10; fragrance, 10.

A variety shall be considered undisseminated which cannot be exhibited other than by the introducer.

All roses shall be disqualified where exhibited with more than two growths (one pinch), except in classes calling for displays and for 100 or more blooms in one vase, on which two pinches are allowed.

Rules for judging groups of rose plants.—Size of group or collection, 20; distinctiveness, 15; cultural perfection, 20; number of varieties, 20; arrangement and effect, 25.

Single specimen rose plants.—Size of plants, 20; cultural perfection, 25; floriferousness, 20; foliage, 15; quality of bloom, 10; color of bloom, 10.

All exhibits of cut-flowers will be judged by points in accordance with the following official scale:

Competitive classes.—Size, 15; color, 20; stem, 20; form, 15; substance, 15; foliage, 15.

Novelties for certificates, etc.—Size, 10; color, 20; stem, 15; form, 15; substance, 10; foliage, 15; fragrance, 5; distinctiveness, 10.

Scale of points for judging displays of cut roses.—Quality, 50; variety, 20; artistic arrangement, 30.

Affiliation of Local Societies with the American Rose Society

Any local organization interested in roses may affiliate with the American Rose Society upon the payment of one dollar for each member, providing that such payment of dues be made to the Secretary of the American Rose Society before February 1 of each year, in order to provide for the required number of Annuals. Such members will receive all rights and privileges received by regular members, and the Society thus affiliating will receive one silver and two bronze medals to be awarded as special American Rose Society prizes at their annual exhibitions. The following organizations were affiliated in 1918, the figures following the names indicating the number of members:

The Syracuse Rose Society, 22; Auburn Rose Society, 9; and the Columbus Horticultural Society, 13.

Members American Rose Society

*Life Member; †Honorary Member; ‡Affiliated Member

Abbott, Donald B., 68 Williams St., New York City.
Acton, Miss Sarah T., Saybrook, Conn.
Adam, Mrs. G. G., 160 St. George St., Toronto, Ont.
‡Adams, Charles G., 10 Nelson St., Auburn, N. Y.
Adams, Mrs. Horatio M., Glen Cove, N. Y.
Adams, Mrs. John D., Box 295, Bayshore, Long Island, N. Y.
Ahern, James J., 218 S. 15th St., Philadelphia.
Alcock, William A., 44 Wall St., New York City.
Alexander, Miss J., 19 Craig Ave., Piedmont, Calif.
Allcott, H. P., 727 Hemlock St., Avalon, Pa.
Allen, G. F., Richmond Hill, Ont.
Allerton, Mrs. S. W., Highland St., S., Pasadena, Calif.
Allyn, O. D., 281 Locust St., Holyoke, Mass.
Alter, Mrs. Louise, 935 N. 29th St., Philadelphia.
Amber, Bertram, 5206a Page Ave., St. Louis, Mo.
Ambruster, Henry, 88 Grant Ave., Brooklyn, N. Y.
*American Florist Co., 440 S. Dearborn St., Chicago.
Amling, Ernest C., Maywood, Ill.
Ammann, J. F., Edwardsville, Ill.
Anderson, Mrs. Edwin, 45 Greene Ave., Madison, N. J.
Anderson, William W., 717 Anita Ave., Houston, Tex.
Andre, H. F., 958 Berkshire Ave., South Hills Branch, Pittsburgh, Pa.
Andrus, Miss Pansy, Dann St., Miami, Fla.
Anspon, B. W., Maryland Agricultural College, College Park, Md.
Araujo, Fausto, Calle 54, Numero 489, Merida, Yucatan, Mexico.
Armfield, C. G., Elkin, N. C.
Armstrong, Dr. J. H., Belding, Mich.
Armstrong, Thos. H., Woodman Road, Rochester, N. Y.
Armstrong, W. J., 749 Beulah Ave., Milwaukee, Wis.
Arthur, J. W., 509 Euclid Ave., Lynchburg, Pa.
Ashton, Miss Antoinette, 30 Buell Place, East Elmhurst, Corona, N. Y.
*Asmus, A. E., West Hoboken, N. J.
Aspinwall, John, Newburgh, N. Y.
Atherholt, Samuel T., Box 923, Narberth, Pa.
Atkins, F. L., Rutherford, N. J.
Atkinson, Mrs. T. O., Doylestown, Pa.
*Auchincloss, Mrs. H. D., 33 E. 67th St., New York City, and Newport, R. I.

Ayer, Mrs. Edward, 2 Bank St., Chicago.
Ayers, Charles H., Peoples State Bank, Detroit, Mich.

Bachman, Frank H., 1512 Chestnut St., Philadelphia.
Bacon, Maurice M., 200 N. Pearl St., Bridgeton, N. J.
Bailey, Frank, 175 Remsen St., Brooklyn, N. Y.
Bailey, J. E., 4549 Ditman St., Frankford, Philadelphia.
Bailey, Joseph, Patchogue, N. Y.
Bailey, Dr. L. H., Sage Place, Ithaca, N. Y.
Bain, Robert E. M., 1101 Locust St., (Southwestern Passenger Agent), St. Louis, Mo.
Bair, George J., 406 Fourth Ave., Haddon Heights, N. J.
Baker, Mrs. Alfred T., Lower Nassau St., Princeton, N. J.
Baker, K. S., 336 Arch St., Marquette, Mich.
Baker, Miss M. A., 12 S. Mole St., Philadelphia.
Bakewell, Roland R., 322 S. Boulevard, Spring Lake, N. J.
Balch, John, 50 Olive St., Boston, Mass.
Balcom, H. Tracy, 1193 Delaware Ave., Buffalo, N. Y.
Baldwin, Penrose, 10 Biltmore Ave., Asheville, N. C.
Baldwin, S. P., 2930 Prospect Ave., Cleveland, Ohio.
Balken, Mrs. Edward Duff, 2 Colonial Place, Pittsburgh, Pa.
Ball, T. Austin, 25 Melrose Place, Montclair, N. J.
Ballinger, John, National Library of Wales, Aberystwyth, Wales.
Bancroft, A. F., Essington, Delaware County, Pa.
Barber, Frank, 822 Berkeley Ave., Trenton, N. J.
Barclay, F. H., 209 E. Fayette St., Baltimore, Md.
Barclay, Hugh, Merion, Pa.
Barclay, W. P., 424 Grove St., Westfield, N. J.
Barlow, Mrs. John W., 127 Federal St., New London, Conn.
Barmore, Charles, 31 Nassau St., New York City.
Barnard, Miss Mary, 288 Burns Ave., Detroit, Mich.
Barnes, Miss Anne H., 1727 Spruce St., Philadelphia.
Barnes, Mrs. George W., 110 Onondaga Ave., Syracuse, N. Y.
Barnes, Miss Katharine, Ridgefield, Conn.
Barron, Leonard, Garden City, Long Island, N. Y.
Barrow, John, 122 E. 83d St., New York City.

MEMBERS AMERICAN ROSE SOCIETY 163

Barry, Charles D., 83 S. Fullerton Ave., Montclair, N. J.
Barry, Mrs. E. T., 447 Audubon St., New Orleans, La.
Barthelenghi, Peter, 1497 E. 15th St., Brooklyn, N. Y.
Bartholomay, Miss Catharine, 1455 North State Parkway, Chicago.
Bartholomay, Henry, 1205 First National Bank Bldg., Chicago.
Bartholomew, Charles P., Orlando, Fla.
*Basset, O. P., Pasadena, Calif.
Bate, W. G., 227 High St., Cleveland, Ohio.
Bates, H. E., Granite Bldg., Rochester, N. Y.
Bates, Mrs. John E., 24 Summit Ave., Mt. Vernon, N. Y.
Baur, Adolph F. J., Indianapolis, Ind.
Baurhenn, A. L., 124 E. 75th St., New York City.
Baxter, Miss Rachel A., Charlestown, Md.
Bayley, R. DeF., 277 Broadway, New York City.
Beach, J. M., 14 Winthrop Place, Maplewood, N. J.
Beal Dr. A. C., Cornell University, Ithaca, N. Y.
Beale, E. M., Lewisburg, Pa.
Beardsley, Mrs. G. A., 73 Prospect St., East Orange, N. J.
*Beatty, H. B., Farmers Bank Bldg., Pittsburgh, Pa.
Beck, Miss Florence E., 213 Forster St., Harrisburg, Pa.
Becker, Mrs. E. A., 72 Ashland Ave., Buffalo, N. Y.
Beckett, Edwin, Ophir Hall, Purchase, N. Y.
Beckley, O. P., Harrisburg, Pa.
Beddall, E. A., Pottsville, Pa.
‡Bee, Mrs. F. G., 866 S. Champion Ave., Columbus, Ohio.
Beebe, Milton E., 2433 G St., San Diego, Calif.
Beer, Mrs. J. A., 90 Oakland Park Ave., Columbus, Ohio.
Beinemann, R., 1530 N. 10th St., Sheboygan, Wis.
Bell, Robert, 172 Woodward Ave., Buffalo, N. Y.
Bell, Roy M., 111 Park Ave., East Orange, N. J.
Below, F. H., 550 Big Bend Road, Webster Groves, Mo.
Belville, Dr. J. Edgar, 5925 Green St., Germantown, Pa.
Benbow, Rev. Earl W., Hersman, Ill.
Benninghofer, C., 807 Dayton St., Hamilton, Ohio.
Bentz, William P., 6th and Walnut Sts., Philadelphia.
‡Benz, Dr. J. C., 416 Euclid Ave., Syracuse, N. Y.
Bense, George, 438 62nd St., Brooklyn, N. Y.
Bergen, Mrs. A. Beekman, Newtown, Bucks County, Pa.
Beringer, George M., 414 N. 5th St., Camden, N. J.
Berkemeyer, W. C., 4209 Virginia St., Kansas City, Mo.

Bernheimer, Eugene, 1531 Ranstead St., Philadelphia.
Bertram, Henry, Glenholme, Dundas, Ont., Can.
Betscher, C., Dover, Ohio.
Betts, S. T., 332 S. Salina St., Syracuse, N. Y.
Bibb, John T., 2131 N. Prospect St., Tacoma, Wash.
‡Bicknell, LeRoy C., 45 Seminary St., Auburn, N. Y.
Biddle, Mrs. Edward W., Ritten House, Philadelphia.
Bidermann, Mrs. Catherine J. E., 11 Bulwer Place, Highland Boulevard, Brooklyn, N. Y.
Bikli, Mrs. C. E., 119 Clarendon St., Syracuse, N. Y.
Billin, C. W., 1716 First Ave., Altoona, Pa.
Binder, Lorma, Mineral City, Ohio.
Bird, Mrs. A. L., 1904 Prairie Ave., Dallas, Tex.
Bird, Charles S., 27 Early St., Morristown, N. J.
Bissell, Miss Mary C., New Rochelle, N. Y.
Bixby, F. A., 5435 Flor Boulevard, Omaha, Neb.
Black, Frank, Oakland, N. J.
Black, Mrs. J. W., 607 E. Gordon St., Kinston, N. C.
Blackburn, Wade, Larimer, Pa.
Blair, Mrs. Edgar, 6321 Wilson St., Seattle, Wash.
‡Blakeley, C. R., 35 S. 4th St., Columbus, Ohio.
Blakiston, Miss Mary, Fort Washington, Pa.
Blanks, W. C., 310 Trust Bldg., San Angelo, Tex.
Blunt, Mrs. A. C., 196 Franklin Ave., Morristown, N. J.
Bobbink & Atkins, Rutherford, N. J.
Boehler, Oscar, West Hoboken, N. J.
Bogaske, C. J., Macedonia, Ohio.
Boit, Mrs. John, 1701 21st. St., Washington, D. C.
Bok, Edward W., Merion, Pa.
Boltz, Miss Clara M., 328 Pelham Road, Germantown, Philadelphia.
Bond, Mrs. Edwin P., 67 Addison Ave., Rutherford, N. J.
Boner, Roy R., 225 Main St., Evansville, Ind.
Bonnewitz, Lee R., Van Wert, Ohio.
Booth, Dr. A. W., 416 W. Water St., Elmira, N. Y.
Borland, W. P., 1806 Kenyon St., Washington, D. C.
Bosch, Joseph, Lake Linden, Mich.
Bott, Mrs. Fred J., 460 Lebanon St., Melrose, Mass.
Bott, Harry F., Volusia, Fla.
Bott, John B., 317 S. Main St., Greensburg, Pa.
Boyle, Neal E., Malden, Mass.
Boyd, James, Haverford, Pa.
Box, Leonard C., F. R. H. S., P. O. Box 937, Fredericton, New Brunswick, Can.
Bracken, E. F., Paoli, Pa.
Brackett, A. H., 970 Denny Way, Seattle, Wash.

Bradley, Mrs. Edgar L., Jr., Glendower, Albemarle County, Va.
Bradley, Walter M., 520 Whitney Ave., New Haven, Conn.
Bradley, Mrs. Winfield S., 157 Central Ave., Dover, N. H.
Brady, J. W., 29 Walter St., Albany, N. Y.
Brady, W. S., Wheeling, W. Va.
Braecklein, Mrs. Ida, 224 E. 18th St., Paterson, N. J.
Brainard, W. F., 142 Ridgewood Ave., Glen Ridge, N. J.
Brawner, J. E., 3115 Fairmount Ave., Dallas, Tex.
Bray, Dr. C. W., 188 State St., Portland, Me.
*Breitmeyer, Phillip, Hon., Detroit, Mich.
Breth, Edward T., Box 175, Fort Johnston, N. Y.
Bricker, Dr. W. H., 1615 N. Broad St., Philadelphia.
Brigante, Rocco, Care of John F. Talmage, Mendham, N. J.
Brigham, H. H., 398 Park Ave., East Orange, N. J.
Brinton, G. Herbert, 218 S. 20th St., Philadelphia.
Brinton, John C., Camp Hill, Cumberland County, Pa.
‡Brister, Mrs. Chas. W., 34 Franklin St., Auburn, N. Y.
Brockenbrough, Mrs. J. M., Richmond, Va.
Brooks, C. Arthur, Monroe, N. Y.
‡Brown, B. L., 729 Ackerman Ave., Syracuse, N. Y.
Brown, Clarence H., 29 Wall St., Wallingford, Conn.
Brown, F. C. W., Care of J. M. Gasser Co., Cleveland, Ohio.
Brown, George, Cornell St., Auburn, N. Y.
Brown, Hubert R., 70 Fifth Ave., New York City.
Brown, Dr. Godwin M., 483 Beacon St., Boston, Mass.
Brown, Melville C., 319 South St., Utica, N. Y.
Brown, W. E., R. F. D. 1, Wilkinsburg, Pa.
Browne, Henry F., 88 Fulton St., Rahway, N. J.
Brubaker, John D., Box "E," Wyomissing, Pa.
Brucker, Wilhelm, Englewood, N. J.
Brunschweiler, Jos. I., 914 30th St., Sacramento, Calif.
Brush, S. B., Grey Bldg., Wellington St. W., Toronto, Ont.
Brutschin, George, 9216 Manor Ave., Woodhaven, Long Island, N. Y.
Brydon, R. P., 3505 Mayfield Road, Cleveland Heights, Ohio.
Buck, F. E., Central Experimental Farm, Ottawa, Ont.
Buckner, Mrs. E. G., 1308 Delaware Ave., Wilmington, Del.
Budell, Miss Hortense, 627 Fourth Ave., Westfield, N. J.
*Budlong, A. H., 37–39 Randolph St., Chicago.
*Budlong, F. L., 564 Pontiac Ave., Auburn, R. I.
*Budlong, J. A., 564 Pontiac Ave., Auburn, R. I.
*Buettner, E., Park Ridge, Ill.
Burgoyne, W. B., 15 Trafalgar St., St. Catharines, Ont.
Burk, Louis, 3d St. and Girard Ave., Philadelphia.
Burke, Paul F., 20–22 Canal St., Boston, Mass.
Burki, Fred, Gibsonia, Pa.
Burnham, John A., 70 Kilby St., Marblehead, Mass.
Burns, Harvey R., 1142 Lincoln St., Milton, Pa.
Burr, C. R., Manchester, Conn.
Burt, Fred W., 81 Carolina Ave., Providence, R. I.
Burton, Alfred, Chestnut Hill, Philadelphia.
*Burton, George Wyndmoor, Philadelphia.
Burton, John A., Chestnut Hill, Philadelphia.
Burton, Mrs. J. H., Cedarhurst, Long Island, N. Y.
Burton, Mrs. M. E., 708 E. Main St., Massillon, Ohio.
Burus, Edward F., 760 First Ave., New York City.
Busey, C. B., 604 Green St., Urbana, Ill.
Bush, Mr. Philo L., 1812 Park Road, N.W., Washington, D. C.
Busk, F. T., 301 Produce Exchange, New York City.
Busk, W. Hamilton, 71 Broadway, New York City.
Butchart, R. P., Tod Inlet, Victoria, B. C.
Butcher, Thomas P., Box 13, Williamstown, W. Va.
Butler, E. K., 938 Centre St., Jamaica Plain, Mass.
Butler, F. Evelyn, Farmington, Me.
Butler, J. W. S., Box 114, Sacramento, Calif.
Byrider, John, 791 E. Market St., Akron, Ohio.

Cabot, George E., 60 State St., Boston, Mass.
Caden, Miss Alice, Maysville Pike, Lexington, Ky.
Cadman, Miss Lilian, 2 Spencer Place, Brooklyn, N. Y.
Cady, Mrs. George W., Clifton Park, Lakewood, Ohio
Cady, Prof. LeRoy, University Farm, St. Paul, Minn.
Caesar, Mrs. H. A., 630 Park Ave., New York City.
Caill, Harry C. M., Hancock's Bridge, Salem County, N. J.
Caldwell, B. M., Winter Park, Fla.
Caldwell, Mrs. J. E., Bryn Mawr, Pa.
Call, Bert L., Dexter, Me.
Campbell, Alfred M., 1510 Sansom St., Philadelphia.
Campbell, Chester I., 5 Park Square, Boston, Mass.
Campbell, George, 34 Marion Ave., Brockton, Mass.
Campbell, George E., Erdenheim, Pa.
Cameron, Mrs. J. R., 31 Grove St., Westfield, N. Y.

MEMBERS AMERICAN ROSE SOCIETY

Canning, John, Ardsley, N. Y.
Caparn, H. A., 220 W. 42nd St., New York City.
Cariveau, Florence, 1139 Dayton Ave., St. Paul, Minn.
Carman, John, Sewickley Heights, Pa.
Carner, H. M., 1327 Birch St., Richmond Hill, N. Y.
Carpenter, Mrs. Hubbard, Lake Geneva, Wis.
Carroll, C. C., 6801 6th St., N.W., Takoma Park, D. C.
Cartledge, A. B., 1514 Chestnut St., Philadelphia.
Casamajor, Robert, 1551 Diamond Ave., S., Pasadena, Calif.
Case, Miss Marion, Weston, Mass.
Cassler, H. A., 1501 W. Broad St., Bethlehem, Pa.
Castle, Mrs. Northrup, Davenport Neck, New Rochelle, N. Y.
Cate, Dr. A. W., Boise, Idaho.
Chaffee, H. Almon, Care of the A. W. Burritt Co., Bridgeport, Conn.
Chalfont, V. E., LeRoy, Ohio.
Chamberlain, A. H., Rahway, N. J.
Chamberlain, Elisabeth, Chappaqua, N. Y.
Champlin, Mrs. Charles A., P. O. Box 747, Falls Station, Niagara Falls, N. Y.
Chance, Mrs. J. S., 3 Webster Terrace, New Rochelle, N. Y.
Chapman, Edward G., Norway Summit Farm, Rushville, N. Y.
Charles, H. H., 23 E. 26th St., New York City.
Chase, Robert, Chase Nursery Co., Chase, Ala.
Chatillon, Mrs. George H., Sea Bright, N. J.
Cheever, James G., 24 Park St., North Attleboro, Mass.
Chenoweth, E. B., Mt. Vernon Nursery, Mt. Vernon, Washington.
Christine, George, 325 E. Walnut St., Allentown, Pa.
Chrystal, Thomas F., Shippen Point, Stamford, Conn.
‡Clancy, Hon. John R., 822 W. Genesee St., Syracuse, N. Y.
Clark, Mrs. A. I., 38 Kensington Road, Edgewood, R. I.
Clark, Mrs. B. S., 14 E. 60th St., New York City.
Clarke, Miss Abby, 105 Garfield St., Watertown, Mass.
Clark, Mrs. Howard F., Great Neck, Long Island, N. Y.
Clark, Mrs. R. L., 717 Bryan St., Chillicothe, Mo.
Clark, W. O., Chillicothe, Mo.
Clarke, A. J., 287 Morrison St., Portland, Ore.
Clarke, Miss Abby, 105 Garfield St., Watertown, Mass.
Classen, Charles H., 218 Roland Ave., Roland Park, Md.
Clegg, Mrs. George R., R. F. D. 3, Box 23B, Youngstown, Ohio.
Clement, Capt. F. H., Hempstead, Long Island, N. Y.
Cleveland Public Library, Cleveland, Ohio.

Clinton, Frank N., 131 Depew St., Peekskill, N. Y.
Clough, A. B., 487 Boyleston St., Brookline, Mass.
Cluett, G. A., 28 First St., Troy, N. Y.
Cobbs, F. J., 707 N. W. Bank Bldg., Portland, Ore.
Cochrane, Mrs. F. E., 741 Wick Ave., Youngstown, Ohio.
Cocklin, Dr. C. C., 126 Walnut St., Harrisburg, Pa.
Coddington, L. P., Murray Hill, N. J.
Coffin, Mrs. H. N., 1403 Franklin St., Boise, Idaho.
Cohen, Max, 31 W. 27th St., New York City.
Cole, W. B., Painesville, Ohio.
Coles, W. W., Kokomo, Ind.
Collamore, Francis, East Bridgewater, Mass.
Collier, H. L., City Treasurer's Office, Seattle, Wash.
Collins, Frederick N., Summit, N. J.
Colson, W. B., Glen Ridge, N. J.
Colt, Mrs. R. C., Garrison, N. Y.
Colville, Mrs., Hilmarton Lodge, Calne, Wilts, England.
Compton, Mrs. Sarah, 1002 Gladstone Ave., Portland, Ore.
Coney, Mrs. George H., Palisade Ave., Windsor, Conn.
Connell, Herbert N., Box 187, Auburn, Wash.
Conner, Miss M. A., 63 Highland Ave., Montclair, N. J.
Conard, C. Wilfred, Lansdowne, Pa.
Consigny, E. F., 307 10th St., Des Moines, Iowa.
‡Constable, T. G., 1275 Wyandotte Road, Grandview, Columbus, Ohio.
Converse, Mrs. C. C., Magnolia, Mass.
Conyers, H. B., 507 N. Main St., Urbana, Ohio.
Cook, C. H., 135 N. Centre St., Merchantville, N. J.
*Cook, John, 318 N. Charles St., Baltimore, Md.
*Cook, Thomas N., 21 Windsor Ave., Watertown, Mass.
Cooke, Mrs. Jay, Stenton Ave., Chestnut Hill, Philadelphia.
Coolidge, Herbert, 77 Garfield Ave., Watertown, Mass.
Cooper, Amos, Collinwood Station, Cleveland, Ohio.
Cooper, Mrs. C. M., Sewaren, Middlesex County, N. J.
Corbett, Mrs. Leah C., 94 Grand Ave., Rockville Center, N. Y.
Cosgrove, Miss Gertrude, Beverly Hall, Quakertown, Pa.
Cottman, L. Warrington, Tiger Bay, Fla.
Cousens, Mrs. John A., 207 Suffolk Road, Chestnut Hill, Mass.
Cowell, Miss Helen E., 2610 Jackson St., San Francisco, Calif.
Coyle, Mrs. D. M., 36 Doremus Ave., Ridgewood, N. J.
Cox, Mrs. J. Elwood, 211 E. Green St., High Point, N. C.
Craddock, C. G., Lynchburg, Va.

Craig, F. M., 1600 Railway Exchange Bldg., Chicago.
Craig, Robert, Market and 49th St., Philadelphia.
Craig, W. N., Faulkner Farm, Brookline, Mass.
Cramer, Emile R., 527 Greeley Ave., Webster Groves, Mo.
Crane, Jasper E., 354 Mt. Prospect Ave., Newark, N. J.
Crane, S. C., 138 Sayre St., Elizabeth, N. J.
Cravens, Mrs. R. O., 1823 "H" St., Sacramento, Calif.
Crawford, William, 205 W. 89th St., New York City.
Crerar Library, The John, Chicago.
Crockett, Charles E., 610 W. Colfax Ave., South Bend, Ind.
Crocker, Mrs. George A., 378 Marlborough St., Boston, Mass.
Crooks, Col. W. E., Keyser, W. Va.
Cross, Whitman, 2138 Bancroft Place, Washington, D. C.
*Crowe, Peter, Utica, N. Y.
Crowell, D. C., Navy Yard, Charleston, S. C.
Crowell, R. Herbert, 227 E. Main St., Moorestown, N. J.
Crowell, S. W., Roseacres, Miss.
Cruden, Burgess A., 238 Ave. A, Bayonne, N. J.
Cullum, J. C., 2752 W. 3d St., Coney Island, N. Y.
Cumming, Alex., Jr., Cromwell, Conn.
Cunningham, Francis A., Merchantville, N. J.
Cunningham, John, 61 Morris St., Ogdensburg, N. Y.
Cuny, Mrs. A. M., 162 E. 36th St., New York City.
Currey, J. A., Portland, Ore.
Curry, Mrs. Thos. W., Buckhannon, W. Va.
Curtis, Mrs. O. A., 185 Ames Ave., Leonia, N. J.
Curwen, John, Berwyn, Pa.
Cushing, Mrs. F. W., Moraine Hotel, Highland Park, Ill.

Dahlstrom, Mrs. C. A., 43 Linwood Ave., Ardmore, Pa.
*Dailledouze, Eugene, Flatbush, N. Y.
Dallam, H. G., 1318 Bolton St., Baltimore, Md.
Daly, John F., 4324 8th St., N.W., Washington, D. C.
Daly, Joseph F., 909 Davis St., Elmira, N. Y.
†Darlington, H. R., Park House, Potter's Bar, Middlesex, England.
Dart, Mrs. Russell, 44 W. 77th St., New York City.
Davenport, Percy C., 29 Union Ave., Belleville, N. J.
Davidson, Fred, R. F. D. 1, Box 132, Traverse City, Mich.
Davis, Mrs. Carl, Morgantown, Ind.
Davis, Ed. O., 244 Oak St., Indian Orchard, Mass.
Davis, Henry J., St. Martin's Lane, Philadelphia.

Davis, Henry J., Jr., Villa Nova, Pa.
Day, Mrs. Walter L., 555 Mountain Ave., Westfield, N. J.
Deal, H. A., Rockville, Conn.
Dean, Mrs. Richmond, 426 Beech St., Highland Park, Ill.
Decker, Arthur N., 145 Passaic Ave., Rutherford, N. J.
DeForest, T. B., 42nd St. Bldg., Madison Ave. and 42nd St., New York City.
Degen, Jacob A., 1288 Park Place, Brooklyn, N. Y.
DeLaMare, A. T., 438 W. 37th St., New York City.
DelCuro, Charles C., 23d and Kansas Sts., San Francisco, Calif.
Dennis, Miss Emma J., Hotel Vendome, Boston, Mass.
Dennis, William A., 19 Randolph Place, Newark, N. J.
Denver Public Library, (Chalmers Hadley, Librarian), Denver, Colo.
Detweiler, J. F., 320 E. Water St., Biloxi, Miss.
Duel, Mrs. W. F., 18 Mountain Ave., Maplewood, N. J.
Diamond, John, 470 N. Third St., Philadelphia.
Dick, Mrs. Fairman R., Coopers Corners, New Rochelle, N. Y.
Dickinson, C. P., Orlando, Fla.
Dieball, Paul, Hubbard Woods, Ill.
Diemond, N. R., Care of Vaughan's Nursery, Western Springs, Ill.
Dietrich, F. S., Clear Lake, Wash.
*Dimock, Mrs. H., 25 E. 60th St., New York City.
Dixon, James, Easton-Talbott Co., Easton, Md.
Dixon, T. H., Chestnut Hill, Philadelphia.
Dixon, Mrs. William A., 207 Wendover Road, Guilford, Baltimore, Md.
*Dodge, Mrs. W. E., Jr., 262 Madison Ave., New York City.
Doemling, August, Lansdowne, Pa.
Dold, J. C., Jacob Dold Packing Co., 145 Williams St., Buffalo, N. Y.
Dorner, F. E., Lafayette, Ind.
Dorner, Prof. H. B., Urbana, Ill.
Dorst, Mrs. J. H., Warrentown, Va.
Douglass, J. S., Bakersfield, Calif.
Douglass, Mrs. F. M., "The Belgravia," 1811 Chestnut St., Philadelphia.
Dowling, Robert, 72 Simmons Place, Port Richmond, N. Y.
Drake, Mrs. F. C., Lake Geneva, Wis.
Drebert, J. F., Boomer, W. Va.
Dreer, Henry A., 714 Chestnut St., Philadelphia.
Dreier, Miss Mary E., 37 Madison Ave., New York City.
Drury, Miss Mary R., Bristol, R. I.
Duffill, E. Stanley, Melrose Highlands, Mass.
Dumont, Mrs. John B., 503 Steele Ave., Plainfield, N. J.
Dunbar, John, Dept. of Parks, Rochester, N. Y.
Dundore, J. H., 972 Belmont St., Portland, Ore.
Dungey, Hugh, "Firenze," Elberon, N. J.

MEMBERS AMERICAN ROSE SOCIETY 167

Dunkle, Eli, Athens, Ohio.
Dunning, D. M., Auburn, N. Y.
DuPont, Mrs. Coleman, 808 Broome St., Wilmington, Del.
DuPont, Mrs. Maurice, 200 Montford Ave., Asheville, N. C.
Durfee, Randall N., 19 Highland Ave., Fall River, Mass.
Dutcher, Mr. Frank J., Hopedale, Mass.
Dutcher, Miss Grace M., Hopedale, Mass.
Dwyer, Mrs. John M., Grosse Point Village, Mich.
‡Dyer, Mrs. Agnes W., 2 Sheridan St., Auburn, N. Y.
Dykeman, William, 305 Glenside Road, South Orange, N. J.

Earle, Courtland, Quidnick Greenhouses, Anthony, R. I.
Earle, Mrs. W. H., Norwalk, Conn.
Easlea, Mr. George B., Graham House, Lake View, Erie County, N. Y.
Easlea, Walter, Pickett's Road, Eastwood, Leigh-on-Sea, Essex, England.
East Lawn Nursery, R. F. D. 2, Box 418, Sacramento, Calif.
Ebel, Otto, Jr., 122 Hawthorn St., Brooklyn, N. Y.
Eberly, W. V., Niles, Calif.
Eccles, Alfred L., 315 S. Clinton Ave., Trenton, N. J.
Echter, George P., Ludlow Greenhouses, Worthington, Minn.
Eddy, Maj. Robert C., U. S. Army, Fort Washington, Md.
Edwards, W. B., Box 102, Erie, Colo.
Egan, W. C., Highland Park, Ill.
Egol, Dr. Chauncey M. F., 219 Elm St., Westfield, N. J.
Eierman, J., Bellflower, Calif.
Eisenhart, E. J., 913 E. A Ave., Oskaloosa, Iowa.
Eisele, J. D., Riverton, N. J.
Elbers, Henry H., South Park Conservatory, Lackawanna, N. Y.
*Elldridge, Miss Isabelle, Norfolk, Conn.
Ellert, Lawrence B., 1352 75th St., Brooklyn, N. Y.
Elliot, Dr. G. T., 128 E. 35th St., New York City.
*Elliot, W. H., Brighton, Mass.
Elliott, Joseph H., R. F. D. 3, Wabash, Ind.
Elliott, J. Wilkinson, Elliott Nursery Co., Pittsburgh, Pa.
Ellis, W. H., Newark, N. J.
Ellison, M. D., 5 The Circle, New Rochelle, N. Y.
Elmer, S. H., Elmer Bros. Nursery, San Jose, Calif.
Engel, George A., Ascot Place, Queens, Long Island, N. Y.
English, William A., 86 Arborway, Jamaica Plain, Mass.
Eprikian, A. G., 656 52nd St., Brooklyn, N. Y.
Epting, F. H., 13 Albertson Ave., Westmont, N. J.
Erb, Lucius L., 1338 Main St., Buffalo, N. Y.
Erb, William, Jr., 122 N. California Ave., Atlantic City, N. J.

Estabrook, Leon M., 1026 17th St., Washington, D. C.
Etz, Miss Katharine, 2110 N. Camac St., Philadelphia.
Evans, W. W., Hamilton, Va.
Evenden, George W., Williamsport, Pa.
Evenden, Geo. W., Jr., 307 E. 3d St., Williamsport, Pa.
Everett, J. E., 1538 Beacon St., Waban, Mass.
Exton, B. N., 157 Major Ave., Arrochar, Staten Island, N. Y.
Eyerdam, Rudolph, 3931 W. 33d St., Cleveland, Ohio.

Fairbairn, Mrs. C. T., Thomas Station, Birmingham, Ala.
Fancher Creek Nurseries, Fresno, Calif.
Fancourt, E. J., 1612 Ludlow St., Philadelphia.
*Farenwald, A., Roslyn, Pa.
Farnham, M. E., Cold Spring Harbor, N. Y.
Farnsworth, H. A., 401 Sigourney St., Hartford, Conn.
Fauver, Mrs. J. C., R. F. D., Yountville, Calif.
Fay, Mrs. Fred Hollister, 63 South St., Auburn, N. Y.
Feickert, Mrs. E. F., Colonial Farm, Dunellen, N. J.
Fendrich, Louis, 29 Daily St., West Nutley, N. J.
Fergus, James, West Newton, Pa.
Ferguson, Thomas, 194 Bradhurst Ave., New York City.
Fernald, Mrs. Gardner G., Wilton, Me.
Fernstrom, Mrs. H., 423 Raleigh Ave., Norfolk, Va.
Fertig, Geo. E., The Deis-Fertig Co., Dover, Ohio.
Ferwerda, Rev. Floris, Dover, Del.
Fesing, H. W., Houghton, Mich.
Fielding, Henry P., 24 Milk St., Boston, Mass.
Fischer, Dr. Henry G., 1411 Walnut St., Philadelphia.
Fish, A. J., New Bedford, Mass.
Fish, John D., 15 Nevada St., Worcester, Mass.
Fisher, Peter, Ellis, Mass.
Fitcher, W. W., R. F. D. 1, Parkersburg, W. Va.
Fitzpatrick, Paul J., Care of Brown, Durrell & Co., Boston, Mass.
Flamisch, Rudolph, 333 E. Union St,. Allentown, Pa.
Flanders, Mrs. Roger Y., 686 Franklin Place, Milwaukee, Wis.
Fletcher, John A., 86 Lincoln Ave., Rutherford, N. J.
Florex Rose Gardens, (Henry Gieger), North Wales, Pa.
Florin, A. L., Fall River Mills, Calif.
Fogg, Hester B., Greensburg, Pa.
Foley, Philip J., 31st St. and Spaulding Ave., Chicago.
Foote, Mrs. F. Stuart, 265 Orchard Hill, Grand Rapids, Mich.
Forbes, H. W., 10 Clinton St., Taunton, Mass.

Ford, Mrs. Bruce, 25 Summit Ave., Philadelphia.
Foreman, Dr. A. W., White Hall, Ill.
Foster, Mrs. A. S., Montchanin, Del.
Foster, W. Edwd., 336 Prospect Ave., Hackensack, N. J.
Foster, William E., Providence Public Library, Providence, R. I.
Foulke, Mrs. William Dudley, Richmond, Ind.
Fountain, W., 30-34 Adelaide St., W., Toronto, Ont.
Fowler, Mrs. Albert E., 17 S. Maple St., Westfield, Mass.
Fowler, Mrs. Anne Bartlett, 19 Hotchkiss St., New Haven, Conn.
Fowler, Elisha, 12 Pearl St., Boston, Mass.
Fowler, E. Clarke, 6155 Webster St., Philadelphia.
Fox, Mrs. Hattie A., Cedar Bluffs, Neb.
Franchot, Mrs. N. V. V., "Fairview," Olean, N. Y.
Francis, Mrs. Edgar S., Durham, Conn.
Francis, James G., 705 Walnut St., Philadelphia.
Franklin, Malcolm, 1438 S. Penn Square, Philadelphia.
Franklin, R. H., 906 D St., San Bernardino, Calif.
Fraser, John, Sr., Huntsville, Ala.
Freeman, Mrs. C. E., 83 Ridgewood Ave., Glen Ridge, N. J.
‡Freeman, L. B., 1437 Madison Ave., Columbus, Ohio.
French, Albert M., Scotland Road, Reading, Mass.
‡French, Mrs. D. E., 123 South St., Auburn, N. Y.
French, Mrs. Stephen L., 262 Underwood St., Fall River, Mass.
Friedlander, William S., 27-33 White St., New York City.
Fritsche, Mrs. Wm. J., 104 W. Delaware Ave., Toledo, Ohio.
Frost, Edwin B., Williams Bay, Wis.
Fuller, Mrs. F. I., 503 Spring St., Portland, Ore.
Fuller, Walter D., 66 Delaware St., Woodbury, N. J.
Fulmer, D. W., 447 Line St., Easton, Pa.

Gager, Dr. C. Stuart, 978 Washington Ave., Brooklyn, N. Y.
Gaiser, Bernard, 710 Princeton Ave., Trenton, N. J.
Gambier, Emilie A., 13 East 124th St., New York City.
Gamwell, Roland G., Bellingham, Wash.
Ganser, Joseph B., 63 E. Main St., Norristown, Pa.
‡Garrett, Thomas H., 103 E. Genesee St., Auburn, N. Y.
George, James I., Fairport, N. Y.
*George, Robert, Painesville, Ohio.
Gephart, Charles T., Valley Falls, Kan.
Gersdorff, Charles E. F., R. F. D. 1, Box 133, Rosslyn, Va.
Gibbons, Mrs. Helen E., 120 Roxborough St., E., Toronto, Ont.
Gibbons, W. R., 150 Commerce St., Rahway, N. J.
Gibbs, Milton E., 22 Wilmer St., Rochester, N. Y.
Gibert, Miss Gertrude, 44 E. 82nd St., New York City.
Gibson, Edward G., Munsey Bldg., Baltimore, Md.
Gibson, James, Fairfield St., Portland, Me.
Gibson, John, P. O. Box 453, Bellingham, Wash.
Gienow, William, River Edge, N. J.
Giesy, Mrs. R. M., High St. and 5th Ave., Lancaster, Ohio.
Gifford, John C., Cocoanut Grove, Fla.
Gilbert, A. F., 505 Market St., Millersburg, Pa.
‡Gilbert, Hon. James M., 737 Comstock Ave., Syracuse, N. Y.
Gilbert, Mrs. Julia B., 155 Summit Ave., Summit, N. J.
Gilbert, Samuel C., 326½ Law St., Allentown, Pa.
Gill, George M., 140 Fifth Ave., New York City.
Gillett, Frank A., Hoquiam, Wash.
Gillett, Lucy D., 31 Court St., Westfield, Mass.
Gillies, Thomas, 17 Garfield Ave., Santa Cruz, Calif.
Gilmore, Mrs. J. C., 1434 Pine St., Philadelphia.
Glasier, Mrs. Frances Holly, Box 966, (127 Wyoming St.), Warsaw, N. Y.
Glasscock, C. W., 3919 Windsor Ave., Kansas City, Mo.
Gleason, Mr. Walter L., 122 Carondelet St., New Orleans, La.
Glen Bros., Inc., Rochester, N. Y.
Glenn, Jos., Box 119, Oyster Bay, N. Y.
Godey, Mrs. Catherine W., Warrenton, Va.
Godfrey, Mrs. Edward A., 447 Laurel Ave., Bridgeport, Conn.
Goetze, Mrs. Otto, 60 Remsen St., Brooklyn, N. Y.
Gohn, Charles, 556 Swaine St., Bristol, Pa.
Goldthwaite, J. O., Chiloquin, Ore.
*Good, John M., Springfield, Ohio.
Goodfellow, A. Z., Box 357, Fitchburg, Mass.
Goodner, Ivan W., 1612 E. 65th St., Seattle, Wash.
Goodrich, Alfred G., 10 Midvale Road, Roland Park, Md.
Goodspeed, Mrs. Geo. F., Wilton, Me.
Goodwin, Mrs. Daniel, East Greenwich, R. I.
Goodwin, George R., 89 Elizabeth St., Hartford, Conn.
Gordon, Joseph H., 1708 N. Junette St., Tacoma, Wash.
Gordon, W. A., 627 Second Ave., S., Minneapolis, Minn.
Gosch, Mary C., R. F. D. 1, Rochelle, Ill.
Goudie, D. O., 56 Cadillac Square, Detroit, Mich.
Graham, W. Pruett, Frankfort, Ky.
Grandin, D. H., 10 Prospect St., Jamestown, N. Y.
Graton, Louis, Randolph, Mass.
Gray, William, Newport, R. I.

Gray, W. R., Oakton, Va.
Greed, Thomas J., 2728 Fenwick Ave., Baltimore, Md.
Greeley, A. P., 2632 Garfield St., Washington, D. C.
Greeley, A. W., 969 High St., Williamsport, Pa.
Greeley, Dr. Jane L., 111 E. 5th St., Jamestown, N. Y.
Green, F. L., Greenwood, Ont., Can.
Green, Miss S. Maud, 2915 O St., Sacramento, Calif.
Greene, Mrs. Wallace, 2024 Hillyer Place, Washington, D. C.
Greenfield, Mrs. Leo. D., 52 Summit Drive, Far Rockaway, N. Y.
Greening, Charles E., Monroe, Mich.
Greenleaf, Miss Anna M., Navarre Apartments, Wilmington, Del.
Greenman, H., 174 Park St., Montclair, N. J.
Gregg, Will W., Earlville, Ill.
Gregory, A. H., 519 Mission St., San Francisco, Calif.
Greve, Charles T., 530 Maxwell Ave., Cincinnati, Ohio.
Gribbel, Mrs. John, Wyncote, Pa.
Griffen, George M., Plainfield, N. J.
Grim, Victor E., 339 N. 16th St., Allentown, Pa.
Griswold, Mrs. Mathew, Jr., 265 W. 10th St., Erie, Pa.
Grob, E. G., Jekyl Island Club, Brunswick, Ga.
Grobbel, Mrs. D. C., 565 Montclair Ave., Detroit, Mich.
Groome, H. C., Warrenton, Va.
Groscup, F. N., 100 Monmouth Road, El Mora, N. J.
Groshens, Victor, Roslyn, Pa.
*Gude, A., 1214 F Street, N. W., Washington, D. C.
*Gude, W. F., 1214 F Street, N.W., Washington, D. C.
Guenther, C. T., Hamburg, N. Y.
Gunn, Mrs. J. B., Cromwell, Conn.
Guthridge, Mrs. Adele F., The Amherst, Washington, D. C.
*Guttman, Alexander J., 115 W. 28th St., New York City.

Haak, John H., 311 Lumberman's Bldg., Portland, Ore.
Haehnlen, Louis F., 21st St. and Bellevue Road, Harrisburg, Pa.
Hage, Daniel S., 80 Wall St., New York City.
Haggin, Mrs. Ben. Ali, 121 Madison Ave., New York City.
‡Hale, Mrs. Frank H., Fayetteville, N. Y.
Hall, Mrs. Sherwood, Jr., 22 Glen Road, Winchester, Mass.
Hall, W. Hunt, Equitable Bldg., New York City.
Hallett, H. H., Davenport Neck, New Rochelle, N. Y.
Hallock, George W., Orient, N Y.
Hambleton, Mrs. F. S., Hambledrive, Lutherville, Md.
Hammer, V. T., Branford, Conn.
Hammond, Benjamin, Beacon, N. Y.

Hammond, W. F., Greenport, N. Y.
‡Hane, Miss Mary E., 84 N. 20th St., Columbus, Ohio.
Hansen, Prof. N. E., Brookings, S. D.
Hanshew, Dr. E., 125 Carlton Ave., Brooklyn, N. Y.
Harde, Mrs. Herbert S., 182 W. 58th St., New York City.
Harding, Mrs. J. Horace, Rumson, N. J.
Haring, Mrs. J. C., 1614 E. Main St., Massillon, Ohio.
Harker, F. F., 2015 Grove Ave., Richmond, Va.
Harkett, W. A., Dubuque, Iowa.
Harris, Frederick A., R. F. D., Amherst, Mass.
Harris, S. G., 63 Hamilton Place, Tarrytown, N. Y.
Harris, Wharton E., Lansdowne, Pa.
Harris, William, Rockwood, Ont.
Harris, W. K., 55th St. and Springfield Ave., Philadelphia.
Harrison, Miss Carrie, 1331 Newton St., Brookland, D. C.
Harrison's Nurseries, Berlin, Md.
Harrison, W. W., 119 N. 11th St., Philadelphia.
Hart, George E., Lynbrook, Long Island, N. Y.
Hart, W. O., 134 Carondelet St., New Orleans, La.
Harte, Mrs. R. H., 1503 Spruce St., Philadelphia.
Harttmann, Mrs. A., 132 Lake Drive, Mountain Lakes, N. J.
Hartranft, John H., 1525 Berkshire Ave., Pittsburgh, Pa.
Hartwick, C. W., 113 Conoy St., Harrisburg, Pa.
Hartwig, C. Fred, 746 Spruce Ave., Niagara Falls, N. Y.
Haug, I. L., 2313 Durant Ave., Berkeley, Calif.
Haupt, Jos. J., 222 Walnut St., Montclair, N. J.
Hauser, Herbert, 4670 San Sebastian Ave., Oakland, Calif.
Haven, Rev. Wm. I., 25 Fernwood Road, Summit, N. J.
Havens, Albert G., Box 182, Mountain Lakes, N. J.
Hawkes, Mrs. McDougall, 8 E. 53d St., New York City.
Hawkinson, Theodore W., Walker, Iowa.
Hawley, Mrs. Flora S., 51 Spring St., Eureka Springs, Ark.
Hawthorne, Mrs. Bayard, 733 Sherman Ave., Plainfield, N. J.
Hayes, George E., Westfield, N. J.
Hayes, Miss Maude, Spiegel Farm, Croton-on-Hudson, N. Y.
Hays, James A., 3211 N. 31st St., Tacoma, Wash.
Hayward, Mrs. Lydia A., Lawrence Park, W., Bronxville, N. Y.
Hayward, Mrs. W. E., Vine Hill, Ipswich, Mass.
Heacock, James W., Wyncote, Pa.
Healey, R. E., 45 Broad St., Plattsburg, N. Y.
Hechler, C. H., Roslyn, N. Y.

Heidtmann, A. W., 15 S. Bleeker St., Mt. Vernon, N. Y.
Heite, Charles E., 1111 E. 63d St., Kansas City, Mo.
Heller, Clyde A., 6471 Overbrook Ave., Philadelphia.
Heller, M. Rudy, 6129 Carpenter St., Philadelphia.
*Heller, Myer, South Park Floral Co., New Castle, Ind.
Helmer, R. H., Supt. Experiment Sta., Summerland, B. C.
*Henderson, Charles, 35-37 Cortlandt St., New York City.
Henderson, Louise MacLeod, Fishers Island, N. Y.
Hendrickson, I. S., Flowerfield, N. Y.
Henn, A. W., National Acme Mfg. Co., Cleveland, Ohio.
Hentz, Henry, Jr., Madison, N. J.
Herndon, Dr. J. S., Roseburg, Ore.
Herring, P., Willemvesgade 42, Copenhagen, Denmark.
Hertzler, John W., 131 E. Orange St., Lancaster, Pa.
Hess, George W., U. S. Botanic Gardens, Washington, D. C.
Hess, J. J., 1415 Farmer St., Omaha, Neb.
Hesson, C. A., St. Catharines, Ont., Can.
Hevesey, Berthold, Jewish Hospital, Logan, Philadelphia.
Hicks, Henry, Westbury, Long Island, N. Y.
Higgins, H. W., 131 Mechanic St., Orange, Mass.
Higgins, Dr. Wm. McK., 616 Madison Ave., New York City.
*Hill, E. G., Richmond, Ind.
Hill, Joseph H., Richmond, Ind.
Hill, W. Gordon, 110 N. 9th St., Newark, N. J.
Hillger, Samuel E., 12 Park Ave., Auburn, N. Y.
Hillman, John E., Delta, Colo.
Hires, Mrs. J. Edgar, Ardmore, Pa.
‡Hitchcock, Charles A., 17 Syracuse Bank Bldg., Syracuse, N. Y.
Hjort, P. J., Thomasville, Ga.
Hjort, S. C., Quitman, Ga.
Hobbie, W. F., 1001 Broadway, New York City.
Hobbs, Edgar E., 87 Greenwood Ave., Rumford, R. I.
Hodge, Harry S., University, Va.
Hodgson, H. W., 14 Minnesota Ave., Richmond Hill, N. Y.
Hoey, Mrs. Clyde R., Shelby, N. C.
Hoffman, A. F., Broadmoor, Colorado Springs, Colo.
Hoffman, Mrs. Charles F., 15 E. 84th St., New York City.
Hoffman, Herrmann, 3320 Graydon Ave., E. W. H., Cincinnati, Ohio.
Hoffman, J. L., 103 Peachtree St., Atlanta, Ga.
Hoffmeier, Dr. E. F., Mauch Chunk, Pa.
Hogansville Nursery, Hogansville, Ga.
Holden, Mrs. Edward P., Madison, N. J.
‡Holland, E. J., Silverdale, Sutton, Surrey, England.

Holland, James H., 172 Dundurn St., N., Hamilton, Ont., Can.
Holliday, George, Marion, Mass.
Hollister, George H., 272 Westland St., Hartford, Conn.
Holman, Frederick V., Chamber of Commerce Bldg., Portland, Ore.
Holman, Mrs. Herbert, 787 Overton St., Portland, Ore.
Holmans, Mrs. Lewis H. P., 1028 W. 55th St., Los Angeles, Calif.
Holmes, H. L., Jr., 224 N. Cleveland Ave., Canton, Ohio.
‡Hommel, Mrs. Edward, 704 McBride St., Syracuse, N. Y.
Hoopes, Bro. & Thomas Co., West Chester, Pa.
Hoover, Mrs. A. H., 2103 Clinton Ave., Alameda, Calif.
Hootes, Alfred C., Ohio State University, Columbus, Ohio.
Hopkins, Dr. A. D., Bureau of Entomology, Washington, D. C.
Hopkins, B. M., 311 N. Washington St., Alexandria, Va.
Hornfeck, Miss Frances, 66 Lakeside Ave., Verona, N. J.
Hough, W. I., 228 S. Carolina Ave., Washington, D. C.
Howard, Mrs. Charlotte S., 92 Caroline St., Ogdensburg, N. Y.
Howard, F. L., Linden, N. J.
Howard, Mrs. Harry T., 3513 St. Charles Ave., New Orleans, La.
Howard, Mrs. R. R., 216 Seminole Ave., Detroit, Mich.
Howard & Smith, 9th and Oliver Sts., Los Angeles, Calif.
Howe, E. W., 378 Washington St., Boston, Mass.
Howe, Mrs. Frank P., 242 S. 17th St., Philadelphia.
Howe, Walter B., Princeton, N. J.
Howe, Mrs. Walter B., Princeton, N. J.
Howland, Mrs. John G., 285 Park Ave., Bridgeport, Conn.
Howell, B. H., Brooklands, Suffern, N. Y.
Hubbard, Mrs. A. T., 1685 Magnolia Drive, Cleveland, Ohio.
Hubbard, S. C., R. F. D. 2, Ithaca, N. Y.
*Hudson, Mrs. C. I., 1 E. 76th St., New York City.
Huebner, Paul, Wayne Junction, Philadelphia.
Huey, Dr. Robert, 330 S. 15th St., Philadelphia.
Hughes, Mrs. E. C., The Highlands, Seattle, Wash.
Hughes, Robert E., 1949 Hertel Ave., Buffalo, N. Y.
Hughey, Mrs. Wm. E., 72 Washington Ave., Clifton, N. J.
Hulst, Mrs. Edward T., 16 N. Parsons Ave., Flushing, N. Y.
Humphrey, Mrs. A. P., Glenview, Ky.
Hunnewell, Mrs. Henry S., Wellesley, Mass.
Hunt, George G., 281 Fairview St., East Allentown, Pa.
Hunt, Mrs. R. A., Amberson Place, Pittsburgh, Pa.

Hunt, R. V., 1761 S. 8th St., E., Salt Lake City, Utah.
Hunt, W. W., 80 Ann St., Hartford, Conn.
Hurley, Irene M., 50 Fairmount St., Marlboro, Mass.
Huston, Miss C. L., 5521 Wayne Ave., Germantown, Philadelphia.
Hutchins, Mrs. Edward W., 166 Beacon St., Boston, Mass.
Hutchinson, C. L., Lake Geneva, Wis.
Hyslop, Frances, Home Spring Farm, Springfield, Ohio.

Ihlder, John D., 264 Fifth Ave., New York City.
Ilgenfritz, T. I., I. E. Ilgenfritz Sons Co., 708 E. Front St., Monroe, Mich.
Ingle, W. O., Box 785, Rochester, N. Y.
Irwin, Roman J., 108 W. 28th St., New York City.
Irwin, Ernest C., 66 St. Nicholas Bldg., Pittsburgh, Pa.

Jackson, Mrs. B. A., Amityville, Long Island, N. Y.
Jackson, John Karl, 320 N. Johnson St., Macomb, Ill.
Jackson, Mrs. John P., 174 St. Nicholas Ave., New York City.
Jacobs, Miss Matilda, Pointed Firs, Aurora, N. Y.
Jacobus, M. R., Ridgefield, N. J.
James, Ellerton, Milton, Mass.
Jamison, Miss Martha A., Sea Girt, N. J.
Jamison, Robert, Woodside, Pa.
Janssen, Miss Helen, Wyomissing, Reading, Pa.
Jardine, Miss Margaret I., Box 118, Mendham, N. J.
Jenks, Mrs. William P., Morristown, N. J.
Jenness, W. H., 32 Cotton St., Roslindale, Mass.
Jerdinston, W. C., 1228 11th St., Moline, Ill.
Johanning, Charles, 4411 Sullivan Ave., St. Bernard, Ohio.
Johnson, Arthur, Esq., Northside, Hockerill Park, Bishop's Stortford, Herts, England.
Johnson, D., 429 Palmerston Ave., Toronto, Can.
Johnson, Mrs. H. M., 542 19th St., E., North Vancouver, B. C.
Johnson, L. A., Guthrie, Okla.
Johnson, Rev. S. Aaron, Leland, Ill.
Johnson, Sadie E., 8 E. 4th St., South Bethlehem, Pa.
Johnston, Miss Mary, Illinois Woman's College, Jacksonville, Ill.
Johnston, R. M., 1061 N. Broadway, Yonkers, N. Y.
Johnstone, Kate A., 703 S. Pasadena Ave., Pasadena, Calif.
Johnstone, Mrs. Robert LeGrand, Thendara, Glen Ridge, N. J.
Jones, B. F., Jr., Irwin and Ridge Sts., N. S., Pittsburgh, Pa.
Jones, Edward B., 218 High St., Mount Holly, N. J.
Jones, George M., 6530 Beacon St., Pittsburgh, Pa.
‡Jones, Hezekiah, 823 Summer Ave., Syracuse, N. Y.
Jones, Mrs. L. C., Falmouth, Mass.
Jones, W. D., 311 N. Windomere St., Station A., Dallas, Tex.
Jones, William J., Box 18, Narberth, Pa.
Jordan, Mrs. E. B., Jr., 129 Hilton Ave., Hempstead, Long Island, N. Y.
Josselyn, E. Howard, 2714 Fenwick Ave., Baltimore, Md.
Jova, Mrs. E. A., North Liberty St., Newburgh, N. Y.
Joy, H. M., Nashville, Tenn.
Judd, Judge, 307 Ridout St., London, Ont., Can.
Judd, Mrs. M. E., "Oneonta," Dalton, Ga.
Julihn, L. G., 208 Ouray Bldg., Washington, D. C.
Jump, John W. D., 109 Goldsborough St., Easton, Md.
Jurgens, Carl, Box 345, Newport, R. I.

Kahle, H. M., 42 Rich Ave., Mt. Vernon, N. Y.
Kalbfleisch, Franklin H., 31 Union Square W., New York City.
Keeble, Glendinning, 1153 Wightman St., Pittsburgh, Pa.
Keeler, B. A., 1450 Railway Exchange, Chicago, Ill.
Keene, P., R. F. D. 1, Box 154, Napa, Calif.
Keenest, E. L., 55 E. Fairview St., Bethlehem, Pa.
Keimel, W. J., Elmhurst, Ill.
Kell, E. J., 5541 Chamberlain Ave., St. Louis, Mo.
Keller, W. L., 25 N. Clinton St., Rochester, N. Y.
Kelley, Mrs. Anthony, 45 Fletcher St., Winchester, Mass.
‡Kellogg, Charles L., 105 Summit Ave., Syracuse, N. Y.
Kellogg, Herbert S., 83 Forest Ave., Glen Ridge, N. J.
Kelly, Miss Julia Z., 114 Orchard Place, Ithaca, N. Y.
Kelsey, Harlan P., 209A Washington St., Salem, Mass.
Kemmerer, Mrs. J. F., Clinton, Wis.
Kendal, H. B., 56 Cadillac Square, Detroit, Mich.
Kenea, Miss Edith L., Thomaston, Conn.
Kennedy, Mrs. John S., 400 Park Ave., New York City.
Kerr, Mrs. Samuel T., 1907 Spruce St., Philadelphia.
Kessler, George E., 423 Security Bldg., St. Louis, Mo.
Kevorkian, Mihran H., 1713 Sansom St., Philadelphia.
‡Kidwell, Mrs. O. L., 277 12th Ave., Columbus, Ohio.
Kiggins, Mrs. W. A., 324 W. Jersey St., Elizabeth, N. J.
Kilbee-Stuart, Capt. R., Wimbold Lodge, N. Newbury, England.
‡Kimball, Mrs. Madison, 53 Smith Place, Columbus, Ohio.
Kimball, Rev. Thatcher R., Brush Hill Road, Hyde Park, Mass.
King, Mrs. Francis, Alma, Mich.

King, John A., 3 W. Craig St., Uniontown, Pa.
King, R. N., Oakwood Village, Dayton, Ohio.
King, William R., 6043 Jenkins Arcade Bldg., Pittsburgh, Pa.
Kingsland, W. J., Derrydale Farm, Goshen, N. Y.
Kirby, James, Huntington, Long Island, New York.
‡Kirkland, R. A., 214 Markland Ave., Syracuse, N. Y.
Kirkpatrick, F. S., 708 Pearl St., Lynchburg, Va.
Kirsch, Mrs. W., 121 W. 61st St., Los Angeles, Calif.
Kleinheinz, William, Ogontz, Pa.
‡Klippert, Miss Josephine, 275 Town St., Columbus, Ohio.
Klosé, Henry K., 65 W. Lacrosse Ave., Lansdowne, Pa.
Knights, Miss Alice L., "The Overlook," Littleton, Mass.
Knoble, H. P., 1836 W. 25th St., Cleveland, Ohio.
Koenig, A. B., 3119 Arsenal St., St. Louis, Mo.
Koerth, Otto, First State Bank, Fredericksburg, Iowa
Kohankie, Henry, Painesville, Ohio.
Kossuth, George J., 139 21st St., Warwood, W. Va.
Krause, J. S., 20 E. Market St., Bethlehem, Pa.
Krenske, Charles, 1943 Michigan Boulevard, Racine, Wis.
*Krippendorff, Carl H., Syracuse and New Sts., Cincinnati, Ohio.
Kuder, Mrs. Paul, 665 Astor St., Milwaukee, Wis.
Kuehne, F. R., Care of A. B. Dick, Lake Forest, Ill.
Kuhn, Fred A., Box 69, Williamsville, N. Y.
Kuhn, John, 5th and Tabor Sts., Philadelphia.
‡Kullmer, Mrs. J. M., 505 University Place, Syracuse, N. Y.
Kuns, Miss Bessie H., 601 W. 110th St., New York City.
Kurts, Thomas C., 699 Schuyler St., Portland, Ore.
Kyle, Harold M., Box 287, Hillsdale, N. J.

Lacey, Mrs. J. M., 6106 Christian St., W. Philadelphia.
Ladd, Charles M., 31 Trinity Terrace, Springfield, Mass.
Lagna, Charles, R. F. D. 2, Box 178, Santa Barbara, Calif.
Lamborn, L. L., Alliance, Ohio.
Lamont, Robert, Quidnick Greenhouses, Anthony, R. I.
Landmann, Miss M. V., Cranbury, N. J.
Lang, George F., 807 Van Buren St., Wilmington, Del.
Lang, William F., Jr., 31 Dart St., Buffalo, N. Y.
Langdon, Clarence Willcox, Southington, Conn.
Langjahr, Alfred H., 130 W. 28th St., New York City.

Latimer, R. E., Thomas Station, Birmingham, Ala.
Lauer, Mrs. Edward, 217 Bouquet St., Pittsburgh, Pa.
Laughlin, Mrs. Alex., Beaver Road, Sewickley, Pa.
Lawlor, Theodore P., Flushing Nurseries, Inc., Flushing, N. Y.
Lawrence, H. V., 599 Bedford Ave., Brooklyn, N. Y.
Lawrence, Miss Alice, 26 Pleasant St., Springfield, Vt.
Lawrence, W. T., 151 Horton St., London, Can.
Lawson, Charles B., Lawson Piano Co., 372 E. 149th St., New York City.
Lay, Henry H., 502 S. Tremont St., Kewanee, Ill.
Leach, Aloysius Anthony, 7012 Thomas Boulevard, E. E., Pittsburgh, Pa.
Leavens, G. McP., Kaycee, Wyo.
Lee, Mrs. Mary E., Glen-Lee, Westerville, Ohio.
Lee, Mrs. W. C., 7 Pine St., Winchester, Mass.
Leedle, Arthur C., Springfield, Ohio.
Leedle, G. D., Springfield, Ohio.
Leister, B. P., 114 Ingram Ave., S. W., Canton, Ohio.
Leonard, Mrs. Frank E., 423 Terrace Ave., S.E., Grand Rapids, Mich.
Leonard, R. W., Foxboro, Mass.
Lester, A. E., 30 E. 57th St., New York City.
Letherman, George M., 1616 Woodland Ave., N. W., Canton, Ohio.
Levis, Edw. H., Mt. Holly, N. J.
Levison, Harry, 2226 Putman St., Toledo, Ohio.
Levy, Mrs. Louis S., Dobbs Ferry, N. Y.
Lewin, Frank, Hawthorne, Calif.
‡Lewis, F. T., 332 E. Genesee St., Auburn, N. Y.
Lewis, Dr. G. G., 600 University Block, Syracuse, N. Y.
Lewis, George W., 144 Midland Ave., Glen Ridge, N. J.
Lewis, Mrs. John L., 1008 Farragut St., Pittsburgh, Pa.
Lewis, S. A., 302 Coulter Bldg., Los Angeles, Calif.
L'Henrinx, Hector P., 24 Grove St., Northampton, Mass.
Library Association, Portland, Ore.
Lichenstein, Isaac, 22 W. 43d St., New York City.
Lidgerwood, Miss Florence V., Speedwell, Morristown, N. J.
Lieb, J. W., 124 E. 15th St., New York City.
Lieder, Chas. J., 1224 52nd St., Brooklyn, N. Y.
Limbert, Clara T., 2002 Robinson Road, Grand Rapids, Mich.
Lindbloom, David, 538 62nd St., Brooklyn, N. Y.
Lindner, Henry G., 48 Blake Ave., Lynbrook, Long Island, N. Y.
Lindsay, Mrs. H. G., 508 North Peters Ave., Norman, Okla.
Lindsay, John M., 716 Lamar Ave., Wilkinsburg, Pa.

MEMBERS AMERICAN ROSE SOCIETY 173

Lippincott, H. Raymond, 6 Merrick Villa, Collingswood, N. J.
Lippincott, Mrs. Robert C., 266 W. Tulpehocken St., Germantown, Philadelphia.
Little, C. A., Box 85, Elyria, Ohio.
Lockey, Dr. R. P., Nacogdoches, Tex.
Logan, Miss M. Dickinson, 4650 Germantown Ave., Germantown, Philadelphia.
Logue, P., 3700 Fairmount Ave., W. Philadelphia.
Long, A. G., 4304 Scott Terrace, Minneapolis, Minn.
Loring, Charles A., 91 Woodland Ave., New Rochelle, N. Y.
Loughlin, Miss Elizabeth, 204 Second Ave., Haddon Heights, N. J.
Lovejoy, J. R., Lenox Road, Schenectady, N. Y.
Lovering, Miss S. L., 10 Dean St., Taunton, Mass.
Low, Clarence F., 204 Carondelet St., New Orleans, La.
Lowe, Mrs. Edward, Holmdene, Grand Rapids, Mich.
Lowell, Edgar L., 415 E. 17th St., N., Portland, Ore.
Lucas, Mrs. Catharine E., Box 125, Howard, Pa.
Luck, Miss L., 62 S. Grove St., East Orange, N. J.
Ludlow, Mrs. Grace F, Palisade, N. J.
Ludwig, M. H., 320 Russell Hill Road, Toronto, Ont.
Lumsden, David, Ithaca, N. Y.
Lundy, Mrs. F. K., 331 High St., Williamsport, Pa.
Lyman, Mrs. J. P., Ashby, Mass.
Lyon, Burt W., Joplin, Mo.
Lyon, H. D., Montrose, N. Y.

McAdow, Dr. Marian, Punta Gorda, Fla.
McBratney, John, 121 Franklin St., New York City.
McCampbell, Mrs. Theron, Holmdel, N. J.
McCarthy, Sarah A., 32 Vesta Road, Dorchester, Mass.
McCartney, Miss Elizabeth, 116 N. 11th St., Philadelphia.
McClain, Frederick, Gibsonia, Pa.
McClure, Richard K., Washington St., Frankfort, Ky.
McConnell, Charles E., 3 Page Terrace, South Orange, N. J.
McConnell, J. H., 1776 Sycamore Ave., Hollywood, Calif.
MacClory, Thomas A., Union, N. Y.
MacConnell, Thomas, 793 Crescent Ave., Buffalo, N. Y.
McCoy, Lester, 1301 Hamilton Boulevard, Peoria, Ill.
McCready, Mrs. Margaret, 237 S. Main St., Cadiz, Ohio.
McCready, R. T., Sewickley, Pa.
McDaniel, John S., St Michaels, Md.
Macdonald, Mrs. H. F., P. O. Box 134, Manhasset, Long Island, N. Y.
McDowell, John W., 52 Wade Ave., Washington, Pa.
McEvan, Mrs. A. F., 1006 E. Garfield St., Seattle, Wash.

McEwen, Mrs. Alfred, "Craig Amel," Tarrytown, N. Y.
†McFarland, J. Horace, Harrisburg, Pa.
McGrady, J. W., 301 S. Rebecca St., E.E., Pittsburgh, Pa.
McGinnis, Prof. N. M., Agricultural and Mechanical College, College Station, Tex.
McGirk, Annie, Phillipsburg, Pa.
McKesson, George C., 91 Fulton St., New York City.
McKie, Miss K. M., Cambridge, N. Y.
McKissock, William, 92 State St., Boston, Mass.
McLaren, George S., 476 Washington Ave., West Haven, Conn.
McLeod, Dr. C. H., Lynden, Wash.
*McMahon, F., Seabright, N. J.
McMurrich, K. D., 140 West 5th St., Oswego, N. Y.
McNaughton, W., 294 Grosvenor St., London, Can.
McQuade, Hugh, Merion, Montgomery County, Pa.
Mack, Eva G., 1330 State St., Alton, Ill.
Mackrille, A., 440 Yale St., New Haven, Conn.
*Macy, V. Everett, 86 Broad St., New York City.
Madlener, William C., 4 W. Burton Place, Chicago.
Magruder, Mrs. H. W., 630 N. Kansas Ave., Liberal, Kan.
Maharg, Howard Feather, 516 Arbutus St., Philadelphia.
Mahon, Joseph E., Glen Head, N. Y.
Malkiel, Leon A., 116 Nassau St., New York City.
Malloy, John D., Washington C. H., Ohio.
Mann, Alan N., Scarsdale, N. Y.
Mann, C. F., 6517 Greenview Ave., Rogers Park, Chicago.
Mann, George R., 1711 Center St., Little Rock, Ark.
Mann, James R., House of Representatives, Washington, D. C.
Manning, Warren H., North Billerica, Mass.
Maple, E. D., Sullivan, Ind.
March, Mrs. A. L., 380 Scotland Road, South Orange, N. J.
Marsalis, Thomas, 15 Crestmont Road, Montclair, N. J.
Marston, Edwin S., 375 Park Ave., New York City.
Marston, Mrs. Edwin S., 375 Park Ave., New York City.
Martin, Mrs. E. P., 1721 Locust St., Chestnut Hill, Philadelphia.
Martin, Miss E. P., 132 Lorraine Ave., Upper Montclair, N. J.
Martin, Gregorio, San Jose, Costa Rica.
Martin, L. B., Lancaster, Ohio.
Martin, Henry C., 25 Madison Ave., New York City.
Martin, Robert Pettit, 270 Midland Ave., East Orange, N. J.
Martini, Albin, Lake Geneva, Wis.
Maschke, Maurice, 17200 Clifton Boulevard, Lakewood, Ohio.

Mason, C. H., The Dansville Gas and Electric Co., Dansville, N. Y.
*Mason, Mrs. J. H., 215 Madison Ave., New York City.
Mason, Mrs. H. J., Avery, Ohio.
Mason, W. H., 3d, 107 Union St., Mount Holly, N. J.
Massenat, Andre, 240 bis Boulevard St. Germain, Paris, France.
Maver, Charles, Box 237, Glen Ellyn, Ill.
May, H. O., Summit, N. J.
*May, John N., Summit, N. J.
Mayer, Ernest, 1851 3d Ave., New Brighton, Pa.
Maynard, Walter E., 501 Fifth Ave., New York City.
Mayo, E. S., 214 Culber Road, Rochester, N. Y.
Meehan, Martin, 892 Campbell Ave., West Haven, Conn.
Meller, C. L., 1010 4th Ave., South, Fargo, N. D.
Mellon, Mrs. T. A., 401 N. Negley Ave., Pittsburgh, Pa.
Mellon, Mrs. W. L., Forbes and Darlington, Pittsburgh, Pa.
Menager, L. C., R. F. D. 4, Jacksonville, Fla.
Merriam, Mrs. E. W., 132 Main St., Newton, N. J.
Merrill, Robert D., 801 Madison St., Chester, Pa.
‡Michael, Mrs. B. R., 508 Estrom Ave., Syracuse, N. Y.
Michell, Frank B., Andalusia, Pa.
Michell, Henry F., 518 Market St., Philadelphia.
Mierswa, Charles, Homestead Steel Works, Munhall, Pa.
Miller, Mrs. A. C., Shelby, N. C.
Miller, A. L., Sutphin Road and Rockaway Boulevard, Jamaica, N. Y.
Miller, Earl S., 30 Lathrop Ave., Binghamton, N. Y.
*Miller, Mrs. Elisabeth C. T., 1010 Euclid Ave., Cleveland, Ohio.
†Miller, Dr. George Norton, 811 Madison Ave., New York City.
Miller, H. H., Box 105, Peapack, N. J.
Miller, Miss Julia, 2034 E. 88th St., Cleveland, Ohio.
Miller, Robert, Miller Floral Co., Farmington, Utah.
Miller, Mrs. S. B., 605 W. 19th St., Wilmington, Del.
Mills, Dr. Edmund M., 823 Sumner Ave., Syracuse, N. Y.
Mills, Mark Packard, 55th St. and Springfield Ave., Philadelphia.
‡Mills, Mrs. S. B., 823 Sumner Ave., Syracuse, N. Y.
Minch, Philip J., R. F. D. 4, Painesville, Ohio.
Minium, Miss Linda, N. Union St., Fostoria, Ohio.
Minns, Miss Lua A., Cornell University, Ithaca, N. Y.
Mitchell, Francis B., Pittsford, N. Y.
Mitchell, George W., 35 Bellevue Ave., Bristol, Conn.
Mitchell, Rev. Jas. F., San Jacinto, Calif.
Mitchell, Percival H., 1003 Traders Bank Bldg., Toronto, Can.
Mitchell, Mrs. Walter, Morewood Place, E. E., Pittsburgh, Pa.
Mitchell, W. G., 5 S. Water St., Rochester, N. Y.
Moffitt, James K., 86 Sea View Ave., Piedmont, Calif.
Mohlman, Mrs. J. H., Brielle, N. J.
Mohney, Delwyn D., 1315 Fourth Ave., Ford City, Pa.
Mohrman, Frederick C., Care Western Union Telegraph Co., 990 6th Ave., New York City.
Molloy Bros., Washington C. H., Ohio.
Monck, W. A., Care of E. J. Trepaguier, 621 Broadway, New Orleans, La.
*Montgomery, Alex., Hadley, Mass.
*Montgomery, Alex., Jr., Hadley, Mass.
Montgomery, Robert, Natick, Mass.
Montour, E. W., 636 W. Lee St., Baltimore, Md.
Moore, J. Turner, Reading, Pa.
Moore, Miss K. T., Scarboro, N. Y.
Moore, Mrs. Kenneth W., 19 Perdicaris Place, Trenton, N. J.
Moore, Miss Laura B., 1717 Avery St., Parkersburg, W. Va.
Morgan, Mrs. F. C., Montgomery Ave., Chestnut Hill, Philadelphia.
Morrill, Mrs. G. N., 11025 Magnolia Drive, Cleveland, Ohio.
Morris, J. G., Millneck, L. I.
Morris, Mrs. A. G., 66 Beechwood Terrace, Yonkers, N. Y.
Morrison, B. Y., 116 Chestnut St., Takoma Park, Washington, D. C.
Morrissee, Miss Althea. Ramapo, N. Y.
Morse, A. B., St. Joseph, Mich.
Morse, Mrs. C. H., 1730 Broadway, New York City.
Morse, Henry, Westfield Nursery, Norwich, England.
*Mortenson, Stephen, Southampton, Pa.
Moss, Milton, Huntsville Wholesale Nurseries, Huntsville, Ala.
Motley, Mrs. Thomas, Jr., 241 Beacon St., Boston, Mass.
Mott, Miss M., Radnor, Pa.
Moulton, W. C., Thomas Station, Birmingham, Ala.
Mueller, Mrs. Frank W., P. O. Box 247, Davenport, Iowa.
Muench, H. E., P. O. Box 229, Stamford, Conn.
Muller, Jean Paul, 5110 14th St., N.W., Washington, D. C.
Mulford, Fanny A., 127 Fulton Ave., Hempstead, N. Y.
Mulford, F. L., Agricultural Department, Washington, D. C.
Mulkey, F. W., Mulkey Bldg., Portland, Ore.
Munsick, G. W., 596 Prospect St., Maplewood, N. J.
Murdock, J. J., 1564 Broadway, New York City.
Murdock, J. Walter, 28 Oak St., Brockton, Mass.

MEMBERS AMERICAN ROSE SOCIETY

Murie, Johnston, Pantorium Dye Works, 970 Denny Way, Seattle, Wash.
Murphey, Roger H., Urbana, Ohio.
Murphy, Miss Katharine E., 6300 Park Ave., Philadelphia.
Murray, Herman S., E. Broadway, Woodmere, Long Island, N. Y.
Murray, Samuel, 1017 Grand Ave., Kansas City, Mo.
Murrell, R., Shepperton-on-Tnames, London, England.
Musser, Rev. James B., 735 Crescent Ave., Ellwood City, Pa.
Myers, C. G., 170 W. Columbia St., Alliance, Ohio.
Myers, F. P., Chestnut Hill, Philadelphia.
Myers, J. S., Chestnut Hill, Philadelpnia.

Nash, Aubrey S., Hentz & Nash, Inc., 55 W. 26th St., New York City.
Nash, Mrs. S. P., Milburn, N. J.
Natorp, William A., Madison Road and Moorman Ave., Cincinnati, Ohio.
Neff, William L., 98 N. 23d St., East Orange, N. J.
Nehrling, A. H., Crawfordsville, Ind.
Nellis, George W., 75 Genesee St., Auburn, N. Y.
Nelson, J. P., 49 Wall St., New York City.
Nelson, N. 400 Washington St., Hartford, Conn.
Nettleboro, Mrs. DeW. B., 245 Broad St., Sewickley, Pa.
Newbold, Miss Edith, 109 E. 73d St., New York City.
Newbold, F. R., 109 E. 72d St., New York City.
Newbold, James B., 2038 Eutaw Place, Baltimore, Md.
Newell, H. G. G., P. O. Box 141, Fellows, Calif.
Nichols, C. A., 21 Townsend St., Worcester, Mass.
Nichols, Mrs. F. C., 112 New Boston Road, Fall River, Mass.
Nichols, Mrs. H. S. Prentiss, 346 Pelham Road, Germantown, Philadelphia.
Nichols, Mrs. J. C., 225 W. 52nd St., Kansas City, Mo.
Nielsen, Einar, "Windy Pines," Glenview, Ill.
Niessen Co., The Leo, 12th and Race Sts., Philadelphia.
Nitchie, Mrs. J. E., Rahway Ave., Westfield, N. J.
Noble, Dr. Joseph W., White Pine Lodge, Hempstead, Long Island, N. Y.
Noe, L. A., Madison, N. J.
North, Miss Clara E., 78 University Place, New Brighton, Staten Island, N. Y.
Northrup, Dr. G. A., 104 Montgomery St., Poughkeepsie, N. Y.
Norton, Harry A., Ayers Cliff, Quebec, Can.
Noye, Richard K., Queenstown, Ont., Can.
Noyes, Frederick B., 122 Michigan Ave., Chicago.
Nusly, S. C., 521 Market Ave., N., Canton, Ohio.

Oakes, Miss Mary, Bloomfield, N. J.
O'Connor, Mrs. Haldeman, 13 N. Front St., Harrisburg, Pa.
Offutt, M. D., Box 141, Midway, Ky.
Ogden, W. B., Lee House Plantation, Lemon City, Fla.
Oglevee, Rev. J. A. B., Edmond, Okla.
Oliver, Mrs. Henry, Woodland Road, Sewickley, Pa.
Olmsted Bros., 99 Warren St., Brookline, Mass.
Olson, Olaf J., St. Paul, Minn.
O'Mara, Patrick, 35 Cortlandt St., New York City.
O'Neill, John J., 552 Washington St., Camden, N. J.
Orlady, G. B., 458 City Hall, Philadelphia.
Ormsbee, Mrs. M. H., Massapequa, Long Island, N. Y.
Orndorff, Miss Lizzie, 201 W. 9th St., Russellville, Ky.
Osborn, Mrs. H. Fairfield, Castle Rock, Garrison, N. Y.
Osman, Fred D., 88 Montross Ave., Rutherford, N. J.
Overley, Mrs. William D., 782 Main St., Danville, Va.
Owens, C. C., Lowville, N. Y.
Owens, Miss Margaret, Care of Dale & Nicholas, Houghton, Mich.

Paar, Frank W., 390 Hancock St., Brooklyn, N. Y.
Paddock, Prof. Wendell, Department of Horticulture, Ohio State University, Columbus, Ohio.
†Page, Hon. Courtney, Earldoms, Ridgeway, Enfield, Middlesex, England.
Palmer, W. J., 304 Main St., Buffalo, N.Y.
Palmer, Dr. W. W., 152 Montclair Ave., Montclair, N. J.
Panabaker, E. A., 100 Bloomingdale Road, Pleasant Plain, Staten Island, N. Y.
Pancoast, Mrs. Annie P., Hancock's Bridge, Salem County, N. J.
Park, Byron B., 904 Clark St., Stevens Point, Wis.
Park, Dr. H. M., 9 E. Main St., Mt. Kisco, N. Y.
Park, Joseph H., Port Murry, N. J.
Parker, A. M., Strafford, Pa.
Parker, A. S., 709 Woodward Ave., Detroit, Mich.
Parker, Charles F., 1205 "F" St., N.W., Washington, D. C.
Parker, Miss Emma H., Hindman Settlement School, Hindman, Ky.
Parker, G. A., Municipal Building, Hartford, Conn.
Parker, Herman, 400 Washington St., Boston, Mass.
Parker, Robert B., 694 Parker St., Newark, N. J.
Parker, Walter M., Manchester, N. H.
Parson, A. E., 404 W. 22nd St., Wilmington, Del.
Parsons, G. F., 21 Carver Road, Watertown. Mass.
Passavant, H. E., 6248 Overbrook Ave., Philadelphia.
Patrick, E. D., Marengo, Ill.

Patten, Fred B., 1102-8 Third National Bank Bldg., St. Louis, Mo.
Patten, I. M., Glasgow, Mont.
Patterson, John N., 86 W. Bean St., Washington, Pa.
Patterson, Morris S., 443 E. Woodlawn St., Germantown, Philadelphia.
Patterson, Mrs. R. A., Route 2, Box 48, Richmond, Va.
Patterson, Mrs. William A., Riverside Drive, Red Bank, N. J.
Paul, A. C., 504 Ridgewood Ave., Minneapolis, Minn.
Paul, Mrs. William K., Belmont, N. Y.
Payn, Mrs. Marion H., Chatham, New York.
Payne, Dr. F. I., 38 Granite St., Westerly, R. I.
Pearsall, Samuel, 86 Woodruff Ave., Flatbush, Brooklyn, N. Y.
Peck, Mrs. A. N., Woodmere, Long Island, N. Y.
Peck, E. C., Macedonia, Ohio.
Peek, S. H., East Aurora, N. Y.
Peer, Mrs. Fred C., 10 Foster St., Lyons, N. Y.
Pegram, Mrs. E. S., New Canaan, Conn.
Peirce, E. A., Waltham, Mass.
Pell, Thorold W., 147 3d St., Newark, N. J.
Pemberton, Rev. Jos. H., Havering, Romford, England.
Penn, Henry, 124 Tremont St., Boston.
Penna, Alfonso, Jr., Bello Horisonte, Estado de Minas, Brazil.
Pennock, Mrs. A. L., Lansdowne, Pa.
‡Pennock, Mrs. John D., 2002 W. Genesee St., Syracuse, N. Y.
Pennock, J. L., 1514 Chestnut St., Philadelphia.
Pennock, Mrs. S. S., Lansdowne Court, Lansdowne, Pa.
*Pennock, S. S., 1612 Ludlow St., Philadelphia.
Pepper, James S., 12 E. 35th St., Kansas City, Mo.
Perin, Mrs. F., Cincinnati, Ohio.
Perkins, G. C., Jackson & Perkins Co., Newark, N. Y.
Perkins, Mrs. J. H., 3264 Stettinius Ave., Cincinnati, Ohio.
Perrine, Mrs. F. A. C., 413 W. State St., Trenton, N. J.
Perry, Joseph H., 276 Highland St., Worcester, Mass.
Persons, Mrs. John C., 782 Main St., Danville, Va.
Perry, Lester, 541 Washington Ave., Ogden, Utah.
Peterson, George H., Fair Lawn, N. J.
Petrosch, Mrs. Carl S., 69 E. 82nd St., New York City.
Pforsheimer, Walter, Hidden Brook Farm, Purchase, New York.
Phillips, Charles S., 4 Lee Court, Lee Place, Cincinnati, Ohio.
*Pierson, F. R., Tarrytown, N. Y.
Pierson, Lincoln, P. O. Box 111, Madison, N. J.
*Pierson, P. M., Scarboro, N. Y.
*Pierson, W. R., Cromwell, Conn.

Pilton, George, 25 Beechwood Ave., Hamilton, Ont., Can.
Pinault, Z. R., 343 Washington St., Fairhaven, Mass.
Piper, Charles, 307 W. Graham St. Pittsburgh, Pa.
Pirkey, Mrs. E. M., 1501 Topeka Ave., Topeka, Kan.
Pitkin, William, 82 St. Paul St., Rochester, N. Y.
Pitt, Mrs. N. R., 254 Cedar Road, New Rochelle, N. Y.
Plumb, Charles E., Ridgeville, Ont., Can.
*Poehlmann, August F., Morton Grove, Ill.
Poffenhols, Wm., General Delivery, Richmond, Calif.
du Pont, Aileen M., Care of Mrs. Chas. Copeland, Wilmington, Del.
du Pont, Mrs. W. K., Box 52, Wilmington, Del.
Pope, Dr. E. S., Corner Braemar Road and North Ave., New Rochelle, N. Y.
Popular, Charles A., 1519 17th St., Galveston, Tex.
Porter, J. M., 13 Burbank Ave., Johnson City, N. Y.
Portman, William, P. O. Box D., Hoosick Falls, N. Y.
Potter, W. F., 15 Stevenson St., Cortland, N. Y.
Powell, Mrs. S. A., Upper Montclair, N.J.
Pratt, Mrs. A. S., 235 W. 75th St., New York City.
Pratt, Mrs. Harold I., Glen Cove, Long Island, N. Y.
Pratt, Percy P., 328 W. Franklin St., Jackson, Mich.
Pratt, Rosalind C., Stony Creek, Conn.
Prentice, Mrs. S. O., 70 Gillett St., Hartford, Conn.
†Preston-Hillary, S. A. R., Gwernant, Northwood, Middlesex, England.
Priest, Mrs. Frank B., Foster St., Littleton, Mass.
Prieto, Ramon F., Princesa 34 O.,Cardenas, Cuba.
Prindle, H. B., Riverside, Conn.
Pritchard, J., Bedford Hill, N. Y.
Providence Public Library, Providence, R. I.
Puller, Gustav, 208 5th Ave., Paterson, N. J.
Purdue University, Horticultural Department, Lafayette, Ind.
Purdy, Mrs. Charles E., Port Chester, N. Y.
Pyle, Robert, West Grove, Pa.

Quereau, C. H., New York Ave., White Plains, N. Y.
Quigley, J. Earl, 800 Green St., Harrisburg, Pa.

Radford, Mrs. G. A., Marshall, Mo.
Rainey, Frank L., Box 96, Danville, Ky.
Rainey, Joseph, Chestnut Hill, Philadelphia.
Ramsperger, H. G., 400 Allaire Ave., Leonia, N. J.
Rankin, Mrs. Ernest, 65 Augustine St., Rochester, N. Y.

MEMBERS AMERICAN ROSE SOCIETY 177

Rasmussen, A., New Albany, Ind.
Rau, Mrs. Alfred, 200 W. 58th St., New York City.
Rawlings, Dr. J. W., 4428 N. 7th St., Tacoma, Wash.
Raymond, W. B., 17 Cliff Road, Toronto, Can.
Redstone, Mrs. Laura, 1705 K St., Bakersfield, Calif.
Reed, Rev. E. A., Edgewood Gardens, Springfield, Mass.
Reese, Miss Ella, 1244 Monroe St., Brookland, D. C.
Reeves, E. A., South Euclid, Ohio.
Rehling, Dr. Martin, 209 E. 61st. St., New York City.
Reid, Miss H. F. H., 100 Broad St., New York City.
Reinberg, George, 35 Randolph St., Chicago.
*Reinberg, Peter, 51 Wabash Ave., Chicago.
Remick, Mrs. J. C., 1614 Valmont St., New Orleans, La.
Remington, Stanley G., 347 N. Charles St., Baltimore, Md.
Reuter, Louis J., 329 Waverly Oak Road, Waltham, Mass.
Rice, Miss Grace E., 214 College Ave., Northfield, Minn.
Rice, Harry L., 10 High St., Boston, Mass.
Rich, Wm. P., 300 Massachusetts Ave., Boston, Mass.
Richards, E. C., Box 1635, Tacoma, Wash.
Richards, E. H., 67 Greenbush Ave., Cortland, N. Y.
Richardson, Hayden, Dennis, Mass.
Richardson, H. A., 420 N. Wall St., Joplin, Mo.
Richardson, J. N., Smithwood Ave., Catonsville, Md.
Ried, Miss H. F. H., 100 Broad St., New York City.
Riegel, A. J., 594 Central Ave., Albany, N. Y.
Riegel, W. H., 240 E. Main St., Mechanicsburg, Pa.
Rieger, Harry, 819 N. 24th St., Philadelphia.
Riley, Frank E., Cumberland National Bank, Bridgeton, N. J.
Ritter, J. A., 1918 N. Charles St., Baltimore, Md.
Ritter, W. Lee, 1018 Appleton St., Baltimore, Md.
Roberts, Eugene H., Bank of Orleans, New Orleans, La.
Roberts, G. Theodore, 121 Madison Ave., New York City.
Roberts, Mrs. G. W., 912 S. Sheridan Road, Highland Park, Ill.
‡Roberts, John T., 538 Roberts Ave., Syracuse, N. Y.
‡Roberts, Miss Louise W., 520 Roberts Ave., Syracuse, N. Y.
Robin, James A., Bank of Orleans, New Orleans, La.
Robins, Mrs. Raymond, 1437 W. Ohio St., Chicago.
Robinson, Dr. Alice, 42 Dartmouth St., Springfield, Mass.

Robinson, A. E., Lexington, Mass.
Robinson, F. W., 390 E. Grand Boulevard, Detroit, Mich.
Robinson, Mrs. Helen J., 328 W. 101st St., New York City.
Robinson, James S., Box 288, Memphis, Tenn.
Rock, William L., 1106 Grand Ave., Kansas City, Mo.
Rockwell, Mrs. A. P., 51 Willard Ave., Bloomfield, N. J.
Rodgers, William T., 27th and Penn Sts., Penbrook, Pa.
Roeding, George C., Fresno, Calif.
Roelker, W., 51 Barclay St., New York City.
Roentgen, A. E., 1315 Manor Park, Lakewood, Ohio.
Rogers, C. B., 11 Ann St., Montgomery, Ala.
Roland, Thomas, Nahant, Mass.
Romaine, Theodore, 421 Park St., Hackensack, N. J.
Rood, Stanley H., 53 Willard St., Hartford, Conn.
Root, John, 412 Lees Ave., Collingswood, N. J.
Rose, Albert N., 701 Summit Ave., St. Paul, Minn.
Rosenberger, Mrs. C. L., 4008 James St., East Syracuse, N. Y.
Rosenberger, Walter Lee, 450 E. Tulpehocken St., Germantown, Philadelphia.
Rosenbluth, E. M., Wallingford, Pa.
Rosengarten, H. B., Malvern, Pa.
Rosenthal, Mrs. H. A., Gypsy, W. Va.
Rosenwald, Mrs. Julius, 4901 Ellis Ave., Chicago.
Rouss, Mrs. P. W., Bayville, L. I.
Rousseau, Thos. G., 3618 Prytania St., New Orleans, La.
Rowe, Mrs. Wallace H., 624 Morewood Ave., Pittsburgh, Pa.
Roy, W. Ormiston, 207 Papineau Ave., Montreal, Can.
Royecs, Jennie, 3109 Hancock Ave., Cleveland, Ohio.
Ruhl, J. W., 120 Blanch St., Houghton, Mich.
Rumford, Dr. Lewis, 1411 Woodlawn Ave., Wilmington, Del.
Rumrill, Mrs. Henry, Jr., 536 Franklin St., Buffalo, N. Y.
Rumsey, Mrs. C. J., 310 W. State St., Ithaca, N. Y.
Rumsey, W. F., 5 Court St., White Plains, N. Y.
Russell, Joseph, 6324 City Ave., Philadelphia.
‡Russell, Mark, 1087 S. High St., Columbus, Ohio.
Rust, David, 606 Finance Bldg., Philadelphia.
Rutherfurd, Livingston, 18 W. 24th St., New York City.
Ryan, John, 1688 Grand Ave., Piedmont, Calif.
Ryder, Clarence H., 109 Montowese St., Branford, Conn.
Ryburn, Robert L., Shelby, N. C.

Sacrey, Louis M., Merion, Pa.
St. John, Mrs. I. E., Orange City, Fla.
St. Louis Public Library, St. Louis, Mo.
St. Paul Public Library, Washington and 4th Sts., St. Paul, Minn.
Samptmann, M., Chestnut Hill, Philadelphia.
Sams, W. J., Stuart, Fla.
Sanborn, A. N., 5301 Boyd Ave., Oakland, Calif.
Sander, Mrs. H. S., 35 S. Raleigh St., Atlantic City, N. J.
Sanders, Herman, 430 Pine St., Brooklyn, N. Y.
Sanford, F. A., 26 Pleasant St., Westfield, Mass.
Saunders, Miss B. C., 1603 Third St., N.W., Washington, D. C.
Saunders, B. Fred, Georgetown, N. Y.
Saunders, Miss Mary Elisa, 260 Warburton Ave., Yonkers, N. Y.
Sawyer, Miss Amelia, Gilman, Iowa.
Saylor, Henry W., Editor "Country Life," Huntington, Long Island, N. Y.
Schalscha, Maximilian, 61 Hobart Ave., Summit, N. J.
Scheffler, Henry H., 94 Best St., Buffalo, N. Y.
Schell, Miss Annie L., Burlington, Mineral Co., W. Va.
Schellentrager, E. A., 540 E. 115th St., Cleveland, Ohio.
Schevick, Mrs. Antonio, 224 Shelton St., Bridgeport, Conn.
Schiele, Charles J., 441 Missouri Ave., East St. Louis, Ill.
Schindler, Theresa E., Graystone House, Cayuga Heights Road, Ithaca, N. Y.
Schlaffer, John G., 414 S. Clinton St., Baltimore, Md.
Schleyer, John A., Fleming and Gay Sts., Roxboro, Philadelphia.
Schmidt, Edward A., Radnor, Pa.
Schmidt, F. A., Kittanning, Pa.
Schmidt, Frederick W., Juniper Hall, Radnor, Pa.
Schmitt, George, R. F. D. 2, Box 167, Ridgewood, N. J.
Scholes, John F., 1213 W. Allegheny Ave., Philadelphia.
Scholle, Herman, Station A., Ames, Iowa.
Schonewolf, Henry W., 188 W. Utica St., Buffalo, N. Y.
Schoonman, Martin, Quidnick Greenhouses, Anthony, R. I.
Schoyer, B. Preston, 304 Union Bank Bldg., Pittsburgh, Pa.
Schreiber, A., East Aurora, N. Y.
Schroeder, Mrs. A., 184 Upper Mountain Ave., Montclair, N. J.
Schulte, E. J., 642 Greenfield Ave., Milwaukee, Wis.
Schultheis, Anton, College Point, N. Y.
Schultz, E. K., Jenkintown, Pa.
Schultz, Joseph K., Barto, Berks County, Pa.
Schumm, Lorens G., 302 "C" St., LaPorte, Ind.
Schuster, Edward W., Crookston, Minn.
Schwartz, E. H., Sharon Hill, Pa.
Scoles, Richard J., Passaic, N. J.

Scott, Alexander B., Sharon Hill, Pa.
Scott, Mrs. Henry P., Delaware City, Del.
Scott, Joseph, 128 Delaware Ave., Charleston, W. Va.
Scott, M. H., P. O. Box 36, Piper City, Ill.
Screaton, Samuel, 26 Craig St., London, Ont., Can.
Scribner's, Charles, Sons, Fifth Ave. and 48th St., New York City.
Scripter, Dr. Otis, 2610 Elm Ave., Zion City, Ill.
Scudder, Lawrence W., 157 E. 81st. St., New York City.
Scull, M. L., Care of American Ice Co., Atlantic City, N. J.
Sealy, Jacob, 50 Washington Ave., Brooklyn, N. Y.
‡Seamans, Dr. Harry, Ashland and Glenwood Aves., Grandview, Columbus, Ohio.
Sears, Mrs. George A., 870 Alameda St., Portland, Ore.
Seaver, Robert, 11 Harris Ave., Jamaica Plain, Mass.
Sechrist, J. F., 245 Hillcrest Ave., Trenton, N. J.
Seeley, Dr. A. C., Roseburg, Ore.
Sessemann, Mrs. H. C., 11 S. 19th St., Harrisburg, Pa.
Sewell, Mrs. Wm. B., 31 Bush Ave., Greenwich, Conn.
Shadbolt, Mrs. Frank, Huntington, Long Island, N. Y.
Shaible, F. G., 61 Locust St., Freeport, Ill.
Shannon, Mrs. R. F., Glenfrew, Sewickley, Pa.
*Sharpe, Mrs. E. M., 80 W. River St., Wilkes-Barre, Pa.
Sharrett, Mrs. Bertha, 492 Villa Ave., Port Richmond, N. Y.
Shaw, Edwin, C., N. Portage Road, Akron, Ohio.
Shaw, H. Clay, Piedmont, W. Va.
Shaw, S. S., Newton, N. J.
Shawhan, John M., 644 15th Ave., Maywood, Ill.
Sheble, Mrs. Frank J., Rumfort Road, Mt. Airy, Philadelphia.
Sheldrick, R., 31 Union Square, West, New York City.
Shepard, W. H., Box 143, Short Hills, N. J.
Shepherd, E. S., Geophysical Laboratory, Washington, D. C.
Shew, E. L., Haddon Heights, N. J.
Shoemaker, B. H., 2nd, 523 Church Lane, Philadelphia.
Shoop, Mrs. Kate, Box 841, Leechburg, Pa.
Shryock, Miss G. A., 225 S. 6th St., Philadelphia.
Siebert, Mrs. M. H., Merriam St., Walla Walla, Wash.
*Siebrecht, H. A., 425 Fifth Ave., New York City.
Silber, Miss Charlotte G., 1044 Webster St., Needham, Mass.
Simkins, Mrs. W. H., 112 Homestead Ave., Collingswood, N. J.
Simmons, H. B., 234 Virginia Park, Detroit, Mich.
Simpson, Harry, 835 Taylor Ave., Scranton, Pa.

MEMBERS AMERICAN ROSE SOCIETY

*Simpson, Robert, Clifton, N. J.
‡Skelton, C. E., 4023 S. Salina St., Syracuse, N. Y.
Skelton, C. W., P. O. Box 217, Jersey City, N. J.
Skidelsky, S. S., 1004 Lincoln Bldg., Philadelphia
Sloan, Mrs. R. S., Woodmere, Long Island, N. Y.
Small, John H., 15 W. 2nd St., N.W., Washington, D. C.
Smalley, J., 611 June St., Fall River, Mass.
Smedley, Wm. W., 3043 Grand Ave., Minneapolis, Minn.
Smith, Mrs. Annie Foote, Lee, Mass.
Smith, James B,. Burlingame, Calif.
‡Smith, P. D., 823 Sumner Ave., Syracuse, N. Y.
Smith, R. E., 279 South Monroe Ave., Columbus, Ohio.
Smith, Mrs. Robert P., 84 Tuxedo Ave., Highland Park, Mich.
Smith, Mrs. T. Hart, 1309 Girard Ave., Philadelphia.
Smyth, James M., 2406 W. 16th St., Wilmington, Del.
Snow, Mrs. Elmer J., Mahwah, N. J.
‡Snow, Mrs. H. G., 807 Court St., Syracuse, N. Y.
Snyder, Dr. F. D., Ashtabula, Ohio.
Sohm, Albert, 19 Brewster Street, Tompkinsville, N. Y.
Spaulding, Mrs. Gale, Sunrise Cabin, Piermont-on-Hudson, N. Y.
Spencer, George A., 418 Lenox Ave., Westfield, N. J.
Spilman, Mrs. B. D., Elway Hall, Warrenton, Va.
Spilman, Miss Elisabeth, Warrenton, Va.
Sprague, R. P., 317 Caroline St., Herkimer, N. Y.
Spreckels, Mrs. C. A., Manhasset, Long Island, N. Y.
Spridgen, May C., Box 221, Yorkville, Ill.
Springer, Mrs. Frank E., South Brownsville, Pa.
Spruance, W. C., Jr., Wilmington, Del.
Squire, Alfred L., 83 Hamilton Ave., White Plains, N. Y.
Stahelin, A. J., Redford, Mich.
Staiti, Mrs. H. T., 421 Westmoreland Ave., Houston, Tex.
Staley, Arthur, Fullerton, Calif.
Stang, Mrs. Clarence, 744 N. 63d St., Philadelphia.
Staples, Harold J., 15 Crescent St., Biddeford, Me.
Stark, William H., Neosho, Mo.
Stark Bros., Louisiana, Mo.
Steele, Dr. Guy, 1 Church St., Cambridge, Md.
Steinburg, Richard W., Box 193, 444 Washington Ave., Grantwood, N. J.
Steinstrup, Mrs. P. S., 1 Hamilton Road, Glen Ridge, N. J.
Stephen, A. L., 703 Chestnut St., Waban, Mass.
Stephens, C. W., 156 2nd St., New Brighton, Staten Island, N. Y.
Stephens, Mrs. T. H., 138 Division St., Hasbrouck Heights, N. J.

Stephenson, Robert S., 2 W. 42nd St., New York City.
Stephenson's Sons, John, Philadelphia.
Stevens, A. F., Ramapo, N. Y.
Stevens, G. A., Mineral City, Ohio.
Stevens, Mrs. H. B., R. F. D. Station A., Syracuse, N. Y.
Stewart, Howard E., 2820 Clifton Ave., Baltimore, Md.
Stewart, Wm. F., Edgewood Road, Lake Forest, Ill.
Stewart, W. J., 147 Summer St., Boston, Mass.
Stich, Mrs. A. C., Independence, Kan.
Stillman, C. C., 9 E. 67th St., New York City.
Stites, Thomas H. A., Hamburg State Sanatorium, Hamburg, Pa.
Stockton, Howard, 31 Commonwealth Ave., Boston, Mass.
*Stoeckel, Mrs. C., Norfolk, Conn.
*Stoeckel, Carl, Norfolk, Conn.
Stolze, Andrew H., 4307 S. Warner St., Tacoma, Wash.
Stone, Miss E. J., 34 E. 50th St., New York City.
Stone, George H., 206 Breaden St., Youngstown, Ohio.
Stonelake, C. A., 144 N. 9th St., Newark, N. J.
Storrs & Harrison Co., The, Painesville, Ohio.
*Stow, W. L., 36 Wall St., New York City.
Straub, Mrs. E., Bayshore Terrace, East Elmhurst, Long Island, N. Y.
Strauss, Mrs. Albert, Oyster Bay, N. Y.
Strawbridge, Miss Anne W., Germantown, Philadelphia.
Strawbridge, Mrs. George, Wissahickon Ave. and Hortter St., Germantown, Philadelphia.
Strayer, Mrs. H. H., R. F. D. 3, Box 61, Middletown, Pa.
Strohecker, S. M., M.D., Kenton Bank Bldg., Portland, Ore.
Stroud, Mrs. Morris W., Jr., Villa Nova, Pa
Struble, Mrs. A. J., Centerville, S. D.
Struckmeyer, Mrs. M. F., Prise, Calif.
Stryker, S. D., Oradell, N. J.
*Stumpp, G. E. M., 761 Fifth Ave., New York City.
Stuppy, Frank X., St. Joseph, Mo.
Sturla, Louis, 3951 Floral Ave., Cincinnati, Ohio.
Sturtevant, R. S., Wellesley Farms, Mass.
Styvers, A. A., 33 Gould Ave., Caldwell, N. J.
Sulliger, Rev. S. S., Kent, Wash.
Sullivan, Elizabeth, 1041 N. Bonnie Brae St., Los Angeles, Calif.
Sunderland, Mrs. C., 94 W. Passaic Ave., Rutherford, N. J.
Swann, Mrs. Sherlock, 908 N. Charles St., Baltimore, Md.
Swenson, P. M., 2526 Polk St., N.E., Minneapolis, Minn.

Tallman, Mrs. F. G., 1401 W. 10th St., Wilmington, Del.

Tanger, Mrs. Charles Y., President Ave., Lancaster, Pa.
Tarnok, Sigmund, 109 W. 10th St., Wilmington, Del.
Taylor, Duncan W., 455 W. 7th St., Plainfield, N. J.
†Taylor, Norman, Brooklyn Botanic Garden, Brooklyn, N. Y.
Terrell, R. A., 503 Title Bldg., Birmingham, Ala.
Thatcher, George, 112 Farm St., Ithaca, N. Y.
Thayer, Clark L., Ithaca, N. Y.
Thayer, Edwin F., Attleboro, Mass.
Thayer, S. Willard, Pawtucket, R. I.
Thilow, J. Otto, Palmyra, N. J.
Thomas, Miss Anne, 312 Washington St., Frankfort, Ky.
‡Thomas, Mrs. C. W., 2585 W. Broad St., Columbus, Ohio.
Thomas, Charles C., Williams & Wilkins Co., 2419 Greenmount Ave., Baltimore, Md.
Thomas, George C., Jr., Chestnut Hill, Philadelphia.
Thomas, Jefferson, 1625 Park St., Jacksonville, Fla.
Thomas, William L., 114 21st St., Warwood, W. Va.
Thomas, Mrs. W. O., Lock Box 578, Clinton, Rock County, Wis.
Thompson, Mrs. Frederick F., Canandaigua, N. Y.
Thompson, Mrs. F. L., Bellows Falls, Vt.
Thompson, F. M., White Plains, N. Y.
Thomson, H. C., 20 W. Fountain Ave., Delaware, Ohio.
Thorburn, C. J., 616 Hatch Ave., Woodhaven, Long Island, N. Y.
*Thorley, C., 562 Fifth Ave., New York City.
‡Thornberg, G. G., 37 W. 2nd Ave., Columbus, Ohio.
Thorne, Jonathan, 43 Cedar St., New York City.
Thornton, L. S., 410 Colwyn Ave., Darby, Pa.
‡Thorpe, George E., 107 W. Newell St., Syracuse, N. Y.
Thorphil, John, 544 E. 115th St., Cleveland, Ohio.
Tillotson, H. S., 5904 Ellsworth St., Philadelphia.
Tipple, Mrs. Ezra Squier, Drew Forest, Madison, N. J.
Todd, George T., Room 37, Federal Bldg., Albany, N. Y.
Tomey, Mrs. J. H., 24 Porter Place, Montclair, N. J.
Tompkins, J. D., Valatie, N. Y.
Totty, Charles H., Madison, N. J.
Towill, Edward, Roslyn, Pa.
Tows, F. H., Norfolk, Conn.
Tracy, Wm. G., 776 James St., Syracuse, N. Y.
Traendly, Frank H., 436 6th Ave., New York City.
Trautmann, F., 73 Barclay St., New York City.
Tregaskis, Mrs. John, 94 Vernon Ave., Brooklyn, N. Y.
Tribuno, M. P., 95 6th Ave., New York City.
Trow, William A., 31 Lowell St., Andover, Mass.
Trutna, Thos. J., Silver Lake, Minn.
‡Tryon, Mrs. O. F., 239 E. Genesee St., Auburn, N. Y.
Tucker, Mrs. Mabel Reid, Winthrop Place, Englewood, N. J.
Tucker, C. J., Manager, Longview Farm, Hickman Mills, Mo.
Turbat, E., 67–69 Route d'Olivet, Orleans, France.
Turnbull, W. R., 42 Ontario Ave., Hamilton, Ont., Can.
Twyeffort, Miss Lillian, 61 W. 90th St., New York City.
Tyndall, David, 104 Main St., Brockton, Mass.

Uhl, L. F., 2692 St. James Parkway, Cleveland Heights, Ohio.
Uhri, Wm. Co., 2163 S. Grand Ave., St Louis, Mo.
Ulrich, A. G., 3966 Arsenal St., St. Louis, Mo.
Underdown, A. R., 141 Mansion Ave., Haddonfield, N. J.
Underhill, F. G., The Laurels, Plough Lane, Croydon, England.
Undritz, Frederick R. M., 188 Greenleaf Ave., West New Brighton, Long Island, N. Y.
Undritz, Reinhold, 188 Greenleaf Ave., West New Brighton, Long Island, N. Y.
Upton, Clarence, Enfield, Pa.

Valentine, John, 707 Riverside Ave., Muncie, Ind.
Van Asdlen, Wilson B., 4603 Woodland Ave., Philadelphia.
Van Bochove, John R., Kalamazoo, Mich.
Vanderbeek, A. B., 174 Broadway, Paterson, N. J.
Van Dervoort, Dr. B. M., 1303 E. Washington St., Bloomington, Ill.
Van Duyn, Mrs. F. W., 81 N. Van Dien Ave., Ridgewood, N. J.
Van Hagen, Miss M. H., 488 Second Ave., Troy, N. Y.
Van Lindley, J., Pomona, N. C.
Van Syckel, Miss Bessie, 425 Greenwood Ave., Trenton, N. J.
Van Winkle, Wm. M., Apawannis Ave., Rye, N. Y.
Vaughan, H. W., Linden Terrace, Rutland, Vt.
*Vaughan, J. C., 84 Randolph St., Chicago.
Vavra, Joseph, Huntington Beach Nurseries, Huntington Beach, Calif.
Velie, Fred A., P. O. Box 160, Marlboro, N. Y.
Verhalen, George F., Scottsville, Texas.
Vert, William, 32 Ridge St., Greenwich, Conn.
Vier, H., 77 Greenedge Ave., White Plains, N. Y.
Vierira de Carvalho, Dr. A., Hospitaes S. Case de Misericordia de S. Paulo, S. Paulo, Brazil.
Volz, E. C., 124 S. Second St., Saginaw, Mich.

MEMBERS AMERICAN ROSE SOCIETY 181

Waddell, M., 30 Church St., New York City.
Wade, Mrs. M. S., 37 St. Paul St., Kamloops, B. C.
Wagner, C. H., 218 Fern Ave., Lyndhurst, N. J.
Wagner, W. D., Dalhart, Tex.
Wakelin, Miss G. V., R. F. D. 1, Quinton, N. J.
Wallace, W. P., Jr., 6159 Webster St., W. Philadelphia.
Waldo, J. F. C., 305 Hennen Bldg., New Orleans, La.
Wales National Library, Aberystwyth, Wales.
Walker, F. Dinwiddie, Narberth, Pa.
Walker, John, P. O. Box 114, N. Diamond Station, Pittsburgh, Pa.
Wallace, Gerald S., 10 Park Ave., Batavia, N. Y.
Wallace, James S., 12 Wellington St., E., Toronto, Ont.
Waller, Elwyn, Morristown, N. J.
Walling, C. Herbert, Rockaway, N. J.
Walsh, J. F., Woods Hole, Mass.
Walsh, M. H., Woods Hole, Mass.
Ward, Mrs. Aaron, Roslyn, N. Y.
Ward, C. W., Cottage Gardens Nurseries, Box 543, San Jose, Calif.
*Ward, C. W., Queens, Long Island, N. Y.
Ward, Elwood W., R. F. D. 1, Southboro, Mass.
Ward, Miss Laura P., 41 Park Place, Bloomfield, N. J.
Warner, C. H., 111 Warburton Ave., Yonkers, N. Y.
Warner, Mrs. Walter, 1211 Stratford Ave., Oak Lane, Philadelphia.
*Washburn, Charles L., Hinsdale, Ill.
Washburn, E. B., Pasadena, Cal.
Watkins, W. H., 12 St. James Place, Buffalo, N. Y.
Watson, George C., Dobson Bldg., 9th and Market Sts., Philadelphia.
Watson, Mrs. H. F., 356 W. 6th St., Erie, Pa.
Watson, Samuel, 501 W. 153d St., New York City.
Waugh, Prof. F. A., Amherst, Mass.
Weak, C. H., 6823 Milton St., Mt. Airy, Philadelphia.
Weaver, Courtney M., 208 Centre Ave., New Rochelle, N. Y.
Weaver, H. D., M.D., 3216 20th St., E., Saskatoon, Sask., Can.
Weavers, Fred C., 130 Chestnut St., Cooperstown, N. Y.
Webb, Mrs. James A., 251 Woodland Road, Madison, N. J.
Webb, Dr. W. S., Warwood, Wheeling, W. Va.
Webber, Samuel S., Charlestown, N. H.
Weber, Miss Caroline U., 101 8th Ave., Brooklyn, N. Y.
Weber, Harry R., 4238 Kirby Road, Cincinnati, Ohio.
Weber, I. H., 289 Main St., Winchester, Mass.
Wedrick, Chester D., R. F. D. 1, Sheridan, Ill.
Weeks, Dr. S. M., 1429 Spruce St., Philadelphia.
Welbank, Charles T., Valley Forge, Chester County, Pa.
Welch, E. S., Sec., Mt. Arbor Nursery Co., Shenandoah, Iowa.
*Welch, Patrick, 226 Devonshire St., Boston, Mass.
Welch, Richard A., Suite 4, Law Bldg., Keyser, W. Va.
Weld, Mrs. Samuel M., Forest Road, Greenwood, Mass.
Welsh, Edward L., 304 Walnut St., Philadelphia.
Wendell, J. R., 521 Wenzel Way, Banksville, Pittsburgh, Pa.
Wenham, R. P., Painesville, Ohio.
Wetterau, W. N., Box 249, Poughkeepsie, N. Y.
Whaley, Mr. E., 74 Roxborough St., E., Toronto, Ont.
Wheeler, Alan R., Beach Road, Newport, R. I.
Wheeler, Alson, Morrisville, N. Y.
Wheeler, E. P., Box 187, Rockland, Mass.
Wheeler, Seymour B., 38 Park Ave., Auburn, N. Y.
Whelan, John F., 44 W. 18th St., New York City.
Whidden, A. J., 2310 Scarff St., Los Angeles, Calif.
Whitcomb, E. M., 12 Lincoln Ave., Amherst, Mass.
White, A. C., Litchfield, Conn.
White, E. A., Cornell University, Ithaca, N. Y.
White, G. Derby, 253 S. Irving St., Ridgewood, N. J.
White, George F., Lansdowne, Pa.
White, Mrs. W. T., Trenton, N. J.
Whitehouse, Mrs. F. M., Manchester, Mass.
Whitford, Samuel, 257 Wisconsin Ave., Long Beach, Calif.
Whitman, C. T., 470 Rugby Road, Brooklyn, N. Y.
Whitney, Vida B., 825 W. 4th St., Plainfield, N. J.
Wicke, Miss Louise, 34 E. 68th St., New York City.
Wicker, W. W., 620 Moffat Bldg., Detroit, Mich.
Wickersham, Thomas, 113 3d St., Aspinwall, Pa.
Wilde, E. I., Box 357, State College, Pa.
Wilkinson, Mrs. Horace, Box 57, Port Allen, La.
Willever, J. C., Wyoming, N. J.
Williams, Mrs. Andrew, R. F. D. 1, Bridgeville, Pa.
Williams, George, New Britain, Bucks County, Pa.
Williams, Miss Helen E., 2030 Sunset Boulevard, San Diego, Calif.
Williams, H. W., 24 Thomas St., New York City.
Williams, John, Haverford, Pa.
Williams, Mrs. Stephen C., 9 E. 75th St., New York City.
Williamson, G. M., Nyack, N. Y.
Willis, W. P., 156 Fifth Ave., New York City.

Wills, John B., 8 Wolcott Terrace, Winchester, Mass.
Wilson, Alice E., 628 Halsey St., Portland, Ore.
Wilson, Mrs. Dale, 327 Pine St., Williamsport, Pa.
Wilson, James A., Lake Forest, Ill.
Windrim, John T., 1501 Commonwealth Trust Bldg., Philadelphia.
Wing, Asa S., 223 E. Central Ave., Moorestown, N. J.
Wing, Franklin R., 12 Harris Ave., Boston, Mass.
Winnett, Henry, Queens Hotel, Toronto, Ont.
Windsor, Robert P., 36 Prospect St., Auburn, R. I.
Wirth, Theodore, Minneapolis, Minn.
Wischman, Herman, 536 N. 4th St., Philadelphia.
Witchell, H., Bank of New Zealand, Otaki, New Zealand.
*Witterstaetter, R., Price Hill Station, Cincinnati, Ohio.
Wittkamp, H. A., Jr., Strathmere, N. J.
Wolf, Earl, Loudonville, Ohio.
Wood, Clarence, Box 315, Danville, Ky.
Wood, Colburn C., Bay View Ave., Plymouth, Mass.
Wood, Mrs. D. V., Birch St., Walla Walla, Wash.
Wood, Miss Marion B., Conshohocken, Pa.
Wood, Mrs. Orrin S., Monroe, N. Y.
‡Woodall, Frank, 2031 Midland Ave., Syracuse, N. Y.
Woodcock, W. P., Spencer, Iowa.
Woodruff, W. T., Thomastown, Conn.
Woods, George H., R. F. D. 4, Bridgeport, Conn.
‡Woodward, George H., 146 King Ave., Columbus, Ohio.
Woodwell, Mrs. Wm. E., 1008 Penn Ave., Pittsburgh, Pa.
Woolson, Mrs. Charles A., Mapledell Farms, Springfield, Vt.
Worcester County Horticultural Society, 18 Front St., Worcester, Mass.

Worker, H., Camillus, N. Y.
Wray, Mrs. Walter, Box 96, Tustin, Calif.
Wray, D. H., Care of Henry Wray & Son, Inc., Rochester, N. Y.
Wright, F. J., 2001 E. 33d St., Des Moines, Iowa.
Wright, M. C., 209 S. LaSalle St., Chicago.
Wright, Z. F., Newberry, S. C.
Wynkoop, C. B., 695 St. Nicholas Ave., New York City.

Yates, L. A., Box 366, Tallahassee, Fla.
Young, C. Edwin, 14 Chestnut St., Newark, N. J.
Young, E. L., Joliet, Ill.
Young, George E., Johnstown, Pa.
Young, Herbert E., 343 Waverly St., Belmont, Mass.
Young, John, Johnson Bldg., 1170 Broadway, New York City.
Young, John W., Germantown, Philadelphia.
Youngson, Mrs. E. A., 689 Alden St., Meadville, Pa.
Younts, C. P., 410 Main St., Houston, Tex.

Zabriskie, Mrs. Andrew C., Barrytown, N. Y.
Zabriskie, Mrs. Charles F., 37 W. 75th St., New York City.
Zeidler, William H., 668 Prospect Place, Brooklyn, N. Y.
Zeilian, Mrs. John J., 916 N. Sycamore St., Santa Ana, Calif.
Zeller, Alfred, 139 Lincoln Road, Flatbush, Brooklyn, N. Y.
Zenger, Joseph P., 168 Woodbridge Ave., Buffalo, N. Y.
Ziedler, Wm. H., 670 Prospect Place, Brooklyn, N. Y.
Zieger, Ernest J. F., 1120 E. Washington Lane, Philadelphia.
Zinnow, G., 2747 E. 27th St., Sheepshead Bay, Brooklyn, N. Y.

INDEX

American Rose Society, 1918 Work, 148; President's Report, 149; Secretary's Report, 150; Treasurer's Report, 152; Executive Committee meetings, 153; Fourth Annual Field Day, 156.
America, Roses Introduced in, 134.
Appleton, W. A., letters from, 82.
Attar, Rose, 15.
Auburn Chamber of Commerce, Wise, 125.
Australia, Roses in, 92.

Back-Yard Bloom Record, Second Year, 71.
Bagatelle Gardens, letter from Director, 53.
Bermuda, Roses in, 89.
Bisset, Peter, article by, 38; note by, 128.
Bloom Records: in Little Rock, 49; Williamsport, 60; Washington, 71; National Test-Garden, 116.
Bud-Variation of the Rose, 36.
Burgoyne, W. B., article concerning, 24.

California is "Different," 133.
Canadian Civic Rose-Garden, 24.
Cant, B. R., new roses, 102.
Caulfeild, Mrs. E. St. G., article by, 89.
Chambard, new rose of, 100.
Cherokee Rose, The Northern, 22.
Climbing Roses, Double Duty, 132; Zephirine Drouhin, 132; Plate facing 137.
Cook, John, Another Rose Coming, 124.
Crawford, Mrs. Andrew Wright, article by, 78.
Crown-Canker, More About, 74.
Currey, Jesse A., article by, 26; letter from, 124, 125.
Cut-Flower Rose Situation, 1918, 104.

Dickson A. and Hugh, new roses, 102.
Dr. Van Fleet's Rose Factory, 126.

Easlea, Walter, new rose, 102.
Egan, W. C., article by, 22; letter from, 123.
England, 1918 Rose Season in, 80.
Experience and Prophecy, 106.

Federal Horticultural Board, letter from Chairman, 115.
Food, Roses as, 125.
Forestier, J. C. N., letter from, 53.
Foreign Roses, The New, 99.
France, Wayside Roses in, 93.
Fragrant Roses, 14.
French Rose Nursery, A Great, 96.

Grafting Roses, stock for, 40.
Gravereaux, M. Jules, mentioned, 17.
Gersdorff, Charles E. F., notes by, 126, 131; list by, 134.
Greeley, Alfred W., article by, 57.
Greeley, A. P., article by, 71.
Guillot, M. Pierre, Memorial to, 85; new rose, 101.

Hammond, Benjamin, tribute by, 52.
Hill, E. G., mentioned, 35; letter from, 51.
Hospital, Flowers Barred from, 129.

Importations of Roses, 114.
International Coöperation, 127.
Italy, Roses in, 85.

Ketten Frères, letter from, 129.
King, Mrs. Francis, note from, 132.

Labor Leader, English, The Roses of, 82.
Leaves—What Good For?, 131.
LeCornu, Philip, new roses, 103, 132.
Local Societies, Affiliation of, 161.
Los Angeles Takes World Honors, 128.
Luxemburg, Hard Rose-Luck in, 129.

Mann, George R., article by, 42.
Marlatt, Dr. C. L., letter from, 114.
Massey, Dr. L. M., article by, 74.
McGredy, Samuel, letter from, 55; new roses, 102.
Medals Awarded 1918, 160.
Medals and Certificates Offered, 160.
Meyer, Frank N., Rose Contributions of, 38.
Minutes Annual Meeting, 148.
Montreal, Riding Rose Hobby in, 67.
Mulford, F. L., article by, 116.
Multiflora Stock, Experience with, 124.
Musk rose, 15.

INDEX

National Rose Society in Wartime, 83.
National Test-Garden in 1918, 116.
Nelles, Harold W., article by, 67.
New Foreign Roses, 99.

Ohio, Rose Advance in, 125.
On a Sun-Dial Wreathed with Roses, 21.
Ophelia, Pedigree of, 35.

Page, Courtney, 83; portrait of, facing 86.
Partial List of Roses Introduced, 134.
Passing of a Great Rosarian, 51.
Paul, A. W., letters from, 35, 54; new roses, 102.
Pemberton, Rev. Joseph H., letter from, 54; new roses, 103.
Pennock, Charles, article by, 96.
Pennock, S. S., article by, 104.
Pernet-Ducher, letter from, 53; new roses of, 100.
Pierson, Wallace R., article by, 106.
Plates, List of, 8.
Poem by Admiral Aaron Ward, 56.
Pomeroy, C. S., article by, 36.
Portland's New Test-Garden, 26.
Prizes, Special, in 1918, 161; for 1919, 161.
Protecting Tender Roses, 128.
Pyle, Robert, mentioned, 83, 129.

Railroad Roses in France, 123.
Red Cross Cash, Turning Roses into, 130.
Registration of New Roses, Rules for, 158; 1918 entries, 158.
Regulations and Scale of Points, 161.
Rockwell, F. F., poem by, 21.
Rosa, species mentioned: agrestis, 20, 34; alba, 17; altaica, 22; Banksiæ, 15; bella, 20; bracteata, 33; canina, 97; carolina, 33; centifolia, 15, 17, 19; chinensis, 19; cinnamomea, 15; damascena, 17; Ecæ, 14; fœtida, 14; gallica, 15, 17, 19; grandiflora, 22; hispida, 33; Hugonis, 16, 29; humilis, 10, 15, 19; Iwara, 30; lucida, 19; lutea, 14, 20, 34; Malyi, 32; Manetti, 97; moschata, 14; Moyesii, 29; multiflora, 14; nitida, 19; odorata, 15, 19, 31; odorata, form, 22, 449, 40; pendulina, 32; persica, 14; Pissardii, 31; rubiginosa, 10, 20; rugosa, 15, 17, 18, 29; setigera, 15, 31; setipoda, 32; Soulieana, 29; spinosissima, 22, 30; virginiana, 15, 19, 31; Wichuraiana, 31; xanthina, 14, 30, 39. (Plates facing 93, 105, 120.)
Rose-Breeding Notes for 1918, 29.
Rose Enthusiast and His Garden, 42.
Rose-Garden, Plan of, 44.
Rose Notes, 123.
Rose Poet, An American, 127.
Rose Premier (colored frontispiece), mentioned, 109.
Roses Cut and Roses Growing, 108.

Save and Use the Roses, 78.
Senni, Countess Giulio, letter from, 85.
Silver Wedding Roses, 9.
Souvenir of Wootton, Climbing, 126.
"Sports" or Bud-Variation in the Rose, 36.
Standing a Hard Winter, 123.
Stanton, Frank, poem by, 91.
St. Catharines, Ontario, garden in, 24.
Stevens, G. A., letter from, 133.
Sweat-box for propagation, 40.

Test-Gardens: Portland, 26; First Texas, 28; Elizabeth Park, 157; National, 115.
Texas, First Rose Test-Garden, 28.
Thomas, Capt. George C., article by, 93.
Thomas Tiplady Story, 128.
Toronto Horticultural Society, 129.
Totty, C. H., article by, 108.
Turbat, Mons. E., article by, 99; new roses of, 101; note from, 133; nursery visited, 96.

Van Fleet, Dr. W., articles by, 14, 29; visited, 126; note of, 130.

Wade, Mrs. M. S., letter from, 130.
Walls, George W., articles by, 92.
Ward, Admiral Aaron, Tribute to, 51; portrait of, facing 56.
Wayside Roses in France, 93.
Wettern, Herbert L., article by, 80.
What's the Use of a Long Name? 127.
Where Are Our Roses Coming From? 111.
White, Prof. E. A., letter mentioned, 129.
Winter Work with Roses, 57.
Wright, Mabel Osgood, article by, 9.

CONARD ROSES BLOOM

For months the thoughts of our people have been far from home. In the emergency, our thoughts have jumped the narrow confines of habit and circumstance and stretched to wherever "our own" were guarding the ideals of civilization.

But now, with the pull of uncertainty released, our thoughts snap back and come to rest at home. Once again we think in terms of home, rather than of the world—in terms of furnishings, paint, seeds, the intimate every-day features of normal life—instead of turmoil, destruction, and death. Change in thought inevitably brings change in interests and in the forms of human activity.

The significance and appreciation of home will be intensified by the sacrifices made to insure its protection. We Rose-growers, in our way, can do much to foster this reborn home interest.

We can define and register on the minds of great people the sound satisfaction and exquisite delight that result from the possession of successful and beautiful Roses. Our part is, first, to make sure our product is in every way better than ever; then we must back it to the end with our written word; and, finally, we must be the friend and advisor of all who buy our wares.

The mere transfer of a certain number of plants to a buyer for a dollar of his coin will not suffice—we must *serve*, not merely sell the American public.

SERVICE must be our slogan and all the people must know it.

> You should own "Hugonis"
> A New Rose of Distinction
>
> First get our book (free)
> *"THE BEST ROSES FOR AMERICA"
> which describes it fully—then get the Rose. Not more than two sent to any one person.
>
> *Many Nurserymen use this book as their authority on Roses.

CONARD & JONES CO. ★ WEST GROVE, PENNA.

Rose Specialists, backed by 50 years' experience

ROBERT PYLE
President

ANTOINE WINTZER
Vice-President

Sold by the Seedsmen of America

For over one-third of a century—that's a good while

USED ON ROSES, CARNATIONS, ETC.

USED ON ROSES, GRAPES, ETC.

Gold Medal from Panama-Pacific Exposition awarded Grape Dust and Slug-Shot, put up in packages from 1-lb. cartons, 5-, 10-, and 25-lb. bags, kegs and barrels in bulk

ASK FOR HAMMOND'S THRIP JUICE NO. 2

Gold Medal awarded for Hammond's Copper Solution used on Roses, etc. Put up in pints, quarts, gallons, 5 and 10 gallons

ASK FOR HAMMOND'S PAMPHLET ON INSECTS AND BLIGHTS

Hammond's Paint and Slug Shot Works, Beacon, N. Y.

HYBRID ROSES
Originated by Jackson Dawson

Dawson   Daybreak
Minnie Dawson   Lady Duncan
Apple Blossom   Arnold
William C. Egan   Pauline Dawson
         Seashell

For Sale by **EASTERN NURSERIES, Inc.**
HENRY S. DAWSON, Mgr.   Holliston, Mass.

Farr's Hardy Plant Specialties

Farr's New Irises

WONDERFUL colors of deepest blue, purple, soft rose, bronzy yellow, crimson and gold are found in this collection of seedling Irises that I have raised at Wyomissing. In addition to these I have gathered a multitude of new varieties and now have the most complete collection of rare varieties in existence.

Farr's Superb Peonies

PEONIES, the aristocrats of the hardy garden, are so democratic in their habits that they bloom in the humblest border, and thrive from north to south. At Quebec the temperature fell to 60 degrees below zero; not a single plant was injured. An Alabama gardener says his Peonies "cannot be surpassed by any in the north."

Farr's Hardy Plant Specialties

Sixth edition (issue of 1918), will tell you about my Gold Medal Irises, my collection of over 500 varieties of Peonies, and many other hardy plants, shrubs, evergreens and roses. If you have not received it, or if it has been mislaid,
A copy will be sent you promptly on request.

Bertrand H. Farr—Wyomissing Nurseries Co.
126 Garfield Avenue   WYOMISSING, PENNA.

Labels and Plant Stakes

AMERICAN MADE OF AMERICAN WOOD FOR AMERICAN GARDENS

The Benjamin Chase Co.
DERRY, N. H.

Cow Manure
For Rose Growing

From the brick-paved cattle pens of the Chicago Union Stock Yards. Sterilized by direct heat drying, screened and pulverized or shredded, conveniently packed in 100-pound bags.

Unequaled for Rose Planting and Mulching. Ask your supply house for Wizard Brand, or write us direct for prices and freight rates.

The Pulverized Manure Company
No. 30 Stock Yards, Chicago, Ill.

Rose Lecture

Our illustrated lecture, "In American Rose Gardens," is made up of one hundred beautifully colored slides of Roses and Rose-gardens in all parts of the United States. This lecture is rented, with manuscript to accompany the pictures. Particularly suited for Garden clubs, Schools, and Church societies.

Our folder, "Educational Prints and Lantern Slides," sent on request.

J. Horace McFarland Co.
Slide Department
HARRISBURG, PENNA.

Roses from the Carolina Hills

WE grow Roses and all the other good plants, shrubs and trees, including fruits, especially for the southern planter.

Let us tell you about them in our beautiful catalog, sent on request. Or, write us about anything in which we can assist in selection or planting.

J. Van. Lindley Nursery Co.
Box R   POMONA, N. C.

Garden Rose Novelties
1919

Hill's Premier

The King of Pink Roses; most noteworthy variety ever introduced of American origin. Price, 4-in. pots, $1 per plant, $10 per dozen.

Dickson's Novelties

As American Agent for Hugh Dickson, Ltd., Belfast, Ireland, we offer his Novelties for 1919, as follows:

Duchess of Abercorn. Creamy white.

E. Godfrey Brown. Deep reddish crimson.

Countess of Lonsdale. Deep cadmium yellow.

Chas. K. Douglas. Intense flaming scarlet.

Climbing H. V. Machin. Climbing sport of the well-known Hybrid Tea variety, H. V. Machin. Color, bright crimson.

All 4-in. pot plants, spring delivery, $2.50 per plant, $25 per dozen

Send for our complete catalogue if you do not have it, including Columbia, Ophelia Supreme, T. F. Crozier, and the other Novelties of 1918 introduction.

TOTTY'S
Headquarters for Novelty Roses
MADISON · NEW JERSEY

MICHELL'S ROSES

POT-GROWN   VIGOROUS
HEALTHY

At our Nurseries, Andalusia, Pa., we make a special feature of two-year-old *pot-grown Roses;* our list embracing the best old and new varieties. Our 1919 Catalogue devotes 4 pages to this department. Our rose plants are vigorous, hardy stock, pot-grown, and certain to give satisfactory results the first and successive seasons.

Write for our Seed Catalogue which lists these plants.

MICHELL'S SEED HOUSE
518 MARKET STREET, PHILADELPHIA, PA.
Nurseries and Greenhouses, Andalusia, Pa.

Breck-Robinson Nursery Co.
LEXINGTON, MASS.

WE specialize in Roses, offering over two hundred varieties. Our collection includes all the leading sorts of Hybrid Perpetual, Hybrid Tea, Climbing Hybrid Tea, Climbing Polyantha, Hybrid Rugosa, etc., etc.

ROSES IN POTS for late spring and summer delivery, guarantees an abundance of bloom immediately

OUR 1919 CATALOGUE NOW READY

T HE Storrs & Harrison's Roses are known everywhere. They cannot be excelled. We sell none but strong, hardy, well-developed plants that have been growing under the supervision of experts.

Our Roses of two years' growth will bloom the first year.

Have 1,200 acres devoted to the growing of ornamental trees, shrubs, vines, seeds, etc.

The Storrs & Harrison Co. has a reputation of 65 years' standing for reliability and fair dealing. 168-page catalog free.

The Storrs & Harrison Co.

NURSERYMEN
FLORISTS
AND SEEDSMEN

PAINESVILLE
OHIO

Dept. B

Los Angeles

THE GREAT AMERICAN HYBRID-TEA ROSE Los Angeles

This Bedding Rose, first sent out in 1917, is continuing to make an enviable reputation for itself in all parts of the country, and has also scored international honors. It was awarded the Gold Medal by unanimous consent of the judges, during the past season's trials at the Bagatelle Gardens in Paris, France, where competitive trials of Roses are made, to which contributions of new varieties come from all the renowned growers of the world, and from these it was singled out as the most meritorious variety shown. This valuable variety is fully described in

Dreer's Garden Book for 1919

which also offers many other desirable Roses, also Plants, Bulbs, Choice Flower and Vegetable Seeds, Lawn Grass Seeds, etc.

A copy will be mailed free on receipt of application

HENRY A. DREER, 714-16 Chestnut Street, PHILADELPHIA, PA.

Schling Service
Nothing Better

CUT ROSES

Schling's quality in cut-flowers means freshness—all seasonable varieties—artistic arrangement and prompt delivery—within two hours we deliver flowers in any city of the United States or Canada.

MAX SCHLING, 785 Fifth Ave., New York

GREEN PLAIN ROSE FARM

YARDLEY, BUCKS CO., PA.

Malcolm Franklin

ROSES FOR THE GREENHOUSE

WHETHER for the big commercial house or for the private greenhouse, we grow plants that will please you and that will start you on the road to success. We have been doing this for years. Ask anyone who knows roses where the best plants can be had, and your answer will be: "A. N. Pierson, Incorporated, Cromwell, Connecticut." We have a reputation for good roses. For years this reputation has been maintained and it will be in the future.

For Your Garden

Roses of all classes and the best stock that can be offered. Strong, heavy, two-year-old plants, budded or grafted to give them strength and flowering ability. If you want a dozen that you can get for a dollar and that will come by mail, don't write us. We don't grow them. If you want good goods for fair money, get in touch with Cromwell Gardens Roses. Our Handbook for the asking! It tells you how.

A. N. PIERSON, Inc.
CROMWELL, CONN.

Excelsior Rust-Proof Trellis

combines beauty with utility. Made of large strong wires with securely clamped joints, it will not sag or get out of shape, and is strong enough to support the heaviest vine. Galvanized after assembling, it makes a rust-proof finish that will last indefinitely. Carried in stock in rolls of 75 and 150 feet each, in 13-inch and 19-inch widths. Galvanized brackets to attach to the house. May we send you our catalog?

WRIGHT WIRE COMPANY
WORCESTER, MASS., U.S.A.

Branch Offices and Warehouses:
Boston   New York   Philadelphia
Chicago   Tulsa   San Francisco

HARDY ROSES
For the Garden

Dormant low-budded, two-year-old, field-grown plants, which include all the leading and popular varieties in Hybrid Perpetual or June Roses, Hybrid Teas, Teas, Rugosas and their hybrids, and Walsh's world-famed Ramblers.

My experience of forty years in rose-growing enables me to advise my clients of the best varieties suitable for the various climates.

M. H. WALSH, *Rose Specialist*
WOODS HOLE   MASSACHUSETTS

YOUR SALESMEN ARE WASTING TIME

if they are attempting to do work that can be done by the printed word—and it's time that *you* pay for!

It's our business to help you save these needless losses by conceiving and executing

Effective Advertising

in magazines and newspapers, and by the preparation of suitable catalogues, booklets, and follow-up plans. Under one roof and management we have all the elements essential to the successful selling of nursery products—plans and copy, photographs and designs, reproductions in natural colors, or printing of a superior quality.

An expression of your interest will bring a prompt response by mail, or a personal interview if it is desired; and without obligation on your part.

J. Horace McFarland Company
Illustrators and Printers

The McFarland Publicity Service
Horticultural Advertising

HARRISBURG, PENNSYLVANIA

The Lovett Sister Roses

Mary Lovett. Pure white.
Alida Lovett. Lively pink.
Bess Lovett. Bright red.

Each by far the best climbing rose of its color.

Full details in our catalogue No. 1—mailed free.

J. T. LOVETT, Inc.
Little Silver, N. J.

WE MAKE THE GROWING OF

FIELD-GROWN ROSES

Our Specialty for the

Wholesale Trade

THE UNITED STATES NURSERY COMPANY
S. W. CROWELL, Mgr.
ROSEACRES, MISSISSIPPI

AMERICAN-GROWN ROSES

FOR AMERICAN CLIMATES

Write for our Beautiful Rose Catalog

Bobbink & Atkins
RUTHERFORD, N. J.

Roses—350,000—Roses
For Autumn 1919 and Spring 1920

WE have in growing the finest collection of Hybrid Tea Roses in America. "Los Angeles," the famous Rose that won the Gold Medal in Bagatelle Gardens in Paris for the year 1918, in competition with the entire world, originated with us (see color illustration in 1917 Rose Annual). Other new seedlings are now under careful observation and will soon be introduced.

Our special Rose Catalogue will be ready during the summer of 1919, and will be mailed on request.

HOWARD & SMITH
LOS ANGELES : CALIFORNIA

PETERSON ROSES

possess the individuality and character that go with superiority, and today they are acknowledged the standard of the world.

They're the result of over twenty years of enthusiastic and—yes, loving effort.

They're born and reared (from 2 to 3 years) out-of-doors—have never even seen a greenhouse. That's *one* of the reasons why they produce such marvelous results.

"A Little Book About Roses"
(A CATALOGUE AND MORE)

a gem of the printer's art, also possessing the stamp of character and individuality, tells you the whole story. It's mailed on request.

GEORGE H. PETERSON
Rose and Peony Specialist

FAIR LAWN   Box 51   NEW JERSEY

MY GROWING GARDEN

is the name of a book in which Mr. J. Horace McFarland, Editor of the American Rose Annual, tells of his garden adventures in making a home out of an old and abandoned vineyard.

It is a plain story of what he did (confessing to "a champagne taste with a beer pocketbook," although hating both fluids!); how he sometimes failed, how he scored some successes, and all the time how much "fun" he had with that garden.

The garden grew month by month through a half-dozen years, from catalogue to fruit, from seed to flower, from the January snows until it was put to sleep before Christmas.

Of course, there are Roses in this Breeze Hill garden, many of them. Mr. McFarland specialized on the hardy climbers particularly.

The book contains plenty of "very different" pictures, some in full color. The difference is that every picture is a picture, and tells something that happened right there.

Many bouquets have been thrown at "My Growing Garden" because it is original, readable, and very helpful to any garden crank. It is also unusually beautiful as a book, because Mr. McFarland happens to be a good photographer and a noted printer as well as a writer. Some like it because it frankly faces the facts of a limited income.

"My Growing Garden" has 230 pages and 37 full-page plates in sepia and in full color. The price is $2 at the publisher's shop (The Macmillan Co., New York), or $2.17 mailed. Any bookseller ought to get it, but it will come promptly if $2.17 is sent to The American Rose Annual, Box 687, Harrisburg, Pa.

THIS BOOK IS DUE ON THE LAST DATE STAMPED BELOW

AN INITIAL FINE OF 25 CENTS
WILL BE ASSESSED FOR FAILURE TO RETURN THIS BOOK ON THE DATE DUE. THE PENALTY WILL INCREASE TO 50 CENTS ON THE FOURTH DAY AND TO $1.00 ON THE SEVENTH DAY OVERDUE.

Printed in the USA
CPSIA information can be obtained
at www.ICGtesting.com
CBHW070002090724
11328CB00003B/61